Tracing your Staffordshire Ancestors

FAMILY HISTORY FROM PEN & SWORD BOOKS

Birth, Marriage & Death Records
The Family History Web Directory
Tracing British Battalions on the Somme
Tracing Great War Ancestors
Tracing History Through Title Deeds
Tracing Secret Service Ancestors
Tracing the Rifle Volunteers
Tracing Your Air Force Ancestors
Tracing Your Ancestors
Tracing Your Ancestors from 1066 to 1837
Tracing Your Ancestors Through Death Records – Second Edition
Tracing Your Ancestors Through Family Photographs
Tracing Your Ancestors Through Letters and Personal Writings
Tracing Your Ancestors Using DNA
Tracing Your Ancestors Using the Census
Tracing your Ancestors Using the UK Timeline
Tracing Your Ancestors: Cambridgeshire, Essex, Norfolk and Suffolk
Tracing Your Aristocratic Ancestors
Tracing Your Army Ancestors
Tracing Your Army Ancestors – Third Edition
Tracing Your Birmingham Ancestors
Tracing Your Black Country Ancestors
Tracing Your Boer War Ancestors
Tracing Your British Indian Ancestors
Tracing Your Canal Ancestors
Tracing Your Channel Islands Ancestors
Tracing Your Church of England Ancestors
Tracing Your Criminal Ancestors
Tracing Your Docker Ancestors
Tracing Your East Anglian Ancestors
Tracing Your East End Ancestors
Tracing Your Family History on the Internet
Tracing Your Female Ancestors
Tracing Your First World War Ancestors
Tracing Your Freemason, Friendly Society and Trade Union Ancestors
Tracing Your Georgian Ancestors, 1714–1837
Tracing Your Glasgow Ancestors
Tracing Your Great War Ancestors: The Gallipoli Campaign
Tracing Your Great War Ancestors: The Somme
Tracing Your Great War Ancestors: Ypres
Tracing Your Huguenot Ancestors
Tracing Your Insolvent Ancestors
Tracing Your Irish Family History on the Internet
Tracing Your Jewish Ancestors
Tracing Your Jewish Ancestors – Second Edition
Tracing Your Labour Movement Ancestors
Tracing Your Legal Ancestors
Tracing Your Liverpool Ancestors
Tracing Your Liverpool Ancestors – Second Edition
Tracing Your London Ancestors
Tracing Your Medical Ancestors
Tracing Your Merchant Navy Ancestors
Tracing Your Northern Ancestors
Tracing Your Northern Irish Ancestors
Tracing Your Northern Irish Ancestors – Second Edition
Tracing Your Oxfordshire Ancestors
Tracing Your Pauper Ancestors
Tracing Your Police Ancestors
Tracing Your Potteries Ancestors
Tracing Your Pre-Victorian Ancestors
Tracing Your Prisoner of War Ancestors: The First World War
Tracing Your Railway Ancestors
Tracing Your Roman Catholic Ancestors
Tracing Your Royal Marine Ancestors
Tracing Your Rural Ancestors
Tracing Your Scottish Ancestors
Tracing Your Second World War Ancestors
Tracing Your Servant Ancestors
Tracing Your Service Women Ancestors
Tracing Your Shipbuilding Ancestors
Tracing Your Tank Ancestors
Tracing Your Textile Ancestors
Tracing Your Twentieth-Century Ancestors
Tracing Your Welsh Ancestors
Tracing Your West Country Ancestors
Tracing Your Yorkshire Ancestors
Writing Your Family History
Your Irish Ancestors

TRACING YOUR STAFFORDSHIRE ANCESTORS

A Guide for Family Historians

CHLOE O'SHEA

Pen & Sword
FAMILY HISTORY

First published in Great Britain in 2025 by
PEN AND SWORD FAMILY HISTORY
An imprint of
Pen & Sword Books Ltd
Yorkshire – Philadelphia

Copyright © Chloe O'Shea 2025

ISBN 978 1 03610 878 6

The right of Chloe O'Shea to be identified as Author of this work has been asserted by her in accordance with the Copyright, Designs and Patents Act 1988.

A CIP catalogue record for this book is available from the British Library. All rights reserved. No part of this book may be reproduced or transmitted in any form or by any means, electronic or mechanical including photocopying, recording or by any information storage and retrieval system, without permission from the Publisher in writing.

The publisher has no responsibility for the persistence or accuracy of URLs for any external or third-party internet websites referred to in this book, and does not guarantee that any content on such websites is, or will remain, accurate or appropriate.

Typeset by Mac Style
Printed and bound in the UK by CPI Group (UK) Ltd,
Croydon, CR0 4YY.

Pen & Sword Books Limited incorporates the imprints of After the Battle, Atlas, Archaeology, Aviation, Discovery, Family History, Fiction, History, Maritime, Military, Military Classics, Politics, Select, Transport, True Crime, Air World, Frontline Publishing, Leo Cooper, Remember When, Seaforth Publishing, The Praetorian Press, Wharncliffe Local History, Wharncliffe Transport, Wharncliffe True Crime and White Owl.

For a complete list of Pen & Sword titles please contact
PEN & SWORD BOOKS LIMITED
47 Church Street, Barnsley, South Yorkshire, S70 2AS, England
E-mail: enquiries@pen-and-sword.co.uk
Website: www.pen-and-sword.co.uk
or
PEN AND SWORD BOOKS
1950 Lawrence Road, Havertown, PA 19083, USA
E-mail: uspen-and-sword@casematepublishers.com
Website: www.penandswordbooks.com

Front Cover Images: John Wayman Keep and Rosabella Mary Barlow, Longdon Church and the headstone of John Shaw at Longdon.

For Robert and Emily
My little dreams come true

CONTENTS

Acknowledgements ix
Introduction x

Chapter 1 Civil Registration 1

Chapter 2 Census Returns 12

Chapter 3 Parish Registers 22

Chapter 4 Parish Records 31

Chapter 5 Wills and Probate 40

Chapter 6 Nonconformist Records 49

Chapter 7 Military Records 59

Chapter 8 Criminal and Court Records 70

Chapter 9 Work and Business Records 80

Chapter 10 Maps 91

Chapter 11 Tax Lists and Oath Rolls 99

Chapter 12 Title Deeds 107

Chapter 13 Newspapers 114

Chapter 14 Manorial Records 121

Chapter 15 Memorial Inscriptions 129

Chapter 16 Other Sources 137

Chapter 17	Staffordshire Archives	152
Chapter 18	Staffordshire Museums	157
Chapter 19	Visiting Staffordshire Parishes	161
Chapter 20	Staffordshire Occupations	167
Chapter 21	Staffordshire Surnames	175
Chapter 22	Internet Sources	184
Chapter 23	Family History Societies	190
Chapter 24	DNA Testing	194

Conclusion   201
Index   203

ACKNOWLEDGEMENTS

With many thanks to:

Mum and Dad
James O'Shea
Staffordshire History Centre
Keith Stanley and the Burntwood Family History Group
Midland Ancestors
Audley and District Family History Society

Credit is also due to:

Ancestry
Findmypast
The Genealogist
British Newspaper Archive
General Register Office

INTRODUCTION

Staffordshire is a county of contrasts. There are areas of great rural beauty and sites of historic urban industry. You may find your ancestors worked the fields in a quaint village or toiled deep in a dark and dangerous coal mine. Some of your ancestors may even have done both. Staffordshire is also a county that has seen great changes over the generations that we will be researching in our family trees. Changes in farming practices and the mechanisation of other industries vastly changed the landscape. Combined with increased urbanisation, our ancestors would struggle today to recognise many of the towns that they once lived in.

County boundary changes mean that certain places, once within its borders, now reside outside of Staffordshire. Others are now found inside the county that previously weren't. To avoid confusion for those researchers who are looking for ancestors in such places, this book will look at the towns and villages that were in the historical county of Staffordshire. Therefore, at times you will read about places that are no longer within the county but previously were.

The biggest county boundary change came as a result of the 1972 Local Government Act which saw the formation of West Midlands county. This took places such as Dudley, Wolverhampton, Walsall and West Bromwich outside of Staffordshire. Other notable changes include when Lichfield ceased to be its own county in 1888 and when Perry Barr was transferred to Warwickshire in 1928.

My ancestors come from across England; from Dorset to Lancashire and several counties in-between. This includes a branch of my maternal line which hails from Staffordshire, hence my interest here. The branch begins with my great great-grandparents Rosabella Mary Barlow and John Wayman Keep who married in Longdon in 1896. Longdon was

Map of historic Staffordshire. (Author's own)

the village where Rosabella was born and resided with her family who ran the post office in Brook End. A majority of her forebears resided in Longdon, Cheadle and Cauldon with others further back from places including Lichfield, Dilhorne, Alstonefield and Kings Bromley.

This book begins with chapters focusing on particular record types, such as census returns and title deeds. The benefits and limitations of each record are explained, as well as where you can find them. The early chapters give examples from the county to demonstrate how the records can be useful for those researching Staffordshire kin. Later chapters look at other sources of information, including family history societies and social media. There is also a section dedicated to Staffordshire surnames which explains their origins and their prevalence in the county.

If you are just beginning your family tree, speak to as many family members as possible. Note down any relevant stories that have been passed down about deceased relatives and ask for copies of any old family photographs they may possess. Secondly, go through any paraphernalia you possess such as diaries, certificates and postcards and extract as much information from them as you can. Remember, family history is not just about finding out names and dates but finding out who our ancestors were as people. Scan any documents and photographs you have and save them in at least two different places to avoid future loss.

I hope this book helps to explain why different record types are useful and how they can be used to trace your tree back further into Staffordshire and beyond. By using the widest variety of documentation possible, we can create a clearer image in our minds of what our ancestors' lives were like and their characters, as well as the trials they faced in their lifetime.

Chapter 1

CIVIL REGISTRATION

About the Record

Records of civil registration are birth, marriage and death certificates available from the General Register Office (GRO). You may sometimes hear them referred to as BMD certificates. They form the backbone of our research, providing essential information about the most important events of our ancestors' lives. Certificates contain the basic information on which we can build our ancestors' stories. You may also be lucky and find extra details supplied, such as a time of birth or a note relating to an inquest on a death certificate. Interestingly, it was a Staffordshire man who helped implement the civil registration system. Thomas Lister (1800–1842) of Armitage Park was the first Registrar General for England and Wales, leading the new General Register Office.

BMD certificates have the same standard format throughout England and Wales and you can find them from July 1837 onwards. To some this may seem fairly recent, but you will quickly realise that the certificates help us to go further back in time than 1837. For example, my fifth great-grandfather Thomas Marshall died in December 1837, but the certificate gives his age as 72, taking us back to 1765.

There are various registration districts across England and Wales which have changed over time. It can be helpful to know which district your ancestors are likely to be found in. Where changes have occurred, it is not always as easy as it seems to know which district applies to you. Stoke-on-Trent registration district existed from 1837 until 1922 when it was added to the new Stoke and Wolstanton district. This itself was abolished in 1934 and was divided into the Stoke-on-Trent and Newcastle-under-Lyme districts. The latter of these was then moved under the title of Staffordshire district in 2008. As long as you are aware of the location of your ancestors at the time and whether this is the district a particular event is recorded in, then this should save you from purchasing the wrong certificates.

In 1837 there were fifteen registration districts in Staffordshire. These were Burton upon Trent, Cheadle, Leek, Lichfield, Newcastle-under-Lyme, Penkridge, Seisdon, Stafford, Stoke-on-Trent, Stone, Tamworth, Uttoxeter, Walsall, West Bromwich and Wolverhampton. There were other districts that partly covered areas of Staffordshire, including Ashbourne, Shifnal and Stourbridge.

This chapter will look at the format of certificates prior to the changes made in 1969. If you are researching more recent relatives, be aware that the appearance is now different. This is a positive as there is more information on the forms and they tend to be easier to understand. They are also typed rather than handwritten, therefore clearer to read.

Locating the Record

The cheapest and quickest way of ordering BMD certificates is directly from the GRO website at **gro.gov.uk**. You will find that other websites offer a certificate purchasing service; however, these essentially act as middlemen who will purchase the record from GRO and charge you extra for ordering it for you. Start by registering for a free account with GRO.

If you are looking for a birth or death certificate, start by clicking 'Search the GRO Indexes'. This is free. Select 'birth' or 'death' and then the year of the event. You can choose to search +/- 2 years if you are unsure of the exact date. This means instead of searching for an event in 1850, the results will show dates from 1848 to 1852. You must enter the person's surname and sex but other details are optional. You may wish to enter further details as, depending on how common the surname is, you may yield too many results to search through. Other options include adding a first name, district, mother's maiden name for birth certificate and age at death for death certificates. For age at death you can choose to search +/- 10 years.

If there are too many results to look through, narrow them down by adding further details. Searching for my distant cousin Edgar Creed born in 1902 (+/- 2 years) gives only one result so it is easy to know which to purchase. If using the same search criteria to look for his Uncle George Barlow's birth in 1867 there are eighty results. The correct George can be found by adding his mother's maiden name of Marshall, which gives just one result.

Some of the detail given in the index is obvious including the person's name, registration district, mother's maiden name and age at death. Other details may appear confusing. The GRO reference becomes easier to understand when you break it down. If we look at Martha Barlow's death in 1849, the GRO reference given in the index is '1849 J Quarter Cheadle Volume 17 Page 22'. This may sometimes be written as 'Cheadle 1849/2/17/22'. The registration district given is Cheadle. The year is the one when the event was registered. This is usually the same as when the event occurred; however, where a birth or death happened in December, you may find that it was registered the following year. The volume and page numbers are needed to order the correct entry.

Lastly, 'J Quarter' refers to the quarter of the year in which the event was registered. Each quarter contains three months as detailed below:

- Quarter 1 (M) – January, February, March
- Quarter 2 (J) – April, May, June
- Quarter 3 (S) – July, August, September
- Quarter 4 (D) – October, November, December

The letter refers to the last month in each quarter. Some genealogy subscription sites will give a 'death date' in their indexes as 'March 1860', when in fact this means that the death was registered in the March quarter of 1860.

In the majority of cases, the information you input into the index will be enough to confidently purchase the correct certificate. There will be other times where you may need to purchase multiple certificates in order to be sure you have the one that relates to your ancestor. For example, there are two William Arthur Smiths born in Burton upon Trent district in 1904. If you do not know the mother's maiden name you may need to purchase both to discover which is correct.

Once you have found the correct birth or death entry in the index there are three formats to choose from:

1. A paper certificate sent through the post. Although it is the most expensive and with the longest lead time, this option has the nicest appearance, looking more like the classic certificates we are used to.
2. A PDF copy of the certificate sent by email. This is only available for births from 1837 to 100 years ago and for deaths from 1837 until 1957, but is cheaper as you will need to print the details yourself – and it does not have the nice appearance of a certificate. The lead time is around a week; a GRO employee crops the details from the register for you.

3. A digital image. This is again only available for births from 1837 to 100 years ago and deaths from 1837 to 1957. This is by far the cheapest option. The cropping of the register is done mechanically and it is not uncommon to find an important part of the record has been accidentally cropped off. In these cases, you will receive a full refund if you fill in GRO's complaint form. Digital images arrive instantly.

The latter two options provide the same information as you would see on a printed certificate, so when you are researching your tree I would advise choosing these two methods to reduce costs –it may be necessary to purchase several of them.

If you wish to order a marriage certificate, this has a different process as there is no index available via GRO. You can use a genealogy website, such as Ancestry or Findmypast, to search for your ancestor's marriage in their marriage index collections. When you have found this, you can use the details given in the record transcript to order the certificate from GRO. For example, looking at the marriage between John Collier and Esther Barlow in Ancestry's 'England & Wales, Civil Registration Marriage Index 1837–1915', we can see that the bride and groom's names are given, the year of the event of 1876, that the marriage occurred in the fourth quarter, the registration district is Stafford and that the volume and page numbers are given as 6b and 9 respectively.

If you then head back to the GRO website, click 'Place an Order' and select 'England and Wales'. Then select 'Marriage' and enter the year of the event. Click 'I know the GRO reference' and enter the details as previously found. If you have been unable to find an event, you can instead opt to select 'I want GRO to search for the registration' and enter the details you have. This option takes longer for the staff to complete so it is better if you can find the correct reference, where possible, to ensure you are purchasing the correct certificate.

Before ordering a marriage certificate, it is worth considering whether to purchase a subscription to Findmypast if you do not already have one. Findmypast currently has the rights to digitised copies of many Staffordshire records, including their 'Staffordshire Marriages' collection. This shows the book entry for the marriage which contains the same information as a certificate from GRO. Using the previous example of John Collier and Esther Barlow, we can see that Findmypast has their marriage certificate entry available to view, telling us they married on 13 November 1876 in Colwich. Always look at the original image rather than relying on the transcription. Findmypast also has a 'Staffordshire

The 1876 marriage certificate of John Collier and Esther Barlow. (Reproduced courtesy of Staffordshire Record Office)

Banns' collection, showing digitised images of the banns book. If your ancestor married by banns, rather than by licence, this book can give you the three dates they were present in church when their banns were read.

Alternatively, you can visit Staffordshire BMD at **staffordshirebmd.org.uk** which is transcribing the local indexes of births, marriages and deaths. The information provided here is similar to the GRO Index. If you cannot find your ancestor in one of these indexes, it is worth checking the other in case one has a transcription error. The site is a collaboration between local register offices and Midland Ancestors.

Values of the Record

It is essential to purchase many records of civil registration to ensure we are tracing the correct line. As we look to grow our tree, this usually means we purchase birth and marriage certificates first, as death certificates tend to be less helpful for this. Never rely on details from other people's online family trees without first seeing evidence in the form of a certificate. Also be wary of using other records to prove parentage. For example, if on a census there is a couple listed as 'Head' and 'Wife' with three children listed, this simply means that the children are the offspring of the head of the household and his wife may not be their mother. There are many cases where the listed 'Wife' is his second wife and the children are the product of his first marriage. In almost all cases, certificates are therefore necessary.

The details given on certificates prior to the changes made in 1969 are listed below.

Birth Certificate

- Registration district and sub-district
- County
- Date of birth
- Place of birth
- Child's name
- Child's sex
- Father's name (if known)
- Mother's name (including maiden name and any former husband's surnames)
- Father's occupation (if name is listed)
- Informant's name, residence and relationship
- Date of registration
- Registrar's signature

Marriage Certificate

- Place of marriage
- County
- Date of marriage ceremony
- Names of the bride and groom
- Bride and groom's age (often noted as 'full age')
- Bride and groom's marital status
- Bride and groom's occupations
- Bride and groom's residences
- Bride and groom's fathers' names and occupations
- Whether they married by banns or licence
- The name of the person who performed the ceremony
- Signature or mark of bride and groom
- Signatures of at least two witnesses

Death Certificate

- Registration district and sub-district
- County
- Date of death
- Place of death
- Name of deceased
- Sex of deceased
- Age of deceased

- Occupation of deceased
- Cause of death
- Informant's name, residence and relationship
- Date of registration
- Registrar's signature

From the above, we can clearly see the value in purchasing BMD certificates for our ancestors; they provide a large amount of information and are among the most reliable records you can use in genealogy. Purchase them in a logical order. For example, if you have your grandfather's birth certificate then use the details of his parents to search for their marriage and then purchase their marriage certificate. From here you can use their father's details given on their marriage certificate to search for their births. It is not always that simple, especially if your ancestor had a common name and lived in a heavily populated area.

If your ancestor was born prior to civil registration in July 1837 but they have younger siblings born after this date, it is worth purchasing their siblings' birth certificates to confirm their parentage. You will need to check that they share the same mother and that the father was not married previously. If your ancestor has a common name, such as William Smith and you are struggling to find their birth certificate, try looking for their siblings in the GRO index first. If they have several siblings then finding them in the GRO index can help confirm their mother's maiden name and, in turn, help you to find the right William Smith in the index.

An often-ignored value of marriage certificates is the name of the witnesses. These people may be unrelated, perhaps friends of the newlyweds, but in the majority of cases, the witnesses are relatives of the bride and groom. This can be particularly helpful where the married name of a sister is given, to help you trace her line. This also means if you are struggling to prove a female ancestor's marriage, you may find her under her married name as a witness to her sibling's marriage. You cannot search by witness name, but it may be worth purchasing her sibling's marriage certificate to see if she is listed as a witness.

You will probably find that many of your ancestors had siblings who died young. This was far more common in our ancestors' day than today. I have found it valuable to purchase these young children's death certificates. It does not often provide you with much more genealogical information, although at times it has helped fill in gaps in a change of residence between the census returns, or a father's changing occupation. The value of these certificates is in the cause of death. You may discover that three young siblings died of whooping cough. It may be they died in a tragic drowning accident, or perhaps suffocated under a blanket. The cause of death can give us a great insight into what their parents and siblings went through at the time and it would have been a huge part of their lives to lose a child in whatever manner. If we are writing up our ancestor's life story, the loss of their children is important to include.

Similar to the above, knowing the cause of death for our direct ancestors helps to conclude their story. Whether they died suddenly in an accident or if they suffered for years from a chronic and prolonged illness can give an insight into what the end of their lives was like, and also hint at the effect on our surviving ancestors. Were they likely to have acted as a carer for them in their last days?

The biggest value of BMD certificates is proving parentage. Rather than copying incorrect online trees, purchasing one certificate can save you years of researching the wrong line. Don't underestimate the importance of viewing all the relevant certificates to your family.

Limitations of the Record

While records of civil registration are among the more reliable documents, they cannot be trusted completely. There are many cases of spelling errors. Some will be because your ancestors were illiterate, so when registering events they would tell the registrar their details and it was up to the registrar how they believed the name to be spelt. This may mean that each child is registered under a slightly different spelling of their surname or their mother's maiden name. There may also be transcription errors, even if the record itself is spelt correctly. GRO has options in their index to search for 'similar sounding variations' and 'phonetically similar variations' of a surname. It is worth using these options if you are finding it hard to trace a birth or death.

A common issue with birth certificates is where no father's name is listed, implying that the child's parents were unmarried at the time of their birth. This can be very frustrating and is the cause of many brick walls. It may be that the mother did not know who the father was, they may have married after the child's birth or the child was the product of a short-lived relationship that had failed to last until the birth. In more recent cases, DNA can often be used to prove paternity.

An often more complex issue is when an incorrect father's name is given on a birth or marriage certificate. This issue is not limited to GRO records, as it was much easier to lie about relationships in the past than it is today where everything is heavily documented. You may find that when searching for a person using the details on a certificate, things don't add up. Or you may find that your DNA results are hinting that a person's parentage is incorrect. If a married woman had an affair, there was nothing preventing her from putting down her husband's name as the baby's father – even if they both knew he was not.

As well as incorrect fathers' names, you may find that other details given are false. A bride or groom may have lied about their age when they married in order to marry without parental consent, or to appear closer in age to each other than they really were. A person may lie about their marital status so that they could remarry without needing a divorce. This was obviously illegal but, as divorce was only an option to the wealthy, it happened more often than you may think. My great-grandfather married three times without ever divorcing, in a rare case of trigamy. For his second marriage he claimed to be widowed and for his third marriage he stated he was a bachelor.

The older the certificate, the less helpful and reliable it is likely to be. Causes of death on early certificates are often given as 'old age' or 'natural causes'. The deceased's age is often incorrect, sometimes several years out, as people were not aware of their real ages the way we are today. If the informant was someone who was not especially close to the deceased, such as a neighbour, this information is more likely to be inaccurate. The more recent the record, the more likely it will be correct. Older certificates are also likely to just give the name of a parish for a person's residence, rather than a helpful address.

For many of us, the biggest limitation of civil registration records is the cost. While in recent years cheaper options have become available, this can still quickly add up. Purchase the certificates in a logical order as discussed and check first to see if the marriage certificate you need is on Findmypast if you have a subscription. You may also save money if a relative already has the original certificate and is willing to share it with you.

Staffordshire Examples

My third great-grandmother Rosanna Sarah Marshall was born on 4 September 1842 in Longdon. Her birth certificate names her father as John Marshall, a butcher. Rosanna's mother is named as 'Ellen Marshall, late Jones, formerly Shaw'. This means she is now known as Ellen Marshall as she is married to Rosanna's father, John, was previously married to a man with the surname Jones and her maiden name was Shaw. Cases like this can help trace a woman's full life story. In Ellen's case she had three children with her former husband, Peter Jones; an illegitimate child with John two years before they married; and five further children with John after they wed.

The 1842 birth certificate of Rosanna Sarah Marshall. (Crown copyright)

My second great-grandparents John Wayman Keep and Rosabella Mary Barlow married in Longdon parish church on 21 October 1896. While John's middle name is not given, the other details are all correct – including their ages, residences and their fathers' full names and occupations. The interesting detail with this register entry is that instead of two named witnesses, they have seven: Samson Barlow, Lily Barlow, Minnie Lacy, James Horton, Laura Creed, John Marshall and Clarice Daft. The majority of these are relatives of the bride and groom.

My fifth great-grandfather Thomas Marshall died on 4 December 1837 in Longdon. Early certificates often give a bit less detail, as in this case where his cause of death is 'natural decay'; however, this is a rare example where his time of death was given as 'around 2 p.m.'. He died at Hill Top, with his son John present at the death and acting as the informant. His age is correctly given as 72.

The 1837 death certificate of Thomas Marshall. (Crown copyright)

Civil registration documents on their own can give us an outline of the major events in our ancestors' lives. Unfortunately, these are not always happy stories. Rosanna and John's illegitimate child, mentioned above, was named Edna. She was born in the first half of 1837, just missing out on having a birth certificate. Her marriage certificate shows she married John Warrallo on 13 October 1857 in Walsall. The next time she appears in civil registration records is her early death less than two years later in Walsall on 21 January 1859. Her cause of death is given as 'fever after confinement', indicating that Edna had recently given birth. Looking through the GRO index leads us to her daughter, Edna Elizabeth Warrallo. Edna Elizabeth's birth certificate tells us she was born in Walsall on 16 January 1859, five days before her mother's passing. Tragically for her father John, Edna Elizabeth was also to pass away at a young age. She died of typhoid on 24 May 1872 in Walsall, aged 13.

Chapter 2

CENSUS RETURNS

About the Record

A census is an official count or survey of a population of people. It acts as a snapshot in time, listing where everybody is on a specific date. A census was taken every ten years in England and Wales from 1801 onwards with the exception of 1941. The returns of 1931 were destroyed by fire, meaning the next census released will be the 1951 census. For the majority of parishes only the census returns of 1841 onwards survive.

The census returns of 1801–1831 were usually headcounts per household or sometimes just headcounts of each parish. These can be of general interest to genealogists who observe how the population of the ancestor's parish changed during that time. In rare cases, more details are given such as the head's name and occupation. The surviving 1801 census returns for Staffordshire are St Michael's parish in Lichfield, Marston township in Stafford, Walsall and Wednesbury. For 1811, the census returns of Colwich, Newcastle-under-Lyme, Walsall and Wednesbury survive. For 1821, only the Walsall and Wednesbury returns survive and for 1831 only Blymhill and Walsall returns survive, with a summary for Yoxall.

Only a minority of researchers will be lucky enough to be able to use the early census returns for their research, but all of us can use the more modern census returns from 1841 onwards. These provide us with much more detail and are an essential record. As with any record, they are prone to errors so should always be used in conjunction with other sources to back up your findings.

It helps to know the date on which each census was taken. For example, if your ancestor died in a census year, you should know whether they died before or after the census was taken so you know whether to look for them or not. These dates are;

- 6 June 1841
- 30 March 1851
- 7 April 1861
- 2 April 1871
- 3 April 1881
- 5 April 1891
- 31 March 1901
- 2 April 1911
- 19 June 1921

The 1921 census was due to be taken on 24 April, a date which confusingly still appears on the returns form, but this was postponed. The information supplied on the form should refer to those staying in each household on the night of 19 June.

For the majority of your ancestors, you will find that working backwards through the census will be the most logical way of tracing them. If your ancestor died in 1856, first find them in the 1851 census and then trace them back to the 1841 returns. There will be times where this isn't the easiest option. It may be that you can find them in the 1841 census easily but a transcription error means that you struggle to find them in the 1851 census. In all cases make sure you are tracing the right family, particularly if the surname is common.

Locating the Record

For the early census returns of 1801–1831, Staffordshire History Centre holds the 1801 returns for Marston, St Michael's in Lichfield and Wednesbury, the 1811 returns for Colwich, Newcastle-under-Lyme and Wednesbury, the 1821 return for Wednesbury and the 1831 return for Blymhill. Walsall Archives holds the returns for Walsall for 1801, 1811, 1821 and 1831.

The modern census returns from 1841 onwards are held at The National Archives in Kew (TNA), although you will not be able to view the original paper documents. The returns up to 1921 have all been fully digitised and are best accessed online via a subscription site of your choice, such as Ancestry or Findmypast. At the time of writing, the 1921 census is only available at Findmypast with an 'Everything' subscription or via Ancestry with an 'All UK and Ireland' or 'All Records' subscription.

Open up the website's search function and filter the page to search for census records only. Then enter the details you know about your ancestor. It is best not to be too rigid with this so keep boxes ticked for spelling variants and widen the location search. Our ancestors moved around more often than you may believe. As a census focuses on one night in particular, you may find that your ancestor is staying the night with relatives, or perhaps staying away for work or holiday reasons. You may find an ancestor is recorded using sometimes just their first name and surname and at other times their middle names may be included. Be open minded as to how they may have been documented. Don't go looking for a person with a specific year of birth. Our ancestors were not as aware of their ages as we are today and even if they were they may have lied, so always widen the date filter.

For some of our ancestors, you may type in their details and all of their available census returns will appear, with no other similar results for other people muddying the waters. At other times, especially for those with common names, there will be a huge number of results. It is common to find people with the same name and of similar age in a locality and you will need to work out which is your ancestor. Take your time with this and stick to what you know. If you know for sure that your ancestor died in 1870, then they cannot be the same person you find in an 1871 return so you can rule that family out. It is often easier to rule people out one by one than go out of your way to prove a certain person is your forebear.

If you accept one wrong census entry for an ancestor this can lead you to research the wrong family in the future. It is important to be sure that you have the correct return; civil registration records and parish registers, among other documents, will ensure you are following the right people. As always, never rely on other people's online family trees. Just because somebody has a census return attached to a shared family member does not make it correct. If you have doubts, research it to prove either them or yourself wrong.

If you receive a large number of results for a person, it is best to narrow it down step by step. Firstly, select a specific census year. Searching for Thomas Hill in Staffordshire in the 1871 census leaves us with 213 results. We can choose to narrow this down further by adding a birth year. Looking for a Thomas born in 1855 +/- five years leaves us with forty-nine results. If we then add a birthplace of Ipstones, this leaves us with one result. What you know about an ancestor will determine which search criteria you can add and in which order. If you still struggle to find the correct person, consider searching for somebody else they are likely to be living with, such as a sibling or a child. It may be that your ancestor's details have been transcribed incorrectly making them hard to find, but another person's may be easier to locate.

Use the details given in a census to make common-sense decisions about whether or not they are your ancestor. For example, if a person is recorded as an agricultural labourer in 1871, they are unlikely to have been a lawyer in 1861. Their place of birth may change dependent on how they remember and report it to the enumerator on the night; however, this is unlikely to change much. If their place of birth is Lichfield in one census, then they are unlikely to have it recorded as Scotland in the next. If you fail to find a certain census, try searching using another website. The transcriptions for these vary, so you may find that while one site has transcribed your ancestor incorrectly, another site will make finding your ancestor much easier.

Values of the Record

The values of the census are huge and mean we can often find it relatively easy to trace most of our lines back to 1841. We can see not only our family's details but also details of their lodgers and neighbours who may be relatives or friends. Each census provides us with slightly different information depending on the year of the record. These details can be seen below.

Year of Census	Details Included
1841	City or parish, sometimes address, names of people in the household, age rounded down to the nearest five years, sex, occupation, whether born in the county and whether born in Scotland, Ireland or 'Foreign Parts'
1851	City or parish, address, names of people in the household, relationship to head, marital status, age, sex, occupation, place of birth and whether a person is 'blind' or 'deaf-and-dumb'
1861	City or parish, address, names of people in the household, relationship to head, marital status, age, sex, occupation, place of birth and whether a person is 'blind' or 'deaf-and-dumb'
1871	City or parish, address, names of people in the household, relationship to head, marital status, age, sex, occupation, place of birth and whether a person is 'deaf-and-dumb', 'blind', 'lunatic' or 'imbecile or idiot'
1881	City or parish, address, names of people in the household, relationship to head, marital status, age, sex, occupation, place of birth and whether a person is 'deaf-and-dumb', 'blind', 'lunatic' or 'imbecile or idiot'

Year of Census	Details Included
1891	City or parish, address, number of rooms occupied if less than five, names of people in the household, relation to head, marital status, age, sex, occupation, whether an employer, employee or neither, place of birth and whether a person is 'deaf-and-dumb', 'blind' or 'lunatic, imbecile or idiot'
1901	City or parish, address, number of rooms occupied if less than five, names of people in the household, relation to head, marital status, age, sex, occupation, whether an employer, a worker or living on own means, if working at home, place of birth and whether a person is 'deaf-and-dumb', 'blind', 'lunatic' or 'imbecile or feeble minded'
1911	Address, names of people in the household, relationship to head, age, sex, marital status, for married woman the amount of years they have been married and how many children they have had and how many of these are still alive, occupation, industry, whether they work from home or not, place of birth, nationality if born abroad and whether a person is 'totally deaf' or 'deaf-and-dumb', 'totally blind', 'lunatic' or 'imbecile or feeble minded' and at what age they first suffered from this, signature of head of household
1921	Address, names of people in the household, relationship to head, age in years and months, sex, marital status, for children under 15 whether one or both of their parents are deceased, place of birth, nationality if born abroad, whether a child attends school full time or part time, occupation, employer's details, work address, number of children aged under 16 and their ages, signature of head of household

The main difference you will see as you browse the census returns are the differences in appearance between the returns of 1911 and 1921 with the earlier records. This is because these are the retained returns filled out by the head of the household, giving us a chance to see their handwriting and signature. We can still browse the records of their neighbours by clicking left and right; however, they do not appear on the same page. Earlier returns were compiled by the census enumerators meaning there is more opportunity for transcription errors, but it is easier to view records for your ancestor's neighbours on the same page who may turn out to be relatives living nearby.

Generally speaking, the more recent the census return the more information it will hold. You are more likely to be given an exact street address with a house number that you can trace in 1921 than you are in 1841. The 1911 and 1921 census returns are also known to sometimes contain unique information that wasn't requested. For example, sometimes the head of the household chose to add their pets' names to the record or the names of their deceased children.

The census records everybody in the household. The details supplied mean we can use the census to find further records for our ancestors, such as their BMD certificates and electoral roll records. Babies' ages are often given in days or months which is helpful in tracing their birth certificates. By viewing all the census records in turn for a person, we can see their changing circumstances including any changes in marital status or occupation. When a person is listed as widowed or suddenly disappears from the records, we know to trace for a death. The 1911 census is especially helpful in listing the number of babies a woman has had and how many had died, helping us trace children who were born and died between census records and who we may have otherwise missed.

Learning an ancestor's address from the census is of great benefit to us as we can use this to trace them in other records too, such as tax records and title deeds. Their place of birth is also very useful, although always be wary as to how accurate this is. You may find that your ancestor remained living in the parish of their birth their whole life, or you may find they frequently moved around the country. This is particularly common with certain lifestyles, such as those living and working on the canals. In this case, you could even find that each of your ancestor's children were born in different counties, something which is hard to prove without a census record tying the whole family together.

The detail given in a census can be used to distinguish between people of the same name in the same area. With other records, such as tax listings this can be impossible to do, but by looking at a number of people you can work out who is most likely to be your forebear. They may have different ages, birthplaces or occupations. Use whatever notable details you know about your ancestor to separate them from the rest.

The information supplied in the 1921 census about a person's occupation can lead us to uncover a lot more about their life. In earlier census records you may have read that they were a factory worker. However, in 1921 the name of their factory should be given and its address, so you can learn about the history of the workplace, discover if any of its occupational records have survived or if the building still stands today.

The census returns take us further back in time than you may think. For example, 101-year-old Rebecca Alcott can be seen in the 1841 census residing in West Bromwich, taking us back to 1740. But remember, sometimes your ancestor's age may be wrong or incorrectly transcribed.

The following extract shows the 1921 census entry for the Axten family of Lichfield. In addition to the details shown, the return reveals that William works at the post office in Lichfield as an overseer. Without referring to other documents, it is not clear from the census return who the 'visitor' is, but this household actually comprises a young couple and their baby and the couple's mothers.

Name	Relationship to Head	Age		Sex	Marriage or Orphanhood	Birthplace
		Years	Months			
Emily Axten	Head	62	11	F	Widowed	Overton, Wiltshire
William Frederick Axten	Son	33	9	M	Married	Chelsea, London
Emma Rosabella Axten	Daughter-in-law	28	11	F	Married	Longdon, Staffordshire
Frederick Ralph Axten	Grandson		Under 1 month	M	Both alive	Lichfield, Staffordshire
Emma Millicent Barlow	Visitor	61	1	F	Married	Eltham, Kent

Limitations of the Record

Despite a census intending to count the entire population, people were still missed. In some cases this may be because they were evading the law, but in most cases there is an innocent reason. They may have been part of a travelling community whose location was missed, or perhaps the enumerator forgot to check the canal boats in his area. Your ancestor may have been a suffragette who refused to complete the form as a protest. If your ancestor is missing from a census, they are likely to appear in the following census as it is very rare for a person to be repeatedly absent. The 1861 census returns for the parish of Tettenhall in Wolverhampton are partially lost which may explain why you cannot find a particular family.

If you cannot find your ancestor in a particular census, don't assume they are one of the missing people. It is more likely that there has been a transcription error somewhere along the way. This could be the fault of the census enumerator who misunderstood a person's answer and recorded it incorrectly, possibly because of our ancestor's accents being misheard. My fifth great-grandmother Anne Brindley's place of birth is recorded as Crakefoot, Staffordshire in the 1851 census. This is an error on the enumerator's behalf as it should read Crateford, near Brewood. More commonly, there are numerous transcription errors where the information has been misread or mistyped. This is frustrating, as despite the census holding the correctly spelt information, the entry may not appear in our search results unless we widen our search terms. Try searching using different websites to see if the right results appear.

Your ancestor may be hard to find if they are recorded under slightly different names. For example, a man named John Joseph Wright may be recorded as John Wright, Joseph Wright, John J. Wright, J.J. Wright or Jos Wright in different returns. Keep your search flexible and think of what pet names a person may have been known as, such as Betty instead of Elizabeth.

You may find that your ancestor's birthplace is recorded differently in some census returns. This is again very common but can be confusing when trying to identify a person or trace their baptism details. Many of our ancestors would have been unaware of where they were born and would have written down the earliest place they could remember living. They may have been born in Shenstone but moved to Tamworth when they were very young, meaning their earliest memories would have been in Tamworth and so that's what they may record. Knowing your place of birth wasn't as important to our ancestors as it is for us today.

It is the same issue with people's ages. A man aged 60 in 1851 would not necessarily be recorded as 70 in 1861. Be flexible with your searches and remember that for the 1841 census those aged 15 and above were supposed to have their ages rounded down to the nearest five. This did not always happen, but a 34-year-old should therefore be listed as being 30 years old. If your ancestor only appears in the 1841 census and was deceased before 1851, this means you should be extra careful when trying to find their baptism record as their age could be very different from that given in the census.

The 1841 census causes a few other issues. Only one occupation was supposed to be listed for each person. If they had two, their main source of income was listed with no mention of their second occupation. This can cause issues with identification where by the 1851 census, their previously unlisted second occupation may have become their only source of income. Relationships between those in the household are also not given. This is arguably the biggest drawback of the 1841 census. Just because a child is living with two adults does not mean that they are his parents. They could be his grandparents, an aunt or uncle or even a family friend looking after the child for the night. The extract below is from the 1841 census from Cheadle showing the few details supplied about my fifth great-grandparents.

Place	Names of Inhabitants	Age and Sex		Profession or Trade	Whether Born in Same County
		M	F		
Longdon Green	William Barlow	65		Ag Lab	Yes
	Martha Barlow		65		Yes

Where relationships are given in later censuses, be careful as labels have changed over time. For example, grandchildren were sometimes referred to as nieces and nephews, and men referred to as sons-in-law may actually be stepsons. This can make searching for family relationships quite complex.

Staffordshire Examples

It is important to view every census in which your ancestor features. For some of these forebears, you may find them in every available census from 1841 until 1921, depending on when they were born and when they died. One such example is John Goodfellow. In 1841, John is aged 1 and is living at Intakes Farm in Heaton. The census shows he was born within the county of Staffordshire. Relationships are not given in the 1841 census, but from this record we can assume he is living with his parents, John and Mary, and six siblings.

In the 1851 census, relationships are stated. John is 11 years old and living with his confirmed parents, John and Mary. John senior is recorded as a farmer of 70 acres at Intakes Farm in Heaton. John junior was born in Heaton and now has four siblings, with John being the youngest. His brother Nathan had left, to live with his wife in Leek, and his sister Mary had left to work as a servant in Bradnop. By 1861, we see a change in the family circumstances. John is now 21 and listed as the son of Mary, a widow. She is the head of the household and has taken over her late husband's farm in Heaton. While they still reside at Intakes Farm, it is now stated to be 75 acres. Also living with John and his mother are two of his siblings and one servant. For the first time, John has an occupation given as farmer's husbandman. The census again states he was born in Heaton.

The 1871 census sees a drastic change for John. He is now the head of the household, aged 31 and lives with his wife Maria and their baby daughter. It appears as though John has done very well for himself as he is recorded as being a farmer of 92 acres at Peck's House Farm in Rushton Spencer. They have three servants. John is again consistently recorded as having been born at Heaton.

1871 Census return for John Goodfellow and family. (With permission from The National Archives)

By 1881, John and his family have moved to Knypersley End Farm in Biddulph. He is aged 41 and lives with his wife and their four children. The farm is 108 acres and he now has four servants, showing this change in location was a good step up for John. John remained living at Knypersley End Farm in the 1891 census although the size of the farm is not given in any further census records. At this time, he remains living with his wife Maria and while their family has increased to five children, his number of servants has halved to two.

The 1901 census shows John and his family have relocated once again. They now reside at Woodhouse Farm in Biddulph. His wife Maria remains with him and they have four children still living at home along with three servants. John is aged 61. In 1911, John is 71 and, for the first time, listed as retired. He is seen living at 93 John Street in Biddulph with his wife Maria, two of his children and his son-in-law. He remains the head of the household. Lastly, we find 81-year-old John in the 1921 census still living at the same address. However, he is now a widower and no longer the head of the household. This title now goes to his son-in-law, Walter Milnes. Also in the house are John's daughter, granddaughter and son. He is still listed as a retired farmer and for the first time his birthplace is stated to be Rushton. This is the only census we see where the birthplace is incorrect. John died in October 1931, aged 91, meaning if the 1931 census had survived he would have also been present in this.

Chapter 3

PARISH REGISTERS

About the Record

Parish registers record the baptisms, marriages and burials within a parish. They are the records we refer to for these events prior to civil registration. It is usually easier to trace a family back through civil registration than it is once you reach parish registers. Parish register entries often contain very little information to help us prove identification of a particular person.

Parishes were instructed to keep registers from 1538, which sounds great for genealogists hoping to trace their family back to the sixteenth century. You will find, however, that very few parishes have a full set of registers kept from this time. Examples from Staffordshire that survive back this far include Alstonefield, Lapley and Mavesyn Ridware. The earliest registers were usually kept on loose sheets of paper. From 1597, the registers were required by law to be bound, which leads to a higher survival rate from this date.

The officials recording the information from 1597 were supposed to input the retrospective entries from 1538. You will often therefore find earlier entries in a bound format where they have been copied and the originals discarded. It is also usual to find the same handwriting over this period where it has been one person's responsibility to enter around sixty years of information. The majority of Staffordshire's parish registers begin in the sixteenth or seventeenth centuries. Exceptions include Quarnford which begins in 1744; Wednesfield which starts in 1751; and Stonnall which begins in 1823.

From 1597, Bishop's Transcripts began to be kept. These are transcribed records of parish registers and are especially useful where the original register has been lost. These transcriptions were ordered to be sent to the bishop within one month of Easter every year. In some cases, the

Bishop's Transcripts have been lost but the original register survives. Where both survive, it is worth seeking out both as sometimes the person who created the lists added extra details in one but not the other.

The information that was requested to be kept in the parish registers changed over time. To begin with, the information for each event tends to be very basic. This will usually just be the person's name and the date of the event. From 1753, a form was used for marriages requiring more information including their marital status, their parish of residence and two witnesses' signatures. From 1812, baptism and burial records were finally given a form to be completed for each event. Whatever year you search for, you may find more information where extra details have been added or perhaps less detail where the form has been filled out incorrectly.

One possible exception you may come across are the books sent to parishes to record births, baptisms and burials due to the Stamp Act of 1783. This was a very unpopular tax that some people tried to avoid by concealing births. As paupers were exempt from paying the tax, some sympathetic clergymen listed many of their parishioners as being a pauper so that they could avoid paying the fee of 3d. This duty lasted until 1793, so if your ancestor was born or died within these years you may find further information on them from the forms, including an ancestor's birth date in a baptism entry, and age at death for a burial record.

Locating the Record

Some counties have had few boundary changes and have one archive where all their parish registers are held. Unfortunately, Staffordshire has a much more complex history, meaning you may need to search various archives to find your ancestors, depending in which part of the county they lived. As you trace your Staffordshire tree branches back, you may find that they dip into other county boundaries that require using a different website or archive.

The majority of Staffordshire parish registers are held by the Staffordshire and Stoke-on-Trent Archive Service and are available to view on Findmypast with a subscription. This includes digitised images of the registers as well as a transcription of each entry. As always, view the original. You may also find an extra piece of information in the original register that has not been transcribed. Findmypast also has the collection 'Staffordshire, Dioceses of Lichfield & Coventry Marriage Allegations and Bonds, 1636–1893'.

Ancestry has transcriptions available of the same Staffordshire parish registers but no digitised images, so it is better to use Findmypast. As the transcriptions are different, you may like to search Ancestry for an event if you cannot find it on Findmypast. If Ancestry helps you to find the event, you can use this information to locate the image on Findmypast. FamilySearch also has the same transcriptions as Findmypast. When you find the correct event on FamilySearch, it directs you to the relevant image on Findmypast.

There are a number of registers held by other archives whose images are not available online. These are largely parishes in historical Staffordshire that have since changed county. Most of these registers are available as transcriptions on Findmypast and Ancestry. The parishes and the archives they are held at are detailed below.

Parish	Archive
Brierley Hill	Dudley Archives
Handsworth	Library of Birmingham
Harborne	Library of Birmingham
Himley	Dudley Archives
Kingswinford	Dudley Archives
Lower Gornal	Dudley Archives
Rowley Regis	Sandwell Archives
Sheriffhales	Shropshire Archives
Smethwick	Sandwell Archives
Upper Arley	The Hive, Worcester
West Bromwich, All Saints	Sandwell Archives

If you are having trouble finding a particular entry, you may wish to try searching on FreeREG (**freereg.org.uk**). This is a free transcription site, whose information you can then use to find the image on Findmypast. The number of transcriptions available for each parish varies and it is down to luck as to what the volunteers have chosen to transcribe.

The Midland Ancestors shop (**https://midland-ancestors.shop**) has transcriptions of many registers available to purchase. There are over 300 different products to choose from in their parish registers section, the majority of which are available to download for a small fee.

Values of the Record

At the very least, parish registers will give us the name of our ancestor and the date of the event in question. This can often be enough information to trace our family tree further. The more details the register provides, the more certain we can be that we are tracing the correct family in the correct parish.

Marriages are particularly useful to trace from 1753 onwards when Hardwicke's Marriage Act introduced a standardised form. From this date, you should find the bride and groom's names, their parish of residence, their marital status, their place of marriage, their date of marriage, whether they married by banns or by licence, the name of the minister who married them, the signatures or marks of the bride and groom and the names of at least two witnesses along with their signatures or marks. Their parish of residence can be used to search for earlier records, such as their baptism or apprenticeship records, although bear in mind they will not necessarily have lived there long.

This new Act aimed to reduce irregular marriages, and new regulations were introduced to do this. The marriage now had to take place by banns, read three times, or by licence, and the marriage had to take place in the parish of residence of either the bride or groom. Only Quakers and Jews were exempt from these new rules, meaning other Nonconformists had to marry in an Anglican church.

A new banns book was also introduced at the same time; some of these are available for Staffordshire at Findmypast. These give the name of the bride and groom, their parish of residence, the three dates their banns were read in church and the name of the minister who read them. You may find that your ancestor had one or two banns read with a partner who they did not end up marrying.

You can sometimes guess as to whether your ancestor was literate or not by whether they signed their name or made a cross. This is not always the case as sometimes an eager minister will fill the names in on the form first and then ask them to sign next to their name. On the other hand, some illiterate ancestors knew how to sign their name but nothing else. Witnesses' names can be useful to trace if they are related to the bride or groom.

George Rose's Act of 1812 introduced printed forms for baptisms and burials. The information given for baptisms included the date of the baptism, the child's forenames, the parents' first names, the family's surname, their residence, the father's occupation and the name of the officiating minister. In cases of illegitimate births, usually only the mother's name is given and if she had an occupation then this is given

When Baptized.	Child's Christian Name.	Parents Name.		Abode.	Quality, Trade, or Profession.	By whom the Ceremony was performed.
		Christian.	Surname.			
1815 May 28 No. 185.	Ann Daughter of	John Elizabeth	Brookes	Marsh Penkridge	Lab.r	Rich.d Slaney Minister

The 1815 baptism register entry for Ann Brookes of Penkridge. (Reproduced courtesy of Staffordshire Record Office)

in place of the father's occupation. The family's given residence will usually be the name of a parish but may give part of an address, such as a street name.

The new burial forms introduced from 1812 are not quite as helpful as the baptism forms but may, nevertheless, give crucial information. The information included the deceased's name, residence, their age, the date of burial and the name of the officiating minister. The details given about the residence are the same as for the baptism forms and the age is often an estimate.

As well as tracking down the baptism and burial details of your direct ancestors, it is advisable to also trace the events of their siblings. This can help you to trace the family's changing residence or a father's changing occupation. It can also give an insight into how many of their children died as infants or children. Likewise, if your ancestors disappear from the registers of their normal parish and you are struggling to track them down, it may be useful to trace their siblings' marriages. Your ancestor may appear as a witness which can give you an idea as to where to search next.

Every event record may provide extra information than was asked for. Prior to 1812, it is not uncommon to find the age of the deceased, particularly if they were very old or very young. At the least, it was often recorded if the deceased was an infant. Noteworthy causes of death were sometimes written in the margins, such as if there was an outbreak of a contagious disease or the cause of death was unusual. My fourth great-uncle William Brindley died in 1837 at the age of 15, a few months before civil registration was introduced. His burial entry states he died

William Brindley No. 158.	Cauldon Grange in Waterfall	March 18th	1¾ 15	R.d Ward
Ann Collis No. 159.	Pitchings in Waterfall	June 27th	7¾ 45	R.d Ward
Francis Phillips No. 160.	Cauldon Low in the Parish of alton	July 19th	M.s 4	R.d Ward

The 1837 burial register entry for William Brindley of Cauldon. (Reproduced courtesy of Staffordshire Record Office)

at Cauldon Grange in Waterfall and that his parents resided at Cauldon. At the bottom of the page, his cause of death is given as hanging and it is noted that jurors could not decide whether the act was intentional.

Another common additional detail you may discover is a date of birth given alongside their baptism date, or their age at baptism if they were an older child or an adult. There are also times where the churchwarden or minister has provided additional details about his parishioners in the front or back of the register. It is worth browsing for any extra information here, as well as at the top and bottom of the pages where your ancestor features.

Limitations of the Record

The trouble with parish registers is the lack of information they provide us with, compared with civil registration. It can be hard to prove we are tracing the right person. If there are two couples called Martin and Joanna Brown within 5 miles of each other who marry within the same year of each other, it is hard to discover the right baptisms for their children. One couple may live in Tittensor and the other may live in nearby Barlaston but if they both married in Stone how can you prove you are tracing the right people?

The answer is to use as many different records as possible and extract as much information from them as you can. For example, the two Martins may have different occupations that you can trace in apprenticeship records with their sons following in their footsteps. One of the families may feature in a settlement examination. The more research you do, the better. Never guess that a family belongs to you without proof.

Very few registers go back to 1538. The further back you go in time, the easier it is to make mistakes. This is because you may be tracing your family in a specific parish but the registers for this parish may be lost beyond a certain date. For example, you may be looking for a baptism entry for Francis Wright born around 1730 in Quarnford. An online search may bring up one result within a ten-year time frame in Staffordshire but it is at Acton Trussell, over 40 miles away. Someone may assume that this must mean this is their ancestor as it is the only successful match that fits. What is more likely is that Francis was born in or around Quarnford but the records have been lost. The registers for Acton Trussell survive back to 1571, whereas Quarnford's earliest entry only dates from 1744. It is therefore important to discover which parish registers have survived for your relevant parish and from which date.

You may find that your ancestors moved around the county. Some of my ancestors moved between Lichfield and Longdon, a 4-mile trip. Others moved from Cheadle to Colwich, an 18-mile journey. Others may move out of the county before moving back into it again. The hardest families to trace are travelling families, such as those that work on the canals. One of my canal-working ancestors, John Blundell, baptised his children in four different counties, including one in Wales, as they moved around. Remain open minded as to where your family may have moved and think about why they may have done so.

During the Period of Commonwealth (1641–1660), many parish registers were not completed, which can explain why many people have gaps in their family trees for this time. After the Restoration of 1660, many families chose to retrospectively baptise their children. Be aware that those being baptised in 1660 and 1661, in particular, may be older than you may expect, if they were not infants when baptised.

As discussed, a number of parish registers have been lost, especially prior to 1600. There is unlikely to be another record of the event where the Bishop's Transcripts have also been lost, except in rare cases. Even where parish registers survive they may be damaged or illegible. As with all records, there is also the possibility that the record has been transcribed incorrectly and will not appear with an online search. It is also fairly common to come across entries that have been missed by the person transcribing – sometimes even whole pages. If you are struggling to find the baptism of an ancestor in the parish you would expect to find them in, try browsing the pages of the baptism entries online. Do this carefully, entry by entry, in case your ancestor is one of the unlucky ones who missed being transcribed.

You must always be wary of the information given in parish registers. Where an age at death is given, take this with a pinch of salt when searching for their baptism. Ages of deceased children are usually more accurate. Don't forget to search for spelling variants also. My Staffordshire-based Horobin family change into the Howrobins and are sometimes transcribed as Morobin.

Staffordshire Examples

My fifth great-grandfather John Brindley was baptised in Cauldon on 16 April 1797, the eldest son of William and Martha. Despite most parishes no longer using the bound forms sent by the government due to the 1783 Stamp Act, the churchwardens of Cauldon had continued to fill these out for each event past the required date. This means that I am able to see that John was born on 25 March 1797.

John married Anne Farnell in Cheadle on 27 December 1817. Looking at the parish register entry for the event, it shows this was the first marriage for both of them and they are both recorded as residing in Cheadle. They married by banns, with John signing his name and Anne leaving her mark. Their witnesses were Mary Brindley and William Chawner.

The 1817 marriage register entry for John Brindley and Anne Farnell of Cheadle. (Reproduced courtesy of Staffordshire Record Office).

The baptism register for Cheadle shows their first child, Mary, was baptised in Cheadle and the family are recorded as residing at Cheadle Mill. They then disappear from the Cheadle registers but reappear in the registers for Cauldon where they spent the rest of their marriage. They had nine further children, all baptised in Cauldon. John's wife, Anne, died in Cauldon and was buried there in 1869.

After his wife's death, John moved in with his son James and his family in Derbyshire. His death certificate shows he died of bronchitis in Grin, Derbyshire on 6 May 1878. The parish registers show that John was buried two days later in Cauldon. This shows if you wish to find an ancestor's place of burial it is always worth trying to trace their burial register entry, rather than assuming they were buried in the parish (or even county) where they died.

Chapter 4

PARISH RECORDS

About the Record

By using census returns, civil registration records and parish registers you can usually confidently build the start of a good family tree. What these records don't tell us much about is who our ancestors really were as people. What were their characters like? Were they hard workers and responsible parents? Did they ever get into trouble? This is where we need to branch out and look at other records.

Parish records were documents created by parish officials and include bastardy records, workhouse registers and settlement examinations. Not only can these records help us to learn more about ancestors who we already have on our tree, they can also help us to break down brick walls and take our family further back in time. They often name the poor of the community, which can fill in gaps where they will not have been named in local tax lists.

From the late 1600s, parishes began to establish workhouses. These initially aimed to reduce the cost to ratepayers of providing poor relief, by creating work for the paupers of the parish. Over time, workhouses were increasingly used as a type of care for the sick and elderly who were unable to work. Surviving workhouse records include admission and discharge registers, vaccination lists, and birth and death registers. It is probable that you will find an ancestor who entered the workhouse at some point in their lives.

Early workhouses were found all over the county, with the largest capacity facilities at Cheadle, Walsall, West Bromwich, Stoke-on-Trent and Tamworth. These had enough space for 80–150 people. Smaller workhouses could be seen in parishes such as Pattingham and Cheslyn Hay, which had spaces for ten and twelve people respectively. After the Poor Law Amendment Act of 1834, parishes were rearranged into unions, resulting in the emergence of union workhouses. In Staffordshire, these were seen at Alstonefield, Burton upon Trent, Cannock, Cheadle, Leek, Lichfield, Newcastle-under-Lyme, Penkridge, Seisdon, Stafford, Stoke-on-Trent, Stone, Tamworth, Uttoxeter, Walsall, West Bromwich, Wolverhampton, and Wolstanton and Burslem.

Parishes also tried to reduce the cost of paying poor relief through apprenticeships. From 1601, overseers could arrange for pauper children be apprenticed. This could be done against the child's and his or her parents' wishes. The apprentice's master was obligated to provide the child with housing and food in return for work, which may have been located in a different parish to the one the child was previously living in. An apprenticeship was usually arranged to last for seven years and an indenture was created as proof of the agreement, which is what often survives today. It is common to find that an apprenticeship was not completed. This was sometimes the fault of the apprentice who refused to work or was deemed to be incompetent but was usually the fault of the master. Due to the vulnerable position the apprentices found themselves in, they were often abused, underfed and overworked by their master. Some cases found their way to the Quarter Sessions.

Lists of names of people in the parish receiving poor relief were kept by overseers in account books. This may be a one-off payment or a regular contribution. You may find your ancestor was donated items such as clothes or fuel rather than given money. Other parish officials who kept account books included waywardens who surveyed the highways of the parish and sometimes named those who provided repairs to the roads. Churchwardens similarly held their own accounts of repairs carried out in the church and the names of who provided the labour. Other items in churchwardens' accounts may include the payment owed to bell-ringers and rat catchers. The latter were often local children.

Parish constables kept their own account books of petty criminals who were caught in the parish, perhaps being locked in the stocks. Constables also had the right to remove certain people from the parish if it was believed that they did not belong there, such as vagrants. Any serious crime was referred to a court, such as the Quarter Sessions or Assizes. The general running of the parish was by the vestry. The vestry was a group of parishioners, usually some of the elders of the parish, who held regular meetings within the church. They wrote minutes, although the detail these go into varies from parish to parish.

Parishes were responsible for raising their own poor relief from residents. In order to try and establish some order regarding the poor relief system, the Poor Relief Act of 1662 stated that a person must have

> Stafford Shire
>
> To wit We whose hands & Seals are hereunto Subscribed & Sett y[e] Church-wardens & Overseers of y[e] Poor of Willenall in y[e] Parish of W.hampton in y[e] County of Stafford aforesaid do hereby own & acknowledge David Price Locksmith — Mary his Wife and four Children (that is to say) David Aged 12 years & Rich.d Aged 10 years & John Aged 3 years & Mary Aged 4 years, to be our Inhabitants Legally Settled in Willenall in y[e] Parish of W.hampton aforesaid in witness whereof we have hereunto Set our hands and Seals this Eleventh Day of June y[e] Fifteenth year of y[e] Reign of our Sovereign Lord George y[e] Second by y[e] Grace of God of Great Britain France & Ireland King Defender of y[e] faith and in y[e] year of our Lord 1741 Ro[bert] Burkett
>
> Attested by
> Ed.d Marston
> John Turner
>
> William his o mark Pery

The Price family settlement certificate dating 1741. (Reproduced courtesy of Staffordshire Record Office)

legal right of settlement within a specific parish to be able to qualify for the receipt of poor relief from them. In some cases, this is clear-cut, such as if a person was born and raised there or if a person completed their apprenticeship in the parish. From 1697, settlement certificates were issued to individuals or families as proof of settlement. This meant the family could move outside of their parish of settlement but they would need to return there if they required the receipt of poor relief.

Other settlement cases were less obvious. If a person or family requested poor relief from the parish but officials doubted their right to settlement there, Justices of the Peace could conduct an investigation. These enquiries were known as settlement examinations and they provide us with some of the most useful documentation for our pauper ancestors. The examination would probe into the person's life history including where and when they were born, if and where they were apprenticed, where and when they married, where they have worked, and where and when their children were born. Names of family members are given, usually their spouse and children but others may also be named. The Justices of the Peace then had to use this information to decide where the person's legal right of settlement was and had the power to send them back to that parish. This was then the only place that they could claim poor relief.

You may discover that your ancestor was forcibly removed from the parish if the Justices of the Peace decided that they had no legal right of settlement there. This created another piece of genealogical evidence known as a removal order. These give the names of the people that were removed, the parish they were removed from and the parish they were moved to.

Parish records also contain records of bastardy. If you have found an illegitimate ancestor in a baptism register where only the mother is named, then you may be lucky in finding out more through these records. Illegitimate children were more likely to become chargeable to the parish due to a lack of father to support the family. This meant that parish officials were keen to find out who the baby's father was so that he could pay for its care. Officials undertook bastardy examinations where the mother was requested to name her child's father. The sex of the child is given and in rare cases its name is also supplied. Witnesses sometimes gave statements regarding the couple's relationship. A bastardy bond was then issued, where the reputed father had to swear to contribute to the costs of raising the child. If the named father refused to pay and there was enough evidence for officials to believe he was the father of the child, he could be imprisoned. If the father was not named or officials were uncertain due to a lack of evidence then another person will be named in the bond. This person would pay for the child's maintenance, often a maternal grandparent.

Locating the Record

The majority of parish records are held by county record offices. This will vary depending on the parish you are looking for. The Staffordshire Archives catalogue can be found at **www.archives.staffordshire.gov.uk** and this contains descriptions of the collections of Staffordshire History Centre, Stoke-on-Trent City Archives, Staffordshire County Museum and the William Salt Library.

If you are researching a parish that was in historical Staffordshire but is now in another county, you may find that a relevant record is held at a different archive. This can be confusing as some are still held at Staffordshire History Centre. A useful way to check is to search via TNA Discovery catalogue. This checks the holdings of all archives in the country and can tell you where a record is held. You may be surprised to find a record relating to your ancestor is held outside Staffordshire. This may be due to an apprenticeship outside the boundaries, for example. Examples of records found elsewhere include a 1792 removal order of John Turner and his wife Epiphany from Laughton to Rowley Regis, which is held at The Keep in East Sussex, and a 1795 settlement examination of James Standyard of Walsall, held at Devon Archives.

To find where Staffordshire workhouses records are held, check the excellent website www.workhouses.org.uk. This lists which records survive for each workhouse, the years they relate to, and where they can be found. It is a comprehensive website that can also give you the history of each workhouse.

Be aware when searching for your ancestor's parish records that not all catalogue entries supply a name. If you search for your ancestor's name, you may discover records such as a removal order or an apprenticeship indenture. However, names from larger records such as vestry minutes and the accounts of parish officials rarely name those included in the text. If you know your ancestor was resident in a specific parish at the time the accounts are dated, it is worth visiting the archive to peruse them page by page.

Values of the Record

Parish records can help us break down brick walls by providing us evidence of positive identification of our ancestors moving from one parish to another, such as in the case of settlement examinations or removal orders. Workhouse records and pauper apprenticeship records can also help us to explain how a person ended up residing in a different parish. Using these records, together with parish registers and tax lists, can give us enough proof to help us be confident that we are tracing the right person.

A bastardy record can also help us break down a brick wall by giving us the name of our ancestor's father. For more recent generations, this can sometimes be backed up with DNA evidence. The baptism register entry for an illegitimate child usually leaves the father's name blank, so a bastardy examination or bond may be the only surviving record with the father's name.

You can find out new information about families through parish records. Settlement examinations tend to name every member of their family and their age. It may also tell you where they were born, where the parents married and where they have lived previously. Pauper apprenticeship indentures usually give the name of the child's father and the child's birthplace. The record is also useful to people who are tracing the master, as it can tell you his name, trade and where he worked. You may find a date of birth or death provided in a workhouse register, sometimes along with a cause of death. The registers also gathered details such as a person's occupation, parish of settlement, marital status and religion. These can all point you to research your ancestor in further records, such as Nonconformist records and occupational records.

As well as breaking down brick walls, parish records can tell us what our forebears' days entailed. The account books of the parish officials are fantastic for reading about the daily happenings in the parish. You may find your ancestor was briefly held in the village stocks by the parish constable or that they were paid to catch rats in the church grounds. Even where our ancestors are not named in these accounts, they can give us a real taste of what their parish life was like. Many parish records were created at a pivotal time in our ancestors' lives, such as removal orders and bastardy records. Knowing that a person went through a difficult situation like this can give us a certain amount of empathy towards them and may explain some of their later actions.

Parish records can hint at how wealthy our ancestors were. You may find that they were frequently given fuel for warmth in overseer's account books or that their child was deemed a pauper and apprenticed in a parish elsewhere from apprenticeship records. Entering the workhouse was a last resort for people, showing evidence of true desperation. Alternatively, you may find that your ancestor contributed regularly to the parish poor rates in the overseer's accounts, telling you that they were wealthy enough to not be deemed poor.

The records are particularly insightful if your ancestor was a parish official. This gives you the opportunity to see the daily events that they faced in their role, as well as the chance to read their handwriting. You can read about decisions that they made and see how they dealt with difficult situations in the parish.

Limitations of the Record

Not all records for each parish survive. Where they survive, there is no guarantee that your ancestor will be named in any of them. It is always worth checking what records survive and reading them to see if there are any mentions of your family name; however, do so with an open mind. Be realistic that you might not find much at all. With this attitude, if you do find something of interest it will make it even more rewarding.

Since many parish records were single slips of paper, such as apprenticeship indentures and bastardy bonds, many have been lost over time. This may be through fire, water damage or deliberate destruction. Where they have survived, damage may have obscured key information.

The reliability of the information given in parish records may be questionable. In a bastardy examination, both the parish officials and the mother of the child were under pressure to provide a father's name. This inevitably led to the wrong man sometimes being named as the child's father. In a time before DNA testing, officials had to go by the word of the mother and the witnesses as proof. This is obviously not always going to be accurate but you may find there is little else to go on when breaking down a brick wall built by illegitimacy. If a man denied that the child was his, you may find evidence of a case being brought to Quarter Sessions. Settlement examinations may also be full of false information. If a person was keen to reside in a particular parish, they could make false claims regarding their previous places of residence, for example.

Full names are not always provided in the accounts of parish officials. These were men who knew the people in their parish well so they were happy to record people as 'Mr Woods' or 'Widow Jones' as they knew who they were referring to. In some cases, no names are given at all. For example, in a churchwarden's account it may simply state that a carpenter was paid £2 for repairing the church pews, or a constable's account may state that a 'poor man' was removed from the parish with no further details.

What is often not clear from parish records is the context behind an event. If you find that your ancestor was claiming indoor relief from a workhouse, you may assume that they have been poor for a long time. This may not be the case. We also do not know why certain people were poor. For many, it was because they were too physically ill to work; however, others were unwilling to work; some may have suddenly found themselves in need due to a house flood and others may have become mentally ill. They may also have recently lost their employment; perhaps their place of work was lost through fire. Certain trades' popularity declined over time meaning your ancestor may have found themselves between jobs while looking for a change in career resulting in temporary poverty. Find as much evidence as you can to see if you can discover what happened to your ancestor.

Staffordshire Examples

Removal orders are great records for discovering two parishes where your ancestor resided; the one that they are being removed from and the one that they are moving back to. The date of the order can help you to know which parishes to search for which date. They can also provide extra information regarding the names and ages of family members. One example of this is the Hodgkins family who were removed by the Overseers of Penkridge back to the parish of Cheslyn Hay, around 7 miles away. Named in the order are Charles Hodgkins, his wife, Mary, and their 14-year-old daughter, Susannah. The standard template is used for the order meaning no reason is given for their removal, other than that they are likely to become chargeable to Penkridge.

UPON the Complaint of the Church-wardens and Overseers of the Poor of the *Parish* —— of *Penkridge* aforesaid in the said *County* — of *Stafford* — unto us whose Names are hereunto set and Seals affixed, being two of his Majesty's Justices of the Peace in and for the said *County* — — of *Stafford* — and one of us of the Quorum, that *Charles Hodgkins Mary his wife and Susannah their daughter aged fourteen years* — — — — — — — — — — — — — — ha*ve* come to inhabit in the said *Parish* — — of *Penkridge* — — not having gained a legal Settlement there, nor produced any Certificate owning *them* — — — — to be settled elsewhere, and that the

The removal order of the Hodgkins family dated 1779. (Reproduced courtesy of Staffordshire Record Office)

It is most likely that Charles had either failed to find work in their new parish or had become unable to do the work he had moved to do. The removal order is dated 14 December 1779. This date can be used by family historians to look in the Cheslyn Hay parish records for the family after this date, as well as the Penkridge records prior to this date. As Cheslyn Hay is their agreed parish of settlement, they will have resided there prior to this date too. No period of time is given as to how long the family had been at Penkridge.

Bastardy bonds will vary in the amount of information they provide and how helpful they are to you. A 1760 bond naming Thomas Harvey of Cotton gives his occupation as a husbandman. The document states he is bound by fellow husbandman James Oulsnam to the amount of £100. The record tells us that Mary Davenport, a single woman of Ipstones, is pregnant with Thomas's child and that Thomas is required to contribute towards the child's upkeep. The document is two pages long and is

The 1760 bastardy bond naming Thomas Harvey of Cotton. (Reproduced courtesy of Staffordshire Record Office)

signed by Thomas. Parish registers show Mary had a son named Samuel in Ipstones a few months after the bond was signed, with no name of the father given in the baptism register.

Chapter 5

WILLS AND PROBATE

About the Record

Many people today talk about leaving a will and understand that this means putting in writing who you would like to inherit your money, belongings and property. In our ancestors' time, they spoke about having a 'will and testament'. Technically, a will referred to bequeathed realty (buildings and land) and the testament described how the personal property of the deceased was to be divided. You will find a will and testament together in the same document and, generally speaking, together they are often referred to as a will.

Not all your ancestors will have left a will. They may have lived to old age and already divided their money and goods among their descendants or they may have been too poor to justify paying somebody to write a will that left very little. It is always worth checking whether each ancestor left a will. Many of the least wealthy of the parish still took the time to have a will and testament drawn up. It was understandably important to many people to know that upon their death their wishes would have been granted.

Wills often give the names of a huge number of relatives and other details such as occupations, residences and marital status. Some are easy to track down online; others take longer to locate. It can also be tricky to know if you have found all the relevant documentation associated with the will. An inventory was often stored separately. These listed a person's belongings in great detail, such as 'one bedstead, three chests, wearing apparel'. You may also find letters of administration (known as admons) if a person died without leaving a will, known as intestate.

The Statute of Wills in 1540 stated that males aged over 14 and females aged over 12 could write a will. The age limit was raised to 21 for both genders in 1837 by the Wills Act. It is more common to find wills written by men as, until 1883, a woman's property legally became her husband's upon marriage. You will, however, find many spinsters and widows who created wills and these are often the most enlightening.

Some wills are a short paragraph, whereas others are several pages long. Some may simply state that they leave everything they own to their spouse. Others will list a huge number of relatives with specifics of belongings they own and details of their land. It can be fascinating to read about what clothing and jewellery they owned, what occupational tools they had and any heirlooms they wanted to pass down. It often isn't just relatives who are named. You may find the names of friends, neighbours and colleagues in their will.

When looking for your ancestors' wills, the important date to remember is 1858. The Court of Probate Act resulted in a huge change with regards to probate jurisdiction. This means that if you are searching for a will from 1858 onwards, there is a different process to follow than if you are looking prior to the Act.

Locating the Record Pre-1858

Tracing a person's will that went through probate prior to 1858 can be more difficult than searching after the date. Your ancestor's will could have been proved at one of many different ecclesiastical courts, largely dependent on where they owned property. For Staffordshire testators this could be the Archdeaconry of Stafford (Diocese of Lichfield), the Prerogative Court of Canterbury (PCC), or a peculiar court.

The first step to tracing your ancestor's pre-1858 will is to find out which year they died and where they owned realty. If your ancestor owned land in more than one area, which sat under two different jurisdictions, the will had to be proven in the higher court. The majority of Staffordshire parishes sat under the Diocese of Lichfield. These records are held at Staffordshire History Centre and have been digitised and made available by Findmypast in its 'Staffordshire, Dioceses of Lichfield and Coventry Wills and Probate 1521–1860' collection. Indexes are also available on Ancestry and FamilySearch.

If your ancestor owned land or property that lay within two different dioceses, then it would be proved by the PCC. This was the highest of the probate courts. PCC probate records are held at TNA but have been digitised and are viewable on Ancestry and The Genealogist. If your ancestor died abroad or held property abroad then their will would also have been proven at the PCC.

Compared with most other counties, Staffordshire has a large number of peculiars. These are outside the jurisdiction of the Archdeacon and

Bishop of the Diocese. Those who died within these peculiars or who had property within them could have their wills proven in the relevant peculiar court. A list of these is given below, along with where they are held and the historical Staffordshire parishes they encompass.

Dudley Archives

Peculiar Name	Parishes within the Peculiar boundary
Manor of Sedgley	Sedgley with Lower Gornal

Staffordshire History Centre

Peculiar Name	Parishes within the Peculiar boundary
Peculiar of the Dean of Lichfield	Adbaston, Brewood, Burntwood, Lichfield St Chad, Lichfield St Michael, Hammerwich, Mavesyn Ridware and Pipe Ridware
Peculiar of the Dean and Chapter of Lichfield	Cannock, Farewell, Harborne, Rugeley and Upper Arley
Prebend of Alrewas and Weeford	Alrewas, Bromley Regis, Edingale and Weeford
Manor of Burton upon Trent	Burton upon Trent
Prebend of Colwich	Colwich and Fradswell
Prebend of Eccleshall	Chorlton and Eccleshall
Manor of Gnosall	Gnosall
Prebend of Handsacre and Armitage	Armitage with Handsacre, Hints and Norton Canes
Prebend of Offley and Flixton	High Offley
Prebend of Longdon	Longdon
Royal Peculiar of Penkridge	Coppenhall, Dunston, Penkridge and Stretton
Royal Peculiar of Tettenhall	Codsall and Tettenhall
Prebend of Whittington and Baswich	Acton Trussell, Baswich and Whittington
Royal Peculiar of Wolverhampton (some are held at Wolverhampton City Archives)	Bilston, Bushbury, Hatherton, Pelsall, Shareshill, Wednesfield, Willenhall and Wolverhampton

Nearly all the wills proved at the above peculiars are available online in Findmypast's collection and will appear with a wills search. The wills for Sedgley with Lower Gornal can be found at Dudley Archives and searched for via its online catalogue.

Locating the Record Post-1858

In 1858, the Principal Probate Registry was established for wills created in England and Wales. When looking for a will from 1858 onwards, the easiest way is to use the National Probate Calendar at **https://probatesearch.service.gov.uk**. It is free to search. Type in the deceased's name and year of death. There are other details you can add if you wish to narrow the search down, such as month of death and year of probate. You can then browse the results page by page to see if your ancestor is listed.

If your ancestor has an entry, this will provide you with a short, typed summary including the deceased's date of death, their residence and to whom probate was granted. The value of the estate will be given and the place that probate was granted. If the person to whom probate was granted is also a relative this can prove useful as their residence is usually given too, often with their occupation.

Once you have found the summary, you can order a copy of the will. This is always recommended. Only the executor(s) will be named in the summary, whereas the will names all beneficiaries and details of specific bequests. When you click the summary book, a side panel will load where you can order the will for a fee. You will receive an email when it has been uploaded. You can then log in to your account and view your orders. These are only kept for a short period, so be sure to download and save them.

Values of the Record

A will can give you information about the deceased at the time it was written. This can include their place of residence, marital status, occupation and where they wished to be buried. The document can also tell you how wealthy they were, with financial bequests detailed and belongings described. You can find out which tools of their trade they are leaving to their children, what property they owned and its location, as well as any charitable bequests.

Usually, the most important value of wills is in the names of beneficiaries. A relationship is usually stated with this, such as 'I leave to my wife Sarah ...' or 'I leave to my eldest son Matthew ...'. Wills can educate us about the deceased's relationships, including children we were previously unaware of, stepchildren, second wives and siblings. We can often find out more about the beneficiaries, including their occupations, places of residence and the married names of females. In some cases, the deceased may name their ancestors. This happened in one of my forebears' wills where he named his grandfather and the property he had inherited from him and wished to pass on.

This is the last Will and Testament of me James Ingram of Hamstall Ridware in the county of Stafford Tailor and Victualler in manner following that is to say In the first place I direct that all my funeral expences and just debts be paid out of my personal estate I give to my Son William Ingram the sum of One shilling only as I have already sufficiently provided for him I give and devise All that my messuage or tenement with the outbuildings garden yard and appurtenances thereunto belonging situate at Hamstall Ridware aforesaid now in my own occupation and used as a public house and all other my real estates whatsoever unto my dear Wife Mary Ingram

The beginning of the will for James Ingram of Hamstall Ridware dated 1816. (Reproduced courtesy of Staffordshire Record Office)

We can also discover more about the type of relationship the deceased had with their beneficiaries. Sometimes a note is added such as 'I leave to my daughter Emily £500 as a gesture of appreciation for her care in the last few years.' Alternatively, if a person has been left a very small sum, such as 1s, this could be a sign of ill feeling between the pair. In this case, the legal advice was to leave a small amount, rather than nothing at all, so that the beneficiary could not claim the testator had forgotten to include him and contest the will.

Where children of the deceased are missing from the will, despite them still being alive at the time that the will was written, this does not necessarily mean there was bad blood between them. Married daughters may be omitted if they received a monetary figure upon their marriage from their parents. Eldest sons may also not be included if they had already taken over the family business upon their father's retirement.

Inventories were compulsory between 1530 and 1782 but not all have survived. Inventories list every item owned by the deceased including the livestock on their farm, the number of beds in their house and items of crockery. The inventory can actually be more useful than a will at telling us exactly how wealthy our deceased ancestor was, giving us a real picture of what their lives were like according to their material goods. Beside each listed item, the estimated value is given.

If your ancestor died intestate, letters of administration do not provide anywhere near as much detail. They should at least give you the deceased's name and the name of their executor. It is important to look for the admons as they could still provide you with a crucial piece of information for your genealogical research.

A type of inheritance tax known as Death Duty was owed on estates over a certain value from 1796–1903. Between these times, will summaries were sent to the Stamp Office. Indexes to Death Duty wills can be viewed online at Ancestry and Findmypast and can tell you the deceased's name, date of death and brief details from the will. The executor's name will also be provided along with the deceased's parish of residence.

If very few of your direct ancestors left a will, it is worth searching for more distant relatives to see if your ancestors are named as beneficiaries. It is not possible at present to search for wills by the names of beneficiaries. The best way to do this is to locate the search page for Findmypast's 'Staffordshire, Dioceses of Lichfield and Coventry Wills and Probate 1521–1860' collection and type in the surname of your ancestor. If this brings up a handful of results then these are fairly easy to scan through for any names of interest. If the surname is more common, try adding the parish name as a keyword. I have demolished several brick walls in my family tree by using this method. If the parish is particularly small, you can also opt to search by parish only rather than surname. Your ancestor could have been left a bequest by someone with a different surname, whether they were a relation or not. When using this method, first ensure there was nobody else with your ancestor's name in the same parish at the same time to avoid identification issues.

Limitations of the Record

The main limitation of probate documentation is that you will not find related documents for each of your ancestors. It can be difficult and sometimes surprising to find who left a will and who did not. As with many genealogical searches, you can lose a lot of time searching for a record that simply doesn't exist.

All wills left by your ancestors will be of some use. The will may tell you the deceased's place of residence, their occupation or the value of their estate and this is all useful information. You will find some wills aren't as useful as others. Sometimes, names of relations are not given, with instructions for bequests to be left to 'my children' or 'my spouse' which is not as helpful. You may also find the opposite and people may be named but no relationship to the deceased is given.

A testator was not required to name their relatives if they did not wish to bequeath something to them. This means if you are aware the deceased had three children called Peter, Simon and John but only Peter and Simon are named in the will, you can't know if John had died by the time the will was written or if he was left out of the will purposefully. There are many reasons why a spouse, child or other close relative

An extract of the will for James Ingram of Hamstall Ridware dated 1816. (Reproduced courtesy of Staffordshire Record Office)

may not be named, but unfortunately the reasons are not stated in the document. You may find other documentation which can explain the person's absence from the will, such as if the will was contested in court.

Some wills are very long and can take a long time to read through, especially if the handwriting is difficult to read. In these cases, it can be easy to miss a key piece of genealogical information. It is easy to accidentally miss a line of text when reading a long document. Take your time and make notes. Make an abstract of the information you find in the will as you come across it.

Generally speaking, the older the will the harder it can be to read. There are exceptions, but seventeenth-century and earlier wills generally take longer to decipher. Not only is the handwriting harder to read but the language used may be unfamiliar. Some words have fallen out of favour more recently, such as wearing apparel instead of clothes and bedstead instead of a bed frame, whereas others are more archaic. Wills tend to use the same phrases and the same rough format so look for these and use them to recognise the letters used elsewhere in the will to translate unknown words. Wills usually start with the date the will was written (sometimes given at the end) and the name, residence and occupation of the testator. The date may be given in the format of a regnal year, such as 'in the fifth year of the Reign of our Sovereign Lord George the Third' rather than simply '1765', but usually both are given.

If a search on Findmypast's probate database draws a blank this does not necessarily mean that a person did not leave a will. Your ancestor may have held property elsewhere or may have moved towards the end of their life, meaning their will could be held in a different archive outside of Staffordshire. Trace as much as you can about their later life to give yourself the best chance of tracking down a will, if it exists.

Staffordshire Examples

My fifth great-grandfather Thomas Marshall was a farmer in Longdon and not someone I would have expected to have made a will. The will gives his residence as Hill Top, Longdon and confirms his occupation. His wife, Sarah, is bequeathed his farm with all stock, implements and crops along with all of the furniture, household goods and money. The will then details how, after Sarah's decease, all the estate should be sold with the resulting proceeds to be split between his five children: Thomas, John, Francis, Charles and Elizabeth. Thomas's wife, Sarah, is named as an executrix with his eldest son Thomas an executor. The will was written on 3 July 1837 and proved in Lichfield on 25 April 1838. From his death certificate, we can see that Thomas died on 4 December 1837 which fits in with these dates.

As a post-1858 example, my third great-grandmother Rosanna Sarah Barlow (née Marshall) died in 1921. Viewing the National Probate Calendar online, the summary shows that Rosanna was a resident of Brook End, Longdon and confirms that she was a widow. Her date of death is given as 10 February 1921. Her probate was granted in Lichfield and her effects amounted to £51 10s. Her executor was Arthur Barlow, a

The 1722 inventory of John Fernyhough of Dilhorne. (Reproduced courtesy of Staffordshire Record Office)

farmer. No relationship is stated here; however, from my own research I know Arthur is one of her sons.

Upon ordering Rosanna's will I was able to uncover further details. She left her piano to her daughter Lily and her housekeeper's cupboard to her son Bertram. Her bedding was to be divided between her children Rosabella, Lily and Charles, with everything else requested to be equally divided between her seven children. This shows the whole will should always be purchased and read carefully to extract as much information as possible.

There is a surviving will and inventory for my ninth great-grandfather John Fernyhaugh of Dilhorne who died in 1722. The inventory lists his possessions and their estimated worth. His belongings included twenty-two sheep, eight lambs, four cows, one long table with four chairs and three spinning wheels. His will names his wife as Alice, his eldest son Thomas and other children John, Alice and Adam. Helpfully, his daughter Alice's married name of Brassington is given as she is my eighth great-grandmother and helps to prove that I am tracing the right line.

Chapter 6

NONCONFORMIST RECORDS

About the Record

People who do not belong to the Church of England are known as Nonconformists. It is common to find Nonconformists in our family tree and this may lead to difficulties in finding them in records created by the Church of England (C of E), such as baptism registers. Many Nonconformist registers are more detailed than those of the C of E, so having an ancestor who belonged to a different denomination can be a good thing and lead to new genealogical discoveries.

It is not essential to understand exactly what your ancestor believed, although it may be interesting. What will help you as a genealogist is knowing which records you can find for each denomination. Some examples of the more common types of Nonconformist that you may come across are Roman Catholics, Methodists, Baptists, Presbyterians, Quakers and Jews. The latter two, in particular, have their own specific records to research. As a result of the 1753 Marriage Act, between 1753 and 1837 marriages were only legally recognised if they were carried out in a C of E church. The exception to this rule were the Quakers and Jews whose marriages could be carried out within their own places of worship and be recognised by UK law. All other Nonconformists who married can be found in the regular marriage registers held in the parish church. Some chose to also marry within their own denomination, meaning evidence of two ceremonies may be found.

When you discover your ancestor in a Nonconformist record, take time to research where else they may be found in the records. Find out where your ancestor's nearest chapel of their chosen denomination was. People often had to travel through several parishes to attend a chapel of their choosing. You may find that your ancestor changed their denomination during their lifetime. Try to keep track of when these changes occurred and look into why this may have happened. An ancestor may have changed their denomination shortly prior to their marriage so that they were accepted by their spouse and in-laws. They may also have changed denomination if their local chapel closed. Look into name changes of the faith that your ancestor followed to make sure you are searching archive catalogues for the right material.

In 1676, Bishop Compton ordered a survey to record the number of Nonconformists in each parish. This is today known as the Compton census, although unfortunately it is far less detailed than the census we are familiar with today. People are rarely named and even the numbers of each different denomination are sometimes not differentiated between. Roman Catholics are usually numbered separately under the heading 'Papists' as the establishment was particularly keen to monitor how many Catholics there were and where they resided.

Roman Catholics were frequently persecuted and life was made very difficult for them to reside in England due to a series of legal restrictions. While England was a Catholic country until 1534, after this date Catholics were viewed with great suspicion for hundreds of years. Understanding some of the different Acts may help you to understand the records where your ancestor may be found. The 1559 Act of Uniformity meant a person could be fined for not attending their local Anglican church. You may therefore find evidence of them still attending their parish church, despite being Catholic. Catholic burial grounds were only permitted in England after the Burial Act of 1853, meaning you may find your Catholic ancestor within the C of E burial registers before this date. Such burial entries often noted that the deceased was a Catholic.

The 1689 Toleration Act allowed Nonconformists to meet for worship and the forced attendance at their parish church was reversed. The exception to this change was the exemption of Roman Catholics, who were still not allowed to meet for worship. They were purposefully made to feel uncomfortable to live within the country. The persecution continued to the point where many Catholic churches did not keep written records until after the Catholic Emancipation Act of 1829.

Another group that faced early persecution was the Quakers, otherwise known as the Society of Friends. This all changed after the 1689 Toleration Act. Nonconformists of other beliefs had to take an oath of allegiance to the king, but Quakers were exempt. They were also able to have their marriage ceremonies legally recognised. Quakers kept highly detailed records of a uniform standard and were known for their organisational skills. For example, Quaker marriage records often named everybody in attendance, rather than just two witnesses as in C of E records. This can

Crop of the 1723 Quakers marriage certificate for Samuel Toft of Leek and Lettice Key of Wolverhampton showing all of the wedding guests. (Reproduced courtesy of Staffordshire Record Office)

provide new leads into familial relationships. Quakers did not perform baptisms, but they were permitted to have their own burial grounds. Due to their belief in equality, all Quaker headstones are of a uniform size and appearance with only the deceased's initials and dates of birth and death given.

Most Nonconformist groups kept their own registers of baptism and marriage. In 1840, it was requested that these registers, as well as any burial registers, were surrendered to the Registrar General. The request was repeated in 1857. The demand was not met by all, particularly by Roman Catholics who remained suspicious of the motives behind the request. Since 1857, some Nonconformists have donated their registers to local archives; others have chosen to retain them.

An ecclesiastical census was taken on 30 March 1851, this time going into a bit more detail than the Compton census of 1676. Unfortunately, once again no names were recorded, but the record is helpful in locating Nonconformist chapels of different faiths. For each chapel, the number of people attending service that day was noted. You can, therefore, see the size of your ancestor's chosen denomination on that specific day. Bear in mind, as with any census, that this is a snapshot of one day in a lifetime. There may have been a contagious illness which kept much of the congregation away that day. Some ministers were also suspected of inflating their congregation size, making it seem more popular than it actually was.

There are many other Nonconformist records in existence. Local archives hold minutes of chapel meetings naming the congregation and the issues they faced. Some account books survive, detailing the incoming and outgoing payments of the chapel. You may discover that your ancestor attended a Nonconformist school. Their records are similar to other schools, so you may find attendance registers, account books and minutes of staff meetings. Faiths often had their own publications which can name congregation members or detail events that they may have attended. These include newspapers and journals such as the *English Presbyterian Messenger* and *The Wesleyan Methodist Magazine*.

As well as the similar records above, each faith had its own specific records, as well as differences in procedure. Baptists, for example, are baptised as adults rather than as infants, which is very important to bear in mind when searching for an ancestor's register entry. Quakers hold yearly, quarterly and monthly meetings across the country. Monthly meetings were of the local congregation and discussed personal matters naming Friends, whereas yearly meetings were held nationally and debated theological matters relating to their beliefs. Some of these meetings have been published and are available to view online for free. Within Jewish records, you may find evidence of circumcision dates and bar mitzvahs.

The Wesleyan Methodist Registry registered births and baptisms of children belonging to the faith in England and Wales between 1818 and 1838. There are also retrospective entries dating back to 1773. The Wesleyan Methodist Historic Roll of 1899–1909 names those who donated to their Millennium Fund to mark the centenary of John Wesley's death. Primitive Methodism is particularly notable to Staffordshire, with the founders Hugh Bourne and William Clowes coming from the county. The first chapel dedicated to Primitive Methodism was in Tunstall in 1811.

Locating the Record

Nonconformist records may be found online, in local archives, in national archives and retained in private chapels. Many have also been destroyed or accidentally lost. Performing an exhaustive search of related records is often very time consuming.

Copies of the published 1676 Compton census are held at the William Salt Library and Stoke-on-Trent City Archives. A microfilm copy is also held at the Staffordshire History Centre. The 1851 ecclesiastical census is held at TNA in Series HO 129. Also at TNA are the Nonconformist baptism, marriage and burial registers that were handed in as a result of the Non-Parochial Registers Act. These are held in Series RG 4–8, with many extracts available to view on Ancestry and Family Search.

Local archives hold a number of Nonconformist records. Search their catalogue or TNA's Discovery website to see what is held. If you are not sure which chapel your ancestor attended, remember that it may not necessarily have been within their parish so there is no use including the parish name in the search field. Examples held at Staffordshire History Centre include records of Tamworth Baptist Church and the Church book of Temple Street Independent Chapel in Wolverhampton. Stoke-on-Trent City Archives holds records of Trinity Presbyterian Church in Hanley and Wolstanton Wesleyan Methodist Chapel baptism register, among others. You may also find Staffordshire Nonconformist records outside the county. Examples of these include Staffordshire Quaker Quarterly Meetings being held at Birmingham Archives and Ettingshall Wesleyan Methodist day school correspondence files held at University of Manchester Library.

Nonconformist headstones are often similar to their Anglican equivalents with some giving a lot of information and others the bare minimum. As mentioned previously, Quaker headstones tend to give the deceased's initials and date of birth and death. Jewish headstones, however, are often very detailed and elaborate. You may find your Nonconformist ancestor buried in their local parish church or a graveyard belonging to their own faith, depending on the laws at the time of their decease and the burial ground local to them.

Records unique to each faith can be found in various repositories across the country. The fifty-volume Wesleyan Methodist Historic Roll can be consulted at the Methodist Central Hall, Westminster. John Ryland's Library at the University of Manchester holds a large collection of literature relating to Methodism, including biographies and journals. The British Newspaper Archive and Findmypast have digital copies of *The Methodist Times* from 1885 to 1902.

For those researching Roman Catholic ancestors, The National Archives holds returns of Papists from 1705, 1767 and 1780 (these were previously held by the Parliamentary Archives). The Catholic Record Society has also published many of its registers and Recusant Rolls. The British Newspaper Archives has digitised a number of related newspapers including *Nottingham and Midland Catholic News* for the years 1908 to 1934. Staffordshire comes under the Catholic Archdiocese of Birmingham with records held at the Birmingham Archdiocesan Archives. Its registers are digitised in Findmypast's collection 'England Roman Catholic Parish Registers'. They include over 150,000 baptisms, nearly 35,000 marriages and around 15,500 burials from Staffordshire's Catholic churches.

Synagogues usually hold their own records relating to Jewish ancestry. The British Newspaper Archive and Findmypast have digitised *The Jewish Chronicle* for the year 1896, *The Jewish Record* for the years 1868 to 1871 and *The Jewish World* for 1877 to 1907. A number of Jewish pedigrees are held at the Society of Genealogists, also in London. To view information about the Jewish Communities of Staffordshire, visit **www.jewishgen. org/jcr-uk/england_geographic.htm**. These include the congregations of Burton upon Trent and Stoke-on-Trent.

Quaker records are often found at the local meeting house, and The Library of the Society of Friends in London. The Quaker Family History Society (**https://newtrial.qfhs.co.uk**) can tell you about the history of the faith and has many resources, including a Quaker wills database. Records relating to Quakers can often be found within local archives, including Quaker marriage certificates and entries in Quarter Sessions records. The meeting minutes held by your ancestor's meeting house are likely to be the most relevant to your research.

Another relevant newspaper available via the British Newspaper Archive and Findmypast is *The Nonconformist* for the years 1841 to 1900; a paper described as 'representing the opinions of the Congregational and Free Churches'. *The Nonconformist Elector* is also available for 1847 and *Dissenter* for 1812.

Some records have been transcribed and published on Midland Ancestors (**https://midland-ancestors.shop**). These are available for download for a small fee. Examples include monumental inscriptions of some Nonconformist burial grounds such as Stoke-on-Trent's Wesley Methodist Chapel and Yoxall's Catholic Church. There are also transcribed Nonconformist registers available for purchase.

Values of the Record

The genealogical potential of Nonconformist baptism, marriage and burial records is the same as with Anglican registers. Some are rather vague, whereas others give fantastic detail. Many non-parochial baptism registers give the mother's maiden name, with some going as far as naming the child's grandparents. The father's occupation is also often supplied. A place of residence is frequently given, especially where a family travelled outside of their own parish to attend a chapel of a particular denomination. Whatever the event, check to see whether it was also registered in their local parish church register.

The Compton census can help you to see how many other people of your ancestor's faith live within their parish, particularly if they were Roman Catholic. The 1851 ecclesiastic census can do the same, as well as show you where the nearest chapel of their faith was. The Wesleyan Methodist Twentieth Century Fund includes the names, addresses and sometimes a death date of more than 1 million donors. Donations were sometimes made in memory of a deceased relative who is also named.

Publications and journals belonging to the faith can provide you with details of events your ancestor may have attended and sometimes find a mention of your ancestor. If there are any surviving minutes of religious meetings these can tell you (depending on the faith) what sermons were read, what hymns were sung and who was in attendance. Quaker monthly meetings can be especially insightful, naming the congregation. The matters raised may include upcoming nuptials, the punishment of someone within the faith who has broken their rules, and the deaths of members. You may also find evidence of a person being punished for 'Nonconformist activities' within Quarter Sessions records. These can help you to see how the wider society viewed people of your ancestor's faith at the time and hint at the level of persecution your ancestor faced.

Values of other records are similar to those featuring Anglican ancestors. Headstones, for example, can provide you with a previously unknown fact such as a date of birth. Newspapers can provide you with useful articles about your ancestors, with many Nonconformist papers having birth, marriage and death columns. You may find out about fundraising events that your ancestor participated in on behalf of the church, and there may be an obituary if they were a long-standing member of their congregation.

Understanding your ancestor's faith can assist you in making new discoveries. Baptist boys were often given their mother's maiden name as a middle name. This can help you to trace the parent's marriage in relevant registers and reassure you that you are tracing the right family.

Biblical names (such as Abraham and Jonah) were popular among Nonconformist groups. Catholics often frequently give their children the middle name Mary, including their sons, whereas Protestant and Jewish names are generally from the Old Testament.

Limitations of the Record

You are less likely to find your ancestors in Nonconformist records than Anglican records. This is partly because some records have been lost and partly because some documents are held privately. Many records were not made in the first place due to the fear of persecution or simply because they did not see the need to record the same information as the C of E was required to. Nonconformists were weary of there being written proof of their faith being anything other than Anglican due to religious tensions within the country. This is especially true for Roman Catholics. Methodists often kept no written record of their marriages and burials, which can result in a gap in your ancestor's life story.

Catholic registers are usually in Latin. If these have been uploaded to a subscription website, such as Findmypast, the transcription supplied is usually accurate but do check the record itself for any errors. The registers may be handwritten or in a pre-printed format. Either way, they tend to follow a similar format so are usually easy to decipher using online translation apps.

You may find retrospective entries in registers, particularly baptisms. These could be added decades after the actual event occurred and provide a birth and baptism date. As recollections may vary after time has passed, be wary that the dates may not be accurate. Many Nonconformist families chose to baptise their children all together at the same time. While a baptism date is usually given for this, the ages of the children are not often provided. We may assume the children's names are listed in order of age, but this is not always the case.

It was common for people to change denominations during their lifetime and keeping track of this is difficult. You may find useful records for your ancestor within Methodist archives but then they disappear. This may mean that they died or changed faiths. You may later find they had converted to a Baptist faith, Presbyterian or perhaps reverted back to the C of E. Your ancestor being a Nonconformist is a common reason for them going 'missing' from records. There may be little, if any, evidence from the records you have that your ancestor was a Nonconformist. The only surviving evidence of their change of residence or burial may be in a Nonconformist record that is not yet digitised and you are, therefore, unlikely to find it without a very thorough search.

Finding your ancestor in a Nonconformist record is not as useful as an Anglican record at proving their parish of residence. The majority of people can be found in their local parish church registers and we can therefore be confident that this was their place of residence at the time of the event. Nonconformist chapels, however, had a much larger catchment area and people were willing to travel a fair distance to get to their chosen chapel. If you find your ancestor in a particular chapel or meeting house's records, firstly check the records to see if their parish of residence is provided anywhere, such as in their children's baptism records. If not, keep an open mind as to how far they may have travelled and look elsewhere to prove their place of residence. Nonconformists are known to have travelled abroad to marry and study so you may even find them in registers outside the UK.

Staffordshire Examples

Viewing Ancestry's 'England & Wales, Non-Conformist and Non-Parochial Registers, 1567–1936' record set held at TNA reveals that many Nonconformist denominations provide similar information regarding the recording of important life events. William Mears was baptised on 25 April 1826 at the Wesleyan Methodist Mount Pleasant Chapel in Leek. His baptism record gives his date of birth as 23 April 1826 and his parent's names are given as Francis and Ann. Francis's occupation is a farmer and Ann's maiden name is Smith. The family reside at Swinesmoor in the parish of Alstonefield; a reminder that families often had to travel to reach the nearest Nonconformist chapel applicable to their beliefs. The baptism was performed by Minister Edward Chapman. This is a great deal more information than we usually find compared with a C of E baptism register entry from the same period.

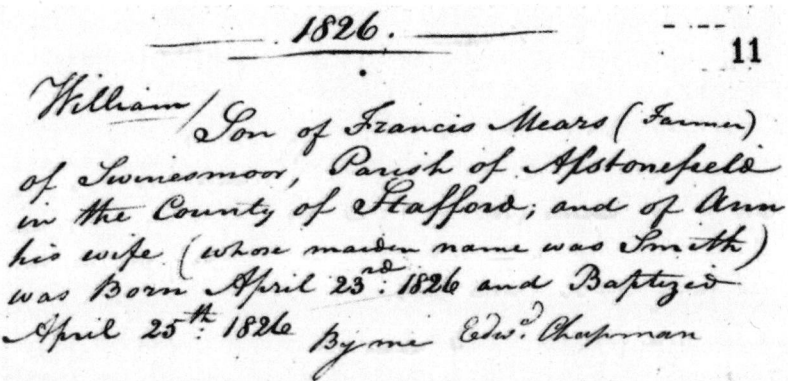

The Wesleyan baptism entry for William Mears of Alstonefield dated 1826. (With permission from The National Archives)

In Findmypast's 'England Roman Catholic Parish Burials' collection, we can see the burial record of Thomas Ashton. The original record is held at Birmingham Archdiocesan Archives. The pre-printed form is written in Latin but is easily decipherable. The register gives his age at death as 77 years old. Thomas's death date is stated as 28 January 1893, with his burial following two days later on 30 January at St Austin's Roman Catholic Church in Stafford.

Chapter 7

MILITARY RECORDS

About the Record

Researching our ancestors' military history has become increasingly popular. Unfortunately, it is not always the most straightforward topic to research. In many cases, no records have survived to tell us exactly where our ancestor fought, and in other cases, where there is plenty of documentation, it can be hard to know if you have uncovered every available source. Nearly everyone will come across a military ancestor in their tree. It may be they fought at sea during the Napoleonic Wars, signed up to the army to fight in the Boer War or were conscripted to join the Second World War.

A common misconception is that during the world wars our fighting ancestors joined the army regiment for their county. Many seek their ancestors in the records of the South Staffordshire Regiment and North Staffordshire Regiment and if they cannot be found there, assume they did not fight. The truth is they may be found in almost any regiment, including non-county-based regiments, such as the Royal Artillery and the Machine Gun Corps, or another county's regiment. My husband's grandfather Vernon O'Shea spent his life in Dorset but was enlisted into the Gordon Highlanders, based in Scotland.

You may find that your ancestor was a patient in a UK-based military hospital during the First World War. In Staffordshire, these were found at Lichfield, Stafford, Stoke-on-Trent, Walsall and Wolverhampton. Your ancestor may have been in a hospital outside of the county before being sent home to recuperate.

The current Mercian Regiment was founded in 2007 as an amalgamation of the Staffordshire Regiment, the Cheshire Regiment and the Worcestershire and Sherwood Foresters Regiment. This Staffordshire Regiment was itself formed in 1959 following a merging of the North and South Staffordshire Regiments, which had been formed in 1881. The history of the changing of regiment titles is complex but can be researched online, through books or by visiting regimental museums.

Your ancestors are likely to have been involved with the Staffordshire Militia. The militia's role was based in Britain, with duties including escorting the king and guarding prisoners of war. Men could be called upon at any time to help with national emergency or to assist the police and initially served for three years, rising to five years after 1786. During a war, the militia were on duty for a majority of the time and were usually sent outside of their home county. A succession of Militia Acts between 1757 and 1762 reorganised all counties' militia regiments using elements of conscription. Staffordshire was one of sixteen counties which did not raise its statutory militia during this time, finally raising its militia in 1773. Each parish was required to provide a set number of able-bodied men aged 18–45 for training.

As there were insufficient volunteers, a ballot system was used. Parish officials made lists of appropriately aged men, a number of whom were balloted for duty. If a man was selected in the ballot to train in the militia but did not wish to participate, he could find and pay a substitute to take his place. Some able-bodied men, including the clergy and teachers, were exempt. These men should still be found listed in the militia records, along with their reason for exemption, the majority of which were due to infirmities. Therefore, even if your ancestor was not balloted to serve in the militia, he should still have been included in the local listings. Conscription via the ballot system was suspended in 1829 due to its unpopularity with the public. Further lists of able-bodied men were taken in 1798 and 1803/4, namely the Posse Comitatus and Levée en Masse. These reserve forces were needed due to the ongoing unrest with France.

You may first learn of a forebear's military past through the discovery of records in your personal collection of paraphernalia. This may include medals, diaries, photographs, items of uniform and various written records. Try to gather as much information from these items before searching elsewhere. They may give you the person's service number, which can help with identifying them in other records – especially if they have a common name.

Military records use a large range of acronyms. Many of these are obsolete and cannot be translated using common sense alone; however, the use of a search engine usually tells you what the letters stand for. TNA has a useful guide for First World War corps acronyms available for free at **https://cdn.nationalarchives.gov.uk/documents/records/abbreviations-in-world-war-one-medal-index-cards-unit.pdf**. This shows some more obvious examples, such as 'S STAFF R' meaning South Staffordshire Regiment, as well as trickier ones such as 'RAPC' for Royal Army Pay Corps. Many other acronyms can be discovered on The Long, Long Trail website dedicated to the First World War at **www.longlongtrail.co.uk/soldiers/a-soldiers-life-1914-1918/common-british-army-acronyms-and-abbreviations-of-the-first-world-war/**. Commonly found examples include GSW for gunshot wounds and PoW for prisoner of war.

Locating the Record

The majority of surviving military records are held at TNA. If your ancestor was in the army prior to the outbreak of the First World War, records you may find include Soldiers' Service Records (1760–1913) held at WO 97, Description Books (1795–1900) and Casualty Lists (1797–1910) held at WO 25, Campaign Medal listings (1793–1949) at WO 100 and Officers' Service Records (1764–1913) at WO 25 and WO 76.

Army officers' records from the First World War were largely destroyed in the Second World War. Many First World War soldiers' records were also lost, meaning sadly there may be very little we can find out about our ancestor's time in service. Of interest to you may be the Medal Rolls in WO 100–102 and WO 390 and Records of Service held at WO 363, WO 364 and WO 400. War diaries for both the North and South Staffordshire Regiments are held at The Staffordshire Regiment Museum in Whittington. You can find various First World War casualty lists online, including on Ancestry, Findmypast and the Commonwealth

An extract from the First World War service record for William Henry Jay of Kinver. (With permission from The National Archives)

War Graves Commission (**cwgc.org**). Ancestry has surviving service records, medal rolls and pension records. They also have registers of soldiers' effects for those killed in action.

For army soldiers who fought after the First World War, only limited information is available. Second World War service records were historically held by the Ministry of Defence, but these are now being transferred to TNA. Some give great detail about where your ancestor was on which date, personal details and medical information. Others give little information. The Commonwealth War Graves Commission also covers the Second World War, and records about Second World War prisoners of war can be found on Ancestry and Findmypast.

You can request military records held by TNA via its website. For ancestors born prior to 1909, visit **https://discovery.nationalarchives.gov.uk/mod-open-foi-request-step1**. For those born between 1909 and 1939, fill in the form at **https://discovery.nationalarchives.gov.uk/mod-closed-foi-request-step1**. Where possible, it is best if you can give as much detail as possible and attach a death certificate to help the process. If you require military records for a person born after 1939 visit **www.gov.uk/get-copy-military-records-of-service**.

Staffordshire Regiment Museum holds over 10,000 items in its collection, including items of uniform and weaponry. The museum offers a research service of its collections to see if there is anything of relevance to your ancestor; although there are no guarantees, it is worth trying. You may also opt to carry out the research yourself using its facilities but this will need to be booked in advance.

There is a great deal of information about Royal Navy Officers available at TNA. Records include Half-Pay Registers (1693–1924) held at ADM 25 and PMG 15, Service Records (1756–1931) at ADM 196, Black Books naming officers guilty of misconduct who were not to be re-employed (1741–1815) at ADM 11–12 and Passing Certificates (1691–1902) at ADM 6, ADM 13 and ADM 106–7. A key source is the Navy List dating from 1782 to the present day available online at Ancestry and Findmypast. Navy Officers' careers can be found summarised in various publications including Marshall's *Royal Navy Biography* and Charnock's *Biographia Navalis*.

Royal Navy ratings' records at TNA include Pension Records (1737–1854) at ADM 6, Continuous Service Engagement Books (1853–1872) at ADM 139 and the Register of Seamen's Services (1873–1924) at ADM 188. Other TNA holdings which contain records about both navy officers and ratings include Medal Rolls (1793–1995) at ADM 171, Ships' Musters and Pay Books (1667–1878) at ADM 36–39 and ADM 41 and Certificates of Service (1802–1894) at ADM 29. You may find information about your navy ancestor online at the Battle of Trafalgar Database (1805) at **www.nationalarchives.gov.uk/trafalgarancestors** or the First World War Lives at Sea Database (1914–1918) at **https://royalnavyrecordsww1.rmg.org.uk**.

Ancestors who served with the Royal Flying Corps (which became the Royal Air Force in 1918) can be found in Service Records (1914–1919) at WO 363–264 and Officers' listings in the Air Force Lists (1914–1919) at AIR 76. They may also be found on the CWGC website and Casualty Lists on Ancestry and Findmypast. RAF Officer Service Records (1918–1919) can be viewed online at Ancestry.

Royal Marines' ancestors may have surviving Attestation Forms (1790–1925) at ADM 157, Description Books (1755–1940) at ADM 158 and Medal Rolls (1793–1972) in ADM 171. Service Records (1842–1925) for the Royal Marines can be found at ADM 196 for officers and ADM 159 for other ranks.

If your ancestors served with the Merchant Navy, they may be found in the Musters (1747–1860) and Crew Lists (1835–1860) at BT 98, Crew Lists (1860–1938) at BT 99, Register of Merchant Seamen's Services (1941–1972) at BT 382, Medal Rolls (1939–1945) at BT 395 and the Register of Masters (1845–1854) at BT 115. There are also records available online, including Register of Seamen's Tickets (1845–1854) and the Register of Seamen (1853–1856) both available on Findmypast. Masters' and Mates' Certificates (1850–1927) are held at the National Maritime Museum but can be viewed on Ancestry. There are many useful websites for tracing Merchant Navy ancestors including 1915 Crew Lists at **1915crewlists.rmg.co.uk** and the Crew List Index Project at **crewlist.org.uk**, the latter of which focuses on 1863–1913.

TNA also holds most of the surviving militia lists for Staffordshire at WO 13. These are not as detailed as many other counties' lists; sometimes a parish of residence is not even provided. Local archives hold a range of militia-related documentation. These include some of the surviving militia listings, such as the 1794 listing for Cheadle and the 1824 list

> NORTH STAFFORDSHIRE REGIMENT.—Blundred 16245 J. H. (Longton); Downing 48143 L.-Cpl. W. W. (Holborn, E.C.); Hewson 41182 W. (Derby); Horne 40374 R. (Bingley); Howle 200550 R. (Smallthorne); Kearsey 202638 F. (Battersea, S.W.); Neate 200851 L.-Cpl. E. (Kidsgrove); Sutton 202847 J. T. (Leek); Taylor 50793 G. A. (Biggleswade).

An extract from Weekly Casualty List dated 7 January 1919 showing the North Staffordshire Regiment's released prisoners of war. (Content provided by THE BRITISH LIBRARY BOARD. ALL RIGHTS RESERVED. With thanks to The British Newspaper Archive (www.britishnewspaperarchive.co.uk))

for Butterton held at Staffordshire History Centre, as well as militia certificates and correspondence. You may also find relevant surviving Tudor and Stuart Musters at TNA and local archives. These include a copy of the 1569 Yoxall muster roll at Staffordshire History Centre.

You will frequently find military-related articles in newspapers which can be viewed at both The British Newspaper Archive and Findmypast. These may include punishments for desertion, notices of casualties and notices for militia meetings. Some local papers printed photographs of soldiers who had recently died.

Values of the Record

We can learn about our ancestors' military service through these records, as well as finding out new personal details about them. For example, we may discover their marriage date or the name of a child we were previously unaware of, as well as brief descriptions of their features, such as hair colour, tattoos and scars. Researchers who take the time to learn about their ancestors' military history can therefore discover much more than their time in service.

Surviving service records can give us a summary of our forebears' time in the military, including what countries they fought in and how long for. These are generally not as detailed as many hope to find, but they are a good starting point to build upon. You can read where and when they enlisted, their previous occupation, their rank, regiment, discharge date and birth information. The name of their next of kin should be provided, usually a parent or spouse. Their marriage date and place may be given as well as the names and dates of birth of any children. You may also come across medical information within the same records. This may list treatment in military hospitals and dates of medical leave, as well as the condition. For First World War soldiers, you will commonly come across shell shock, gunshot wounds and typhus.

Service summaries for Royal Navy officers can be best discovered through the previously mentioned publications by Marshall and Charnock, as well as through passing certificates. Officers' and ratings' service summaries can also be seen in certificates of service, registers of seamen's services and continuous engagement books.

Casualty lists can tell us when and where our ancestor died during service. Some go into more detail than others. If the information is brief, try using a search engine to discover what battles happened in the country they were in on the day your ancestor died. Information given by websites such as CWGC can include the soldier's service number, age at death, name of his next of kin and place of burial or memorial.

The World War One Memorial in Cauldon church. (Author's own)

Pay lists and pension records can give us financial details about our ancestors, including their salary, pension rate and when they were awarded their pensions. For the Royal Navy, pay books can tell us the name of the ships they served on.

Medal rolls do not usually give much away other than the soldier's name, regiment, regimental number and the medals awarded. Many medals were automatically given to each soldier such as the 1914–15 Star, presented to military personnel who served between 5 August 1914 and 31 December 1915. Others, such as the Victoria Cross, were only given to a select number of recipients for extreme bravery in the face of the enemy. Since its introduction in 1856, the Victoria Cross has been awarded to those in the Staffordshire Regiments thirteen times. This includes Lieutenant George Albert Cairns VC who led his men in an attack on 12 March 1944 even after he lost his arm at the hands of a Japanese officer. His injuries sadly resulted in his death the following day.

War diaries hold information regarding where a unit was on which date. If we know that our ancestor was present, this can help us to understand more about what they encountered day to day. They do not often go into great detail; however, it is interesting to read about the unit's movements, how many soldiers were lost and any other notable points, such as mentions of a contagious disease.

Militia listings and musters can act as a census of the adult male population of a parish. Identification can be hard in the case of common names; however, there may be a clue as to who they were, such as an occupation or the inclusion of 'Jr' and 'Sr' (Junior and Senior), hinting at a father and son within the same parish. If our ancestor was exempt from duties, the reason should be given. This may tell you that your ancestor was missing fingers, suffered from blindness or walked with a limp.

With every new piece of information you gather from military sources, be sure to research this further elsewhere. For example, if you find they were present in a particular battle then research what happened there or if your ancestor was on board a specific ship then look up the details of the ship to discover what it looked like. If your ancestor's previous occupation is given, see if you can find out anything about this previous work or if they returned to it after they had finished in service.

Limitations of the Record

Military records are often seen as some of the more trustworthy sources; however, care still needs to be taken to double-check information where possible. My great-grandfather Ernest Taylor lied on his second attestation form saying he had not served previously. He changed certain details about himself, such as omitting his middle name, and lied about his place of birth to avoid being caught out. He was quickly discovered, however, and was taken to court charged with making false attestations. He had previously served with the Grenadier Guards at the age of 18 before being discharged as medically unfit with hysteria. He was discharged and was allowed to serve during the First World War. As with census records, a person's birthplace should only be used as a guide from military sources in case it is incorrect. The most common lie to find on an attestation form was regarding a person's age. Many older boys claimed to be adults as they wished to fight, so again take a person's age as a rough guide.

It can be frustrating to discover that very little has survived to tell us about our ancestor's military career. So many records, such as most First World War service records and some Merchant Navy muster rolls, have not survived. A huge majority of Staffordshire's militia lists were also destroyed. These records are irreplaceable. If you know that your ancestor served in the military, exhaust all possible sources of material. This includes reading war diaries and regimental histories to get a generalised view of what your ancestor may have been up to during service.

Even where we manage to find our ancestor in several military records, it can still be difficult to paint a picture of their time in service. The best sources by far are if the person left a diary or a recorded oral history. Relying on written records from the Ministry of Defence alone means we are left to make assumptions about their service. The places they served are recorded in service records simply as countries and do not detail their exact movements from town to town. Medical information can be fairly detailed but sometimes it may simply note that they suffered a gunshot wound. We may never know where on their body the wound was, whether it affected their mobility or exactly how the wound was received.

With some of the medical information, we need to be aware that the understanding of the psychological effects of warfare were less understood in times gone by. My great-grandfather Ernest Taylor suffered from shell shock and the details of his symptoms of mutism, temporary paralysis and hysterical emotion are not sympathetically recorded. They describe how he 'walked spastic' which was cured with 'encouragement' and his inability to talk was cured with 'vigorous persuasion'. Today, the treatments received for both mental and physical illnesses are often vastly different. The hardest medical records to read are of those who died from diseases that are now easily preventable or curable, whether with vaccinations or antibiotics for example. Ultimately, we need to remember the time that they were written in, and also have the breadth of mind to realise that in another hundred years, with medical advances having occurred, our descendants will probably be shocked at the current treatments for certain conditions.

Staffordshire Examples

The service record of Richard Jervis, available to view on Ancestry, begins with his attestation form. This tells us that Richard resided at 3 Grafton Street in Hanley, Staffordshire. At the time of enlistment, he was 24 years and 3 months old and his trade was a potter. He was unmarried and had not been in service previously. His regimental number was 19280 and he enlisted into the North Staffordshire Regiment. Richard measured at a very specific 5ft 3⅜in tall and his chest was 33½ inches round. He had a fresh complexion with brown eyes and brown hair. Richard's next of kin is his mother Emma Jervis, living at the same address in Hanley.

The exact details of Richard's service from the record are minimal, as they often are. He was stationed at Wallsend until 5 June 1916. The following day, he was sent to fight in France. While the date of his embarkation to France is given as 6 June 1916, the column requesting his date of departure from France is left blank. The following page explains why.

The next document in Richard's record of service is Army Form B.103, otherwise known as a 'Casualty Form-Active Service'. This confirms his previous personal details. It shows Richard joined the 1st Battalion in France on 18 June 1916 but was killed in action on 28 June 1917. The next document of note is a slip signed by James Jervis, acknowledging that he had received Richard's British War and Victory Medals on his behalf. This is dated 31 October 1921.

Army Form W.5080 provides us with a wealth of genealogical information. These were only filled out if the soldier died in action. There is a section for details of Richard's wife and children; however,

			Age	
Father of the Soldier ...		James Jervis		26 Jervis St Hanley
Mother of the Soldier ...		Emma Jervis		26 Jervis St Hanley
Brothers of the Soldier	Full Blood ...	Edward Jervis	20	26 Jervis St Hanley
	Half blood ...			
Sisters of the Soldier	Full blood ...	Eliza Jervis	32	26 Jervis St Hanley
		Florence Jervis	18	26 Jervis St Hanley

Extract of Form W.5080 of Richard Jervis of Hanley. (With permission from The National Archives)

this is left blank, showing he never married. His mother and father are named as James and Emma Jervis of 26 Jervis Street, Hanley. His siblings are named as 32-year-old Eliza, 20-year-old Edward and 18-year-old Florence all of whom are listed at the same address. The form was signed by Richard's mother, Emma, in 1919.

Using the information found in Richard's service record, we can conduct further searches for more records. Richard's 'dependant's pension' card can be seen on Ancestry. This confirms his date of death with the location given simply as 'France' with no further specifics. His mother, Emma, is listed as being his dependant and received his pension from 5 February 1918. She was entitled to receive this for the rest of her life.

Also on Ancestry is the Register of Soldiers' Effects. This confirms Richard's regiment, service number and date of death. His place of death is given only as 'in action'. His medal card can also be viewed, confirming the information we discovered previously. Richard's entry on the CWGC website adds that his name features on The Menin Gate memorial in Ypres, Belgium on Panel 55. A newspaper entry in *The Staffordshire Sentinel* on 11 August 1917 states Richard's memorial service would take place on 12 August 1917 at Hanley Parish Church at 6.30 p.m.

Chapter 8

CRIMINAL AND COURT RECORDS

About the Records

It is not uncommon to find you have ancestors who committed crimes. These are sometimes minor offences that today would not even be considered criminal acts. If your ancestor committed a crime, this may leave you feeling conflicted depending on the severity of the offence. The good news is that being charged with a crime left documentation that we can now use for genealogical purposes. You may also discover that your ancestors were victims of crime, called as witnesses to a court case or worked in crime prevention. In my own family tree, I have ancestors who were charged with either drunkenness, smuggling or poaching. All the offences have led me to new discoveries about them.

There are many different types of court where your ancestor may have appeared. If a person was accused of a moral sin, rather than any illegal activity, they may have been brought before the ecclesiastical courts run by the Church. This practice would be unthinkable today, with the accused being forced to stand in front of their parish congregation to state their sins and apologise or receive a fine for such crimes as premarital sex, adultery and defamation. Some local offences were heard by the manorial courts, discussed further in Chapter 14.

Minor offences were heard at Petty and Quarter Sessions, with more serious cases referred to Assizes. There is some overlap between the courts; for example, theft or assault could be heard at either. There was also some overlap between criminal courts and ecclesiastical courts, with drunkenness and bastardy heard at both. Petty Sessions were the lowest court in the judicial system and as well as dealing with crime, they also approved alcohol sale licences. No jury was involved, with the decision of whether the accused was guilty or not resting on the magistrate. Punishments dealt by Petty Sessions included fines and short-term imprisonment with hard labour.

Quarter Sessions were traditionally held at four set times each year, meaning your ancestor may have appeared due to an offence committed a few months prior. The cases heard here were typically more serious than those discussed at Petty Sessions. Offences included child cruelty, embezzlement and burglary. There were also many cases where people were found guilty of attempting suicide, previously viewed as a criminal offence. The usual punishment issued by Quarter Sessions was imprisonment with hard labour. The cases were presided over by two Justices of the Peace. Quarter Sessions also issued licences, such as for gamekeepers and alehouses.

Records that may survive include minute books giving brief outlines of each case and lists of attendance in court; bonds requesting a person attend the next session; order books listing verdicts and sentences for each case; and session rolls detailing recognizances, witness statements and jury lists. Calendars of Prisoners can provide additional information, including whether the accused was literate and their age. In Staffordshire, Quarter Sessions were held at Stafford. Hanley held Quarter Sessions from 1880.

Assize courts were organised in circuits and heard more serious criminal cases. Staffordshire was part of the Oxford Circuit, with the court session being held at Stafford. The records tend to be more detailed than those of the more minor courts. Cases were heard before a judge and jury, with the court meeting twice a year. Offences heard at Assize courts included treason, murder and forgery. Punishments included long-term imprisonment, transportation and the death penalty. By the 1800s, there were over 200 offences carrying the death penalty. You could be sentenced to death for sheep stealing, pickpocketing or shoplifting. The records can make for shocking reading, with children under the age of 16 liable for execution until the enforcement of the Children's Act of 1908. The Assize court records include witness statements (known as depositions) and court minute books which give a summary of each case. There are also surviving calendars of prisoners which were made prior to trial. This means they include the names of people who were found not guilty, as well as those who were charged. Petty Sessions, Quarter Sessions and Assizes continued until 1971, when they were replaced by the current court system.

Imprisonment used to be at local lock-ups. These could hold people awaiting sentencing at court, as well as vagrants and drunks. Many were released without charge, often leaving no record or just a small mention in a parish constable's account book. Larger gaols were seen in towns, including Lichfield and Stafford. The latter was referred to as the 'county gaol' and opened in 1793, with a women's prison added in 1852. Prisoners could be held here for longer sentence periods. The Prison Service, as we now know it, has only been run by the Home Office since 1877. The Home Office Register of Criminals gives the person's offence, whether or not they were found guilty and their sentence. The list is in date order according to when they were admitted.

Early offenders were sent to an Industrial School, such as the one at Werrington, or a reformatory ship as young teenagers, usually for three years or until the age of 16. Records of these tend not to survive well but if you find your ancestor was sent to a ship, you may be able to find out more via census returns, newspaper records or records held at TNA.

Until 1793, most executions in the county took place at Sandyford near Stafford, thereafter being carried out at Stafford Gaol. These were carried out in public until 1872. The majority of people sentenced to death had their sentence reduced to a lesser punishment, although in the eighteenth century death sentences were typically carried out quickly. For example, Mary Saunders of Cannock was sentenced to death on 24 March 1763 for murdering her illegitimate daughter. She was executed just four days later. It was rare for children to be hanged and there are few cases in Staffordshire. One example is 17-year-old Joseph Wilkes accused of murdering Matthew Adams in Wednesbury in 1842. The last hanging in Staffordshire was of Josiah Davies on 10 March 1914, who was convicted of murdering his landlady in Wolverhampton.

Locating the Record

Before heading to the archives, it is advisable to begin your search for criminal ancestors online. One method is to check newspaper records for evidence of your ancestor committing a crime or appearing in court as a victim or witness. By searching for your ancestor's name via the British Newspaper Archive (BNA) (**britishnewspaperarchive.co.uk**) or Findmypast's newspaper collection, you may receive relevant results. You may need to add an additional search term if they have a common name, such as their parish of residence. Minor crimes appeared regularly in local papers – so narrow your search to these – whereas serious crimes also made it to national newspapers. You may find several similar accounts of a crime or court case. It is worth checking them all to see which have any additional information. This is most likely to be found in the local papers.

To discover if your ancestor appeared at Quarter Sessions, you can check the Staffordshire Name Index (**staffsnameindexes.org.uk**), created by Staffordshire and Stoke-on-Trent Archive Service. Their online search for Quarter Sessions Indictments dating 1581–1733 gives names of defendants, names of complainants, the offence the defendant was accused of, the location and the year of the Session. In some cases, additional information is provided in the index, such as a convicted woman's husband's name and occupation. At the bottom of each transcription is the option to 'add to basket'. For a small fee, you can receive a copy of the document, which is advisable in case of errors and to gain additional information.

Also available from the Staffordshire Name Index is the Quarter Sessions Jurors Lists Index, 1811–1831. These can give you the person's name, occupation and parish. There is also an index to the Calendar of Prisoners at Staffordshire Quarter Sessions, 1779–1921. The index gives limited information including the prisoner's name, age, year of offence and the type of crime and where it was committed. If you believe from this information that you have found an ancestor, you can pay a small fee to access a longer transcript via a link at the bottom of the page. This additional transcript can give extra detail including the prisoner's occupation, literacy level and the jury's verdict.

Ancestry's 'England & Wales, Criminal Registers, 1791–1892' collection includes scans of Staffordshire registers from 1805–1892. There are also entries for Staffordshire in Ancestry's 'Licences of Parole for Female Convicts, 1853–1871, 1883–1887' collection. Staffordshire has over 9,000 entries in Findmypast's 'England & Wales, Crime, Prisons & Punishment, 1770–1935' collection. This collection comprises information from various sources including criminal petitions and the habitual criminals register. Some entries just give name and location, whereas others provide a wealth of detail. Findmypast's 'Prison Ship (Hulk) Registers' collection contains over 300 cases of prisoners convicted at Staffordshire between 1812 and 1842, although only transcriptions are available.

Assize records are held at TNA. Some of these records have been digitised and are available online. In Series HO 27 is the Home Office Register of Criminals which is available on Ancestry, Findmypast and The Genealogist. Records relating to transportation are also held at TNA, such as convicts transported to Australia 1781–1870 in HO 11, also available at Ancestry, Findmypast and The Genealogist. Also at TNA are Criminal Entry Books in SP44, correspondence regarding those who received the death penalty in PCOM 8–9 and Assize records after 1858 in the ASSI series.

Transcripts of Old Bailey proceedings can be read at the Old Bailey Trials website (**oldbaileyonline.org**) with many Staffordshire folk appearing. Blacksheep Ancestors (**blacksheepancestors.com**) provides links to free searches for your ancestor in court records, execution lists and biographies of infamous criminals. The Australian National Archives (**naa.gov.au**) has great information for researchers interested in transportation to the country.

Staffordshire History Centre holds records relating to Petty Sessions, Quarter Sessions, ecclesiastical courts and prison records. These relate to Stafford Prison, including prisoner photographs dating 1876–1899, visitor books and admission and discharge registers dating 1878–1911. Search the catalogue for a relevant term, such as 'Rugeley Petty Sessions' to view the results. Wolverhampton City Archives holds records relevant to the city, including Quarter Sessions record books dating 1864–1967 and appeal books dating 1864–1955.

Values of the Record

The amount of detail given in criminal records, and the value of this, varies from document to document and can depend on the severity of the offence, whether the crime was reported in the newspapers and if the person was a repeat offender. Some prison records and newspaper reports will include a photograph of the accused and many will give a description of their appearance. Ancestry's 'England & Wales, Criminal Registers, 1791–1892' collection generally gives the defendant's name, the date they were tried, their alleged offence and the sentence they received. For example, John Brewer was tried for larceny on 1 July 1885 in Stafford and received a punishment of two months' imprisonment. Ancestry's 'Licences of Parole for Female Convicts, 1853–1871, 1883–1887' collection gives the prisoner's name, their crime, the date of conviction, the court where they were convicted, their sentence and sometimes additional information including their birth year.

Findmypast's 'Prison Ship (Hulk) Registers' collection gives good detail, including the prisoner's name, age, marital status, occupation, literacy level, date and place of conviction, year of incarceration, their offence, the sentence they received, the hulk where they were imprisoned, details about their character and how they were discharged, such as transportation or death. One example is that of Richard Parr, a 13-year-old boy convicted at Stafford on 4 January 1842. He was sentenced to seven years for stealing pork and it is noted he associated with thieves. He is recorded as having a very bad character and was imprisoned on the *Euryalus* hulk at Chatham. The record states he was transported to Tasmania, then known as Van Dieman's Land, in 1843.

Convict transportation registers give the name of the prisoner, where and when they were convicted, the sentence they received, the name of the ship, the date it departed and the country they were transported to. Sometimes the prisoner's birth year or other details are also given.

In Findmypast's 'England & Wales, Crime, Prisons & Punishment, 1770–1935' collection are Calendars of Prisoners. These again give a wealth of detail including the prisoner's name, age, occupation, date of warrant, the date they were received into custody, their offence, the date they were tried, the jury's verdict, notes of previous convictions and the sentence they received. One example is that of 23-year-old serial offender Ethel Rose tried on 22 October 1897. Her offence this time was regarding intent to defraud two men in Walsall, to which she pleaded guilty at Stafford Assizes. She received no punishment. Ethel's previous convictions include thefts of clothing, a pony trap and a suitcase.

The information provided on the Old Bailey Trials website (**oldbaileyonline.org**) varies. In some cases, it may just be the person's name, the fact they are originally from Staffordshire and why they are there, such as the crime they committed, witnessed or were victim to. In other cases, they can provide very valuable details. One example is within an Ordinary's Account, dated 16 June 1693, regarding prisoners who were executed that day in Tyburn, Middlesex. One of the unlucky

Extract of Quarter Sessions conviction for John Darlastone, William Marshall and John Marshall of Longdon for unlawfully killing a deer in 1791. (Reproduced courtesy of Staffordshire Record Office)

prisoners was Joseph Stitch, a shoemaker born in Staffordshire who was convicted of housebreaking in Middlesex. A brief biography of his life describes how he moved to Ireland to serve in the war after people disapproved of his marriage.

Petty Sessions records can tell you the name of the offender, the name of the prosecutor or complainant, the offence they were accused of, in which parish they were committed, whether the defendant attended the hearing, the date of the proceedings, the magistrate's decision (such as convicted or discharged) and the name of the magistrate. Quarter Sessions give similar information.

You may come across crimes involving the family. These can include child neglect, abuse of a spouse and murder, among others. On 18 March 1812, Benjamin Mycock was hanged at Stafford Gaol for murdering his brother Joseph in Ilam. There are numerous cases of women murdering their newborn babies, who may have gone unregistered, and family feuds that got out of hand and ended up in criminal court. Sometimes witnesses called to a case will be family members, such as the accused's spouse or parent.

Criminal records can help explain a person's disappearance from a particular parish or from the records altogether. Someone may have been imprisoned, transported or executed, but also a family may have simply felt the need to move away after the shame of one of them being accused of a crime. When a man was incarcerated, his family were not usually given any financial support in his absence, meaning they are likely to turn up in the parish poor records, such as workhouse registers or receiving aid from the parish overseer.

If your ancestor's crime reached the press, you are likely to gain more information. The accused's, the victim's and witnesses' court statements are often quoted, offering a unique insight. Some of those accused may appear extremely remorseful; others may come across as unrepentant. Information in newspaper articles may also include the location of the crime, the parish of residence of the accused, victim and witnesses and further details about the crime and the events leading up to it.

Uncovering as much information about an ancestor's crime as possible will help you paint a picture of what their life was like at the time. You may have found their spouse supported them throughout a trial, or perhaps friends turned their backs on them as witnesses? A person may claim they committed crimes such as theft or forgery due to living in poverty. If a person was imprisoned for a long period of time this may also explain a gap in the births of their children. Census records usually recorded prisoners by their initials only, making them much harder to find.

Limitations of the Record

Many criminal records are vague and it may be hard to be certain you have correctly identified your ancestor in a record. Some will give just a name and their place of residence. If you are searching for a John Smith of Stafford then this will make it more difficult! Uncover as much information about the incident as possible; a newspaper record that gives a street address or occupation can help you to positively identify your forebear.

When researching a crime, try to approach it sensibly and with caution. It can be difficult to separate fact from fiction. Witnesses gave false statements; victims and the accused lied; and newspapers sensationalised details. If your ancestor protested his innocence and he or she was found guilty, this does not necessarily mean that they carried out the crime in question. In many cases, guilt is difficult to prove even today with the latest modern technology so this was certainly harder in our ancestor's day before CCTV and mobile phone tracking.

If your ancestor was a prolific criminal then they are more likely to have used an alias to evade authorities. Some people used several different names and moved around the country to escape justice. If they were caught, then criminal registers often give a list of their known aliases, which can be used to try to trace their past convictions. Many were unemployed, meaning we cannot use a given occupation to help identify them, and they may also have lied about their marital status or parish of residence.

It can be difficult to gain much context from criminal records about why our ancestor may have committed a crime. Newspapers and verbatim records can sometimes make this clear. For example, the accused may state they committed theft due to poverty; however, for most cases, the reasoning can never be discovered. It can be difficult to learn much about an ancestor's character if they committed just one crime in their lifetime, perhaps a one-off bad judgment where they were punished and learnt their lesson and moved on with their lives.

We must be aware when reading about criminals in the past that there was previously a huge gap in understanding how mental health impacted on our actions. There are a large number of cases where people are clearly in a vulnerable state due to a personal situation, such as being recently bereaved or having just given birth, who are found guilty of a crime and punished severely. Today there is much more understanding about how our mental health can impact on our decision making.

As with most genealogical records, many criminal records have been lost or damaged. These particularly include records such as reformatory ships' documentation, parish constable's accounts and Petty Sessions records. Some were purposefully destroyed, such as some Assize records. Where they do survive, some can be hard to read and understand – largely due to the legal jargon used – and some are in Latin, such as Quarter Sessions order books from the seventeenth century.

If you cannot find a criminal record for an ancestor, this usually means that they abided by the law. Of course, we can never rule out that they actually did commit a crime but escaped justice for it.

Staffordshire Examples

There are thousands of Staffordshire folk in the Calendars of Prisoners held by TNA in Series HO 140. One such example is Enoch Baggaley. In the 1879 register, he is described as a 35-year-old stoker. The register states that in January that year he was found guilty of stealing a pair of scales in Hanley. He pleaded guilty and was imprisoned for nine months with hard labour at Stafford. The supposed harsh punishment is most likely due to a catalogue of previous convictions listed in the register. These include two occasions of drunkenness, four incidents of theft and six occurrences of acting like a 'rogue'.

Enoch can be seen again the 1886 register, listed as a 42-year-old potter. His previous convictions are again noted, this time with additional convictions for vagrancy in Burslem in 1884 and for theft under which he used the alias 'George Turner' and received a sentence of twelve months' imprisonment. This time around, in 1886, Enoch was accused of stealing a shirt belonging to John Bloor at Longton at the end of the previous year. Enoch again pleaded guilty and received punishment of six months' imprisonment at Stafford with hard labour.

Using this register and the information it contains, we can find many records about Enoch's crimes. He features in the Habitual Criminals Register, under his alias, where additional details are given. His birthplace is given as Bilston and he is stated to be unmarried. He is

Name and aliases (Surname, Christian Names)	Date of Birth	Place of Birth	Married or Single	Trade or Occupation	Complexion	Hair	Eyes	Height (without shoes) ft. in.	Build	Shape of Face
Turner, Ellen	1853	Manchester	M	factory hnd	sl	br	gr	4 11	prop	oval
Turner, Ellen see Sutton, Amy										
Turner, George alias Baggaley, Enoch	1843	Bilston	S	labourer	fr	gr	gr	5 2¼	slendr	oval

Extract from the Habitual Criminals Register for Enoch Baggaley. (With permission from The National Archives)

described as having a fair complexion with green eyes and grey hair. He had a slender build and measured 5ft 2in tall. His face shape is given as oval and he had a birthmark on his back. His destination upon his discharge in 1881 is given as Longton, where we know he went on to commit further crimes.

Multiple entries for Enoch exist in further criminal registers, as well as in newspaper reports. The *Staffordshire Sentinel* on 25 May 1861 reports that Enoch pleaded guilty to fighting John Gaskill in Tunstall and was ordered to pay a fine of £1. The *Birmingham Daily Post* on 29 December 1885 gives rather amusing detail regarding the shirt theft of John Bloor, stating that Enoch was wearing the shirt at the time he was arrested. Caught red-handed, one might say!

Chapter 9

WORK AND BUSINESS RECORDS

About the Record

Our ancestors' occupations are often revealed to us through sources such as the census and parish records. Knowing what an occupation involved at the time they were doing it is certainly valuable. People spent huge portions of their lives working, as we still do today, and occupational records can help us to gain a true insight into their working lives, as well as provide us with new information.

There is likely to be an array of occupations in your family tree – potters, smiths, thatchers and millers for example. In more recent times, a larger range of occupations became available to us, our parents and grandparents. It is not possible to cover the location of every possible specific occupational record here, therefore, though it will be explained generically how to do so. You may find that you had an ancestor in the learned professions – the clergy, medicine and law. You should find an entry for them in a university alumni source, most likely from Oxford or Cambridge, but possibly also Dublin. All are also likely to feature in newspaper records.

Ancestors in the clergy should be searchable via **theclergydatabase.org.uk** and this is a great place to start. Results here usually give a brief biography and direct you to further sources to help research their career. Further sources include the *Clerical Guide* (1817), the *Clergy List* (from 1841) and the *Clerical Directory* (from 1858). You may find their ordination papers have survived in diocesan records, some of which contain genealogical records including baptism certificates. You can see their daily goings on via parish registers and parish records, such as vestry minutes. Ecclesiastical court records may also give you new information, such as if they were accused of a wrongdoing.

> Dickenson, Edward, s. Joseph, of St. Mary's, Stafford (city), cler. WORCESTER COLL., matric. 16 March 1769, aged 18; B.A. 1772, M.A. 1775, B.D. 1792, rector of Stafford.

Edward Dickenson's entry from Alumni Oxonienses.

Ancestors in the medical profession can be found in many records including the *Medical Directory* (1845), in the records of the Society of Apothecaries or in the Roll of College Physicians. If they worked in the forces, such as the Army Medical Department, you may find them listed in the Army List or Navy List.

The last of the learned professions was the legal route. If your forebear was a barrister they would have studied at university before continuing their training at the Inns of Court in London. If your ancestor was a solicitor, then attending university was not necessary as many were apprenticed. Legally trained men's details may be published in the Law List (from 1775) and Men at the Bar (Foster 1885).

The majority of our ancestors will not have worked in the learned professions so finding out about their occupation and training may not be as straightforward. From 1563, all apprentices entering a trade needed a written contract, known as an apprenticeship indenture. This was an agreement between the apprentice and their master (or more rarely, a mistress) who would teach them their craft. Two copies of the same document were created so each party could keep one as evidence of the agreement. Indentures are recognisable by the wavy line at the top or bottom of the document where they were cut in half. If there was a dispute, each party would need to provide the indenture to ensure that the wavy lines met in the middle so that a document could not be faked. The indenture was proof of legal settlement for the apprentice.

Apprenticeships normally lasted for seven years. The apprentice was usually aged between 14 and 21, although this may vary. The master was often a relative or friend known to the family; commonly a father would apprentice his son. A person may be apprenticed to a master previously unknown to them and outside of their parish, so keep an open mind as to an apprentice's movements across the county. When you discover the name of your ancestor's master, check to see which other apprentices they had before and after your forebear as they may also have been relatives.

If your ancestor owned a business, they may appear in a local trade directory. For a fee, they could enter brief details as a form of advertisement. Directories are usually subcategorised by parish with the surnames of tradesmen and women listed alphabetically by surname. Others are grouped by business type, such as wheelwrights and butchers. Examples of trade directories are *Kelly's Directories* and *Pigot & Co*. You may also find your business-owning ancestor in newspapers, perhaps in the form of an advertisement or perhaps accused of wrongdoing in the workplace.

Your Staffordshire ancestor may have worked on the canals or railways that run through the county. Both involved a wide range of jobs. I have ancestors who worked as lock keepers, as well as train drivers and railway carpenters. Canals and railways both required large amounts of maintenance and management and it is common to find an occupation based around these.

Depending on when and where your ancestor worked, you may discover a whole catalogue of related records or there may be nothing. Occupational records include staff registers of attendance, wage books, absence and disciplinary records, accident reports, training certificates and staff magazines. All can give different information including a person's wage, workplace injuries and their reason for leaving the job.

Once you know your ancestor's occupation, you can use this as an additional search term on subscription websites. Searching newspaper records for 'John Shaw' yields a lot of results, whereas searching for 'John Shaw, miller' narrows the field considerably. A person's occupation is not always noted in reports but it may help to find a specific article. If you know where your ancestor worked, you can use this as a search term instead of your ancestor's name. While this is unlikely to bring up records specific to your ancestor, it can tell you what it was like to work there and any notable events that occurred.

Some occupations carried a higher risk than others. If you discover your ancestor was a quarryman for example, you may find an article about a workplace accident in the papers from your ancestor's time there. Certain occupations also carried increased long-term health risks. These include women hired to carry out intricate stitching, who often suffered from headaches or lost their sight, and milliners (hat makers) who suffered from mercury poisoning. The latter condition was even termed 'mad hatter disease' due to the number of milliners who were afflicted.

As well as finding out what your ancestor's occupation involved day to day, research where they worked on a map. This can help you imagine their daily commute. You may also be able to find photographs or your ancestor's workplace, or even be able to visit it today.

Locating the Record

An increasing number of occupational records are being made available online. This includes records relating to how our ancestors trained for their job, such as through university. Alumni records from Oxford and Cambridge, known as *Alumni Oxonienses* and *Alumni Cantabrigienses*, are both available on Ancestry. The alumni records from Dublin, known as *Alumni Dublinenses*, are digitised on Findmypast. All are easily searchable. The original record should be viewed, since the majority of the information provided in the text has not been transcribed.

Masters had to pay a tax known as Stamp Duty, enforced between 1710 and 1811. The registers are held at TNA in Series IR 1. These have been digitised and are available to view on Ancestry. Transcriptions are available on Findmypast. The registers can tell you the name of the master and their apprentice, their parish and their trade.

Those researching ancestors from the three learned professions can find out a great deal online. These include the publications *Clerical Guide* and *Men at the Bar*, both freely available via Google Books. Medical Directories for 1845–1942 can be searched via Ancestry and *The Clergy List* (1896) can be viewed on Findmypast. You may find publications mentioning your professional ancestor by searching for their name on The Internet Archive (**https://archive.org**). This is a free search facility containing much historical documentation. The clergy, for example, sometimes created short publications discussing their views on religious and local matters. You may also find your lawyer or doctor ancestor named.

Newspapers are best viewed via The British Newspaper Archive whose collection is also available at Findmypast. Any occupation may be mentioned from any walk of life. There are articles about workplace accidents, business liquidation, crime within the workplace and advertisements. You may find articles about the closing of a workplace and any notable people that worked there. Sometimes there are even reports about royal visits.

A variety of trade directories are available on Ancestry, Findmypast and The Internet Archive. There is also a good collection on Leicester University's page **http://specialcollections.le.ac.uk**. For Staffordshire, these range from 1818 to 1914. Local archives also hold a good selection of relevant trade directories, some of which are not available online. The William Salt Library holds the largest collection for Staffordshire with others available at Wolverhampton City Archives.

Also online, you will find a good range of specific occupational records. Ancestry has collections relating to Electrical Engineers

1871–1930, Postal Service Appointment Books 1737–1969 and Railway Employment Records 1833–1956. Findmypast has records sets regarding Trade Union membership registers, a list of mining disaster victims, Teachers' Registration Council Registers 1914–1948 and the Dentists' Register dating 1887–1906. There is a wide range available so check their holdings online to see what is relevant to your research. You can narrow these results down to Staffordshire as there are many county specific collections that will not be applicable to your ancestors. Keep an open mind, however, in case they worked over the county border.

TEACHERS REGISTRATION COUNCIL
REPRESENTATIVE OF THE TEACHING PROFESSION
(Established by Act of Parliament and Constituted by Orders in Council).

E.

S

Register Entry concerning: JARVIS, ALICE MAUD.

Date of Registration: 1st August, 1931.   Register Number: **83263**

Professional Address: Polesworth Nethersoles Infants' School,
                        Polesworth, TAMWORTH, Staffs.

Attainments:

Board of Education Certificate.
Certificates in Elementary Drawing, Physical Education, Advanced Hygiene and Advanced Physiography.

Teachers Registration Council Registers entry for Alice Maud Jarvis of Tamworth. Register number 83263. (Published with the permission of the Society of Genealogists)

Many occupational records are retained in archives and are not available online. TNA has a broad range, including civil service and coastguard records. Local archives also hold occupational records. Stoke-on-Trent City Archives holds documents relating to Royal Doulton and Spode, among other pottery companies. Staffordshire History Centre holds records for companies including locomotive manufacturer Baguley-Drewry of Burton upon Trent, the National Coal Board and Lichfield craft guilds. Try searching archives online catalogues for your ancestor's work place to see if any records are held there. Some occupational records are still retained by the workplace if it is still in operation.

You may find details about your ancestor's occupation given in parish records, such as churchwardens' accounts, as well as any diaries or letters created locally. Churchwardens' accounts often named a person, their trade and the amount the church paid them to carry out a particular task. This may be a carpenter repairing church pews or a mason required for stonework.

There are many occupations that required a licence to practice and these sometimes survive within the archives, including Staffordshire History Centre and TNA. From 1617, a person needed a licence to be an innkeeper. An increase in pubs followed a relaxation in the laws in 1830. You can find details about licences in Quarter Sessions records and newspaper articles. Other innkeeper records survive, including a register of public house licences for Kingswinford and Wordsley for 1872–1958 held at Dudley Archives and Quarter Sessions records containing alehouses recognizances for the county dating from the mid-sixteenth century onwards held at Staffordshire History Centre. Licences were also required for midwives and gamekeepers.

To discover more about your ancestor's occupation, what it involved and what records survive, search online for any books on the subject. Pen & Sword has excellent titles, including *Tracing Your Coal Mining Ancestors*, *Tracing Your Textile Ancestors* and *Tracing Your Canal Ancestors*.

Values of the Record

Occupational records can tell you more about the working life of your ancestor as well as give you information about their personal lives. Finding out about our ancestors' working lives can help explain why they moved parishes or hint how they came to contract a disease. Comparing their weekly wage to others of the same time period can tell us how comfortable their standard of living would have been.

Your ancestor was more likely to have moved far from home if they were in the learned professions. It is common to find clergy in England who attended the University of Dublin. Professionals were often allocated roles where they were needed and would often end up somewhere they had never been before. It may be that your ancestor was born and trained in another county but settled to work in Staffordshire. Alternatively, it may be the case that your ancestor was born in Staffordshire, attended university and never returned to the county.

People in jobs that required less education can also be seen moving further afield. This is most commonly seen with people moving to London for better prospects. Many relocated for work, including moving abroad, only to return to their home county after a few years. If you cannot find your forebear in a particular census, consider that they may be found elsewhere.

Apprenticeship indentures can help prove an ancestor's change in parish. They are useful to people researching both the apprentice and the master. You can find out their trade, where the apprenticeship was carried out and what the agreed term was. Once you have found the name of your forebear's apprentice or master it may be worth spending some time researching them. There are examples of bequests being left in wills, an ongoing friendship between the two or alternatively a disagreement during the term leading to an appearance at Quarter Sessions. Further details may also be given in parish records. I have a settlement examination for my 80-year-old ancestor, Thomas Bugden, where he named his master, the dates he worked for him and described how the two changed parishes during his training. Only Thomas's name is transcribed in the catalogue meaning anyone researching his master's life would be unlikely to find this record.

Some occupations are described in great detail in books and research journals. These can be fascinating to discover further information about your ancestor's day at work, such as their working hours, what they wore and how popular their trade was in the period they were alive. Occupations such as agricultural labourers, railway workers and the learned professions all have a great deal written about them. You will be able to find out something about most occupations via a search in the newspapers.

You are more likely to find useful records if your ancestor worked for a company. If they were self-employed then any specific records have probably been destroyed. Company records can tell you an employee's start and finish date, their reason for leaving, their wage and how often they were paid, any disciplinary action taken against them and any injuries that occurred at work. You may also find registers giving their full name, address, date of birth and next of kin. Every company is different as to what information was requested and retained.

Trade directories are useful to find an address for your ancestor's business (which was often the same as their home address) and to find out dates when they worked there. You may find that a business was handed down through the generations of the same family, such as a shoemakers or wheelwrights. You can also see what competition they had within the same parish. Extra information is given for some occupations.

For every occupational record that you find, ensure you have extracted as much information from it as possible. When this is done, piece together your ancestor's working life to see what you can learn from this. They may have changed jobs several times and moved around the county. They may have remained in the same trade all their life, becoming a renowned expert within their town. An ancestor may have been clever enough to follow good opportunities and worked their way up the job ladder. Alternatively, they may have had bad luck following a job loss or period of ill health that lead to them living in poverty. Researching their working conditions and their likely wage is important. If you think about your own life and how your job has impacted on your happiness and your family's standard of living, you can start to appreciate how it was for your ancestors. Remember that they also had very little time off and worked long hours in conditions where an employee's health and safety was seldom considered.

Limitations of the Record

Researching occupational records can be time consuming. There are many different avenues to consider and it is not easy to know what records survive and where they are held. While an increasing number of occupational records are being digitised, the majority remain in the archives. It is well worth a visit if the archives' catalogue clearly shows a particular company's records are held there for the time period you are interested in. Many occupational records have been destroyed and some collections are held privately and are therefore inaccessible.

You may be disappointed to find that some occupational records provide very little detail. Some employee registers record their employees' names only with a first initial and surname. Most do not include middle names, which can make identification more difficult. Some records use a lettering or coding system whose meaning has now been lost.

Information may not always be as accurate as it seems. Trade directories, for example, are generally about a year out of date at the time of publication. This is particularly deceiving if your ancestor changed jobs, moved parishes or died in the time between supplying the information to the directory and it being published. When you find your ancestor in a trade directory, make a note of the date of its publication but also note down this is likely to refer to the previous year to avoid future confusion.

Apprenticeship indentures can also be misleading. Just because your ancestor was apprenticed to learn a trade does not mean that they finished their apprenticeship. Indentures were often broken. This may have been due to mistreatment of the apprentice, the death of the master or a lack of commitment from the apprentice. It may be possible to find out more in Quarter Sessions records or parish records. Even if your apprentice forebear completed their apprenticeship, it does not mean they went on to work in the trade.

There is much that we are unlikely to discover about our ancestors' working lives. If they left any first-hand evidence such as letters and diaries then this is the richest source of information. Otherwise, it is improbable that we will know whether an ancestor enjoyed their job, whether they were good at it or why they chose a particular career path. We can find out names of their colleagues but probably won't know who their friends at work were or how they were viewed by their contemporaries. Volunteer work also often goes unrecorded and may have been an important part of a forebear's life. If you are writing up your ancestor's life story be careful about making assumptions. Your ancestor may not have liked their work or been very good at it despite working in the same position for many years. They may not have relocated for a more secure job offer but for other personal reasons. Life was as complex for our ancestors as it is for us today so try to stick to the facts.

Staffordshire Examples

My ancestor Samson Barlow (1838–1919) frequently changed his job. During his life, his roles included a coachman, porter, post master, coal miner, cab proprietor and a groom. The majority of these do not leave many records behind. While he worked as a post master for Longdon, Samson appears in a selection of trade directories. These include the following extract from Kelly's Directory of 1900 which gives information as to when the mail arrived from Rugeley and when it was dispatched. A further directory entry on the same page tells us that Samson was also working as a fly proprietor as well as a post master. It was common for men to have two jobs.

Reverend John Horatio Cotterill was the son of Charles and Harriett Ann, born in Cannock in 1805. From viewing various records, we can put together a picture of John's life. Burial registers show John was buried in Oakamoor Church on 5 December 1833 aged 28. The previous four burial entries on the same page show John was the officiating minister prior to his death. There are several reports in newspapers on his death. The *Staffordshire Advertiser* of 7 December 1833 notes that John died on 30 November at the house of fellow Reverend C.S. Hassell. Affectionate wording is used: 'his parishioners have lost a zealous and faithful pastor.' The most enlightening article was published on 21 December 1833 in the *Staffordshire Advertiser*. Here a lengthy article describes how he suffered an epileptic fit three months prior to his death from which he never fully recovered. He spent the weeks prior to his death being

> Post & T. Express Delivery Office, Brook End. – Sampson Barlow, sub-postmaster. Letters arrive from Rugeley at 7.15 a.m. & 1.5 p.m. week days; Sundays 7.40 a.m. to callers only; dispatched at 7.30 p.m. week days; Sundays, 11 a.m. Postal orders are issued here, but not paid.

Samson Barlow's entry in Kelly's Directory, 1900.

cared for by Reverend Hassell. Despite his short period in the position, John was highly regarded by his parishioners and all who knew him. The article states he was 'simple and engaging in his manner' and that his funeral procession was attended by 'nearly the whole population of the district'. John was clearly very much missed. The article finishes by giving personal information about John's family including that his father was C. Cotterill Esquire of Cannock and his uncle was Reverend T. Cotterill of Sheffield. John died unmarried and in his will he bequeathed his belongings to his brothers and sister.

The Clergy Database tells us that John attended Cambridge University and was the minister of Cotton and Oakamoor. He was ordained in Norwich Cathedral on 18 October 1828, with his ordination record giving his date of birth as 2 September 1805. He worked as an assistant curate in Newcastle-under-Lyme from October 1829, prior to his appointment at Cotton and Oakamoor.

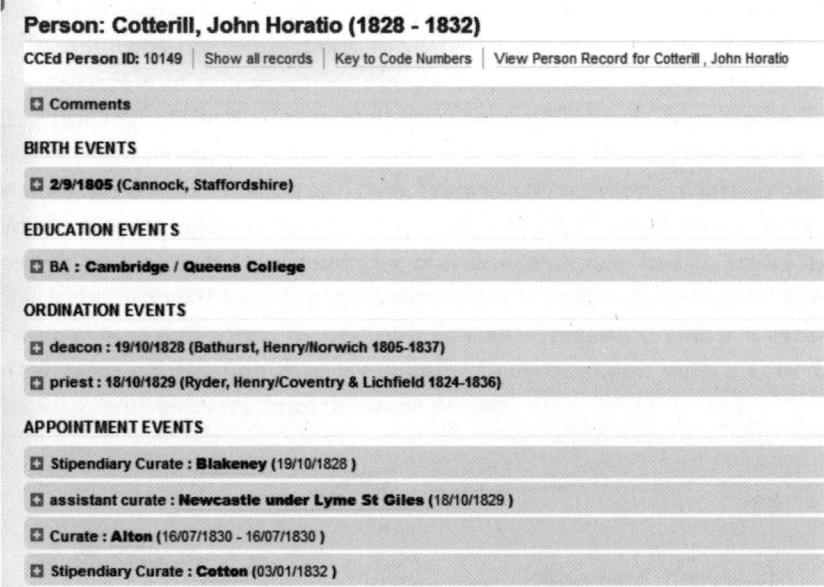

Screenshot of The Clergy Database showing John Horatio Cotterill's entry. (With permission from The Clergy of the Church of England Database Project)

Alumni Cantabrigienses shows John was admitted to Queens College at Cambridge on 15 March 1824, achieving his BA there in 1828. The personal details state he was Charles's second son. The record confirms John's birth and death years, his ordination information and his place of ministerial work.

Searching the newspapers for articles about John's time as a minister reveals why he was so highly praised within his parish. The *Wolverhampton Chronicle* on 22 August 1832 reveals that John had promoted the building of Oakamoor parish church and helped raise funds for the cause. The church's ceremony of consecration took place on 13 August 1832 with the bishop leading and John as the assisting minister. Further details about John's work and daily working life are provided in the parish registers and records for Cotton and Oakamoor.

Chapter 10

MAPS

About the Record

Maps can not only show the location of your ancestors' property but also tell us who their neighbours were, whether they lived close to other relatives and how close they lived to their workplace. The documents attached to maps can tell us the acreage of our forebears' land, the rent they paid and the estimated value of their home.

Gather as many maps as you can for the parish where your ancestors lived. When you have a collection, this can show you the changes that occurred within a parish during the time your ancestors lived there. This will likely involve an expansion of housing areas, the introduction of Nonconformist chapels and the loss of surrounding farmland. Your ancestors may have lived in the same house all their life but have seen many changes. Perhaps their house started out at the edge of a village before being gradually swallowed up by surrounding housing development? They may also have seen the implementation of the railways and canal systems, which would have drastically changed their surrounding environment. We can all think of our own examples of how our home village, town or city has changed since we have lived there. Our job is to put ourselves in our ancestors' shoes and think of how certain changes may have affected them.

The oldest map that you may find for your parish of interest is an estate map. While these are not applicable to all areas, when they are found they can be very enlightening. A landowner may decide to have a map drawn of their estate if they need evidence of the extent of their land, to help value their property or to assist with establishing rent payments from tenants. The reason the landowner wished to have the map drawn will affect the detail given. Some maps will show every property and outbuilding along with geographical features. Others will be more basic and less precise.

Tithe maps are often the first maps that family historians use as they are fairly easy to find. Tithes were a tax paid to the parish church, paid as one-tenth of the produce of a person's land. This could mean a person had to give the church a tenth of their eggs or timber, for example. As you can imagine, there was much confusion in establishing whether a person was paying a tenth of their produce or not and so the system was changed to a monetary tax instead. The Tithe Commutation Act of 1836 meant tithe maps were created so that the new monetary system could be established. Many parishes had already switched to a monetary system several years prior to the Act, but the maps formalised the matter and ensured people were being charged fairly. Alongside the maps, apportionments were created. Apportionments are required to make sense of the tithe map, providing the names of the landowners and occupiers.

When you are familiar with tithe maps, enclosure maps are a good source to follow up with. You will not necessarily find both for a particular parish. They are of a similar appearance, so where both survive they can be useful for comparison. The land in a parish used to be divided up into strips, giving a vastly different appearance to the rural landscape of today. These strips were eventually deemed not to be the most profitable way of using the land, with preference towards larger fields as we see

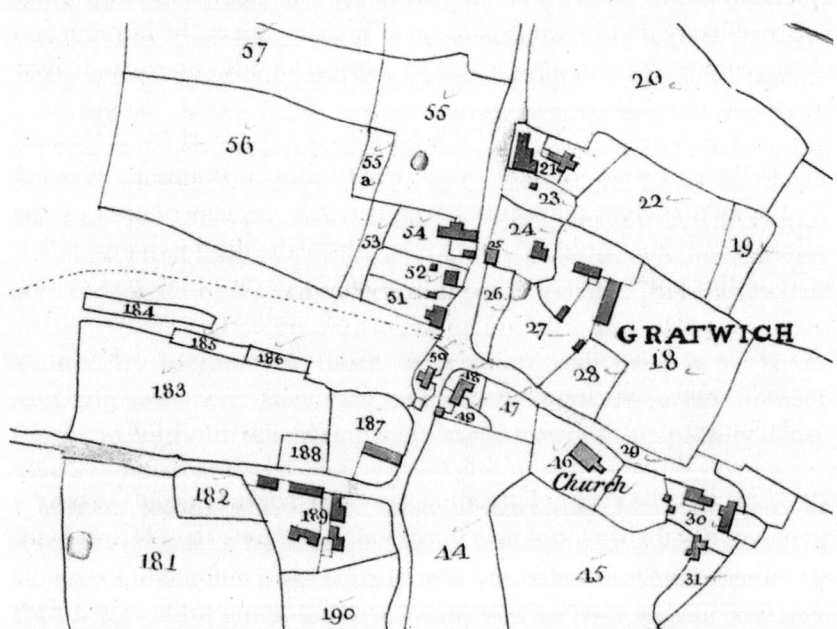

Tithe map of Gratwich dated 1843. (Reproduced courtesy of Staffordshire Record Office)

now. Parishes could opt to undergo 'enclosure' via an Act of Parliament to achieve this new field system, which was a complicated process. The system was simplified by the General Enclosure Act of 1801, meaning we see more enclosure records after this date. At the time of enclosure, a map was drawn to demonstrate who owned each plot of land and its extent. Each plot was given a reference number with details written into an 'award'. The later enclosure maps from the nineteenth century are usually very detailed, with footpaths, drains and some properties featured.

There are fantastic maps in archives that were created to show plans for a new service, such as a railway or a housing estate. These are usually very detailed and used by engineers and architects to carry out works within a parish. When we are viewing these maps, we must bear in mind why they were created. For example, a plan for a canal or railway is likely to only show detail for the land close to the building proposals and is unlikely to show the whole parish. They are great to demonstrate how our ancestors' landscape changed, especially where the work was close to their home. We can use public utility plans and fire insurance schedules in a similar manner. The latter showed the properties that were covered by their policy and give details about the building and the householder.

You are almost certain to be familiar with Ordnance Survey (OS) maps. It was only fairly recently that we used them on car journeys to help us navigate, in a time before we could access maps on satellite navigation systems. The OS is Britain's official map maker, meaning the company has high standards of accuracy, detail and consistency in presentation. The OS was first established in 1791, although its maps were not mass produced until 1914. Prior to this date you will still find maps for your parish of interest, but they were not created on a regular basis as they are today. The scale is always clearly marked on the map, along with points of interest such as schools and churches.

After the 1910 Finance Act, the Lloyd George Domesday records, otherwise referred to as Inland Revenue Valuations, were created between 1910 and 1915. This Act introduced a new tax on property sales, which resulted in every property being assessed and located on a map. Another record from the twentieth century is the National Farm Survey dating from the 1940s. Due to agricultural problems during the Second World War, the government decided each farm needed to be assessed according to its land use, size and utility provision. This is a fantastic resource for researchers whose parents or grandparents owned a farm during the war.

There are, of course, many other miscellaneous maps of Staffordshire that you may come across. These may include archaeological maps, valuation maps and those created by parish officials for various purposes. Never forget the importance also of a county map. It can be crucial to view a map to see the distance between two parishes. This can help us to see how far our ancestors travelled and can be especially useful to those researchers who are not familiar with the area. If you cannot find a baptism for your ancestor in the parish you would expect, try looking at the map to see the surrounding parishes to give you a lead as to where you could search next.

Locating the Record
The tithe records for Staffordshire are available online in two ways. You can view the maps online for free at Staffordshire Past Track website (**staffspasttrack.org.uk**). This site has an excellent feature for zooming in and the images are clear. You can opt to pay a fee to download the map if you want your own copy. To the right of the page under the 'Resource Links' heading is a hyperlink to the Staffordshire Name Index website (**staffsnameindexes.org.uk**). This site holds transcriptions of the relevant tithe apportionments. You can do a name search for your ancestor to see the relevant land or property number and use this to refer back to the map. Some people held several plots of land; others had none. You can also view tithe maps with a Diamond subscription to The Genealogist website. If there are a large number of maps you wish to purchase then this may be the cheaper option for you.

Also available to view for free on the Staffordshire Past Track website are enclosure maps for Staffordshire. Some maps have the names of landowners written on the document, such as the 1780 map of Ipstones. Most do not and use a reference number system like the tithe maps. Unfortunately, the attached documents have not yet been transcribed or digitised. This means for many records we cannot simply use the online resource to know where our ancestors owned land. If you cannot visit the archives to see the documents, you can ask the archives to research this for you. Once you have a reference number and the associated details for your ancestor's plot of land, you can then refer back to the free map online to see where in the parish they owned land.

A majority of other maps are held in local archives, including estate maps and service plans. Search the online catalogue for each archive, or by using TNA's Discovery page, using the term 'map' or 'plan' along with your parish of interest. Some parishes will have many maps, which are useful to compare, whereas others may only have one or two surviving. It is worth viewing any maps for the parish you are interested in as even the amateur-drawn maps with few details on may just hold a key piece of new information.

TNA holds further estate maps, the National Farm Survey and Lloyd George's Domesday records. The records of the National Farm Survey are held in Series MAF 32 while the maps are in MAF 73. These are currently being digitised due for completion in March 2027. The Lloyd George Domesday field books are held at IR 58, with plans in IR 121 and valuation books at IR 91. The field books tend to be the most useful. These records are being digitised by The Genealogist and are available to view with a subscription; however, at the time of writing, Staffordshire is not yet available. To order a specific record for a property from TNA, you will first need to order the relevant plan to discover the reference number for your ancestor's house. This is different from their house number. Once this has been noted from the plan, you can order the correct field book.

Ordnance Survey maps are held at Staffordshire History Centre, TNA and the British Library. You can view a large collection of maps online at the National Library of Scotland, which also covers England and Wales (**https://maps.nls.uk**). The Genealogist's Map Explorer is very useful for subscribers, with the ability to select from a range of maps for an area and overlay them to see the changes to a place easily. You can also purchase some old OS maps from the late nineteenth and early twentieth century at **https://midland-ancestors.shop/Staffordshire/Staffordshire-Maps**.

Values of the Record

Tithe maps clearly show the boundary of your ancestors' property and it is easy to use the reference number to then find out more about their plot in the attached apportionment book. This lists both the occupiers' names and the landowner's name so you can either see where they resided or what they owned. The size of the plot is given in the old measurement system of acres, roods, perches. A perch is equivalent to $30¼$ square yards, a rood equals 40 perches and 1 acre is 4 roods. The apportionments give a brief description of the land (such as garden or orchard) and the monetary tithe amount the occupier was expected to pay.

Enclosure maps are similar but are more useful to researchers with landowners in their family tree, rather than tenants. The extent of their plot and its situation in the parish will be clearly marked along with good geographical details. Where a tithe map does not exist for a parish, you may find that an enclosure map can fill in some gaps for you and vice versa.

Public utility maps and builders' plans can shed new light on how the landscape was altered. We can sympathise with an ancestor whose home once faced farmers' fields only to find it faced a factory in their later years. We can, alternatively, see improvements that were made around them, such as the introduction of a village shop or the expansion of a school. Some developments, such as railways, were seen as a fantastic source of work and means of travel by some but hated by some parishioners who loathed the destruction of local land. Be careful not to assume how your ancestor might have reacted to these changes.

OS maps are well known for their accuracy and so using these can be an insightful way to view changes to a parish as they are easy to interpret. You may find that some estate maps are more detailed, showing every property in an area with field names. Additional information can be gained from the Lloyd George Domesday field books which give the property owner and occupiers' names, the house address, the number of rooms, the property's estimated value and the amount of rent due.

Limitations of the Record

It is unlikely that every parish will have each different type of map. For example, many parishes, including Longdon and Rushall, have no enclosure map. All you can do is search to see what maps do exist for your parish and go from there. There will always be OS maps for your place of interest so these are a good starting point. Used on their own, however, they are slightly limited. There is no written documentation attached, meaning what you see on the map is all the information you can get from it. Not all properties are outlined clearly on OS maps and no house owners or occupiers' names are provided. They are best used in conjunction with other surviving maps to see the changes in the parish.

The quality and reliability of hand-drawn maps vary considerably. This includes tithe maps, enclosure maps and estate maps. Tithe maps are classified as either first or second class depending on their accuracy, with only approximately one-sixth judged to be precise enough to be first class. They are almost always neatly presented and easy to understand, however, with the standard of accuracy largely erring on the side of caution in case the maps were requested for legal reasons, such as boundary disputes.

The amount of detail you will find on each map can be unpredictable. Most enclosure maps are useful to view in some way, but there are many which have no properties drawn on them, and some estate maps and utility maps will only show a small section of a parish. Consider why the map was originally drawn before concluding your ancestor's house had not yet been built at the time the map was created. It may well have been there but deemed unnecessary for the map creator to include.

Maps and their associated documents will often name the property or landowner and its occupier; however, it is very rare to find anyone else from the household listed. It is sometimes easy to assume that because the main householder is present in a property that his spouse and children would be there too, but this is not always the case. As with a census return, maps are a snapshot of what was happening at that time. You may find a family in the Lloyd George survey and think they had lived there a while, whereas they may have only moved into the property the previous week. Somebody listed as an occupier may have become a property owner soon after the map was drawn. The information we gather from maps, as with most sources, are only true at the time they were made.

Staffordshire Examples

My fourth great-grandfather John Marshall (1803–1871) lived in Longdon his entire life, so it is not surprising to see him featured in the 1843 tithe map for the parish. The apportionment for John tells me that he was the occupier of property reference 778. The property is a house and garden owned by John Rushton, with the extent of the land listed as 17 perches. John was recorded as due to pay 4d in tithes. Looking at property 778 on the tithe map shows us that John was resident in the Brook End part of Longdon. We can see that the parish church was within easy walking distance of his property. As with all tithe apportionments, only John is listed with no other inhabitants named. Looking at the 1841 and 1851

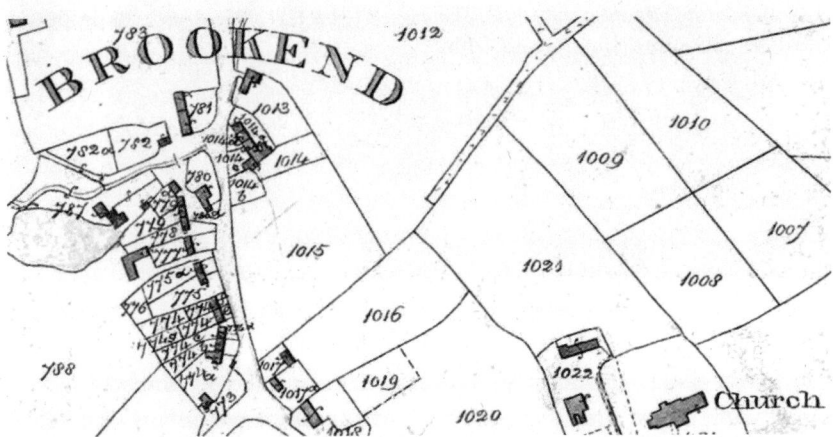

John Marshall's property on the 1843 tithe map of Longdon. (Reproduced courtesy of Staffordshire Record Office)

census returns shows that John was living at Brook End in both and working as a butcher. Both returns show his brother Charles living in the same street, working as a publican. The tithe map and apportionments show that Charles was actually living next door to his brother, in plot 779.

The 1782 enclosure map for Dilhorne is particularly interesting to view. This is a 1930s drawing by R. Thomas and is a hypothetical map created from the text of the award. No original enclosure map was made at the time. The landowners are usually named with their first initial and surname, as in the case of S. Harris and J. Hyatt. There are other examples, including Widow Heath and John Daniel, the vicar of Dilhorne. Also of note are M. Phillips and J. Phillips who own adjacent plots. Anyone interested in researching the Phillips family would therefore be wise to look into both people, in case they may be related. Dilhorne School and Blythe Marsh School are clearly marked and the roads are all named.

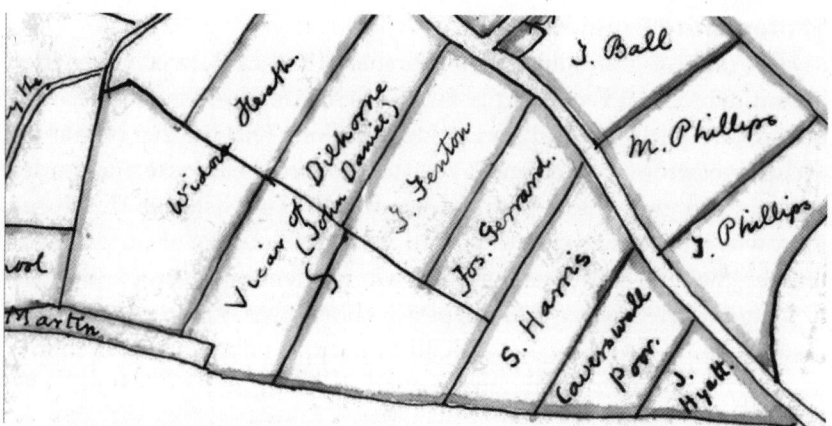

A 1930s map of Dilhorne drawn by R. Thomas using the text of the award. (Reproduced courtesy of Staffordshire Record Office)

Chapter 11

TAX LISTS AND OATH ROLLS

About the Record

Tax lists and oath rolls don't sound like exciting records to view, but you may be surprised what information you can find out by looking at them. You can pinpoint where an ancestor was living at a particular time, discover more about their standard of living or find other relatives living within the same parish. While not quite as enlightening as some other records, they are still necessary to view to gain a full picture of our forebears' lives. Their survival rate is generally low, but when they are found they can act as an early census substitute, giving us the names of householders in a parish.

The oldest tax lists you may come across are the lay subsidies, dating back to the thirteenth century. Each payment was decided depending upon a person's 'moveable goods', rather than property. These are more than likely to pre-date your genealogical research; however, they can be interesting to view local surnames and see where yours may have originated. Names were recorded until 1332, after which parish totals were given instead. This is of some interest to see how your parish of interest grew or declined over time.

Poll tax was first taken in 1377. This was a sporadic rather than regular tax, with the tax being taken subsequently in 1379, 1381, 1513, 1641, 1660, 1677, 1694 and 1698. Very few of the earlier lists survive, although there are good examples for some Staffordshire areas in the seventeenth century. The tax was seen as highly controversial as it taxed a wider range of the population, regardless of wealth or status, including servants and married women. This makes the record more useful to us as it features people who otherwise do not appear in other records.

In 1662, the hearth tax was introduced. The more hearths a person had, the more tax they had to pay. This tax was taken twice yearly at Lady

Day (25 March) and Michaelmas (29 September). Duplicate copies of the tax lists were sent to the Exchequer, although there are known errors and omissions within these copies. Property owners were required to inform parish officials of how many hearths and stoves they had. If the officials wished to query this, they had the right to enter the property to check the accuracy of the property owner's claims. As this was rather invasive and a confronting job for the parish officials, the hearth tax was eventually replaced by the window tax. Officials could check how many windows a property had without the need to enter the person's house. Window tax was payable by the occupier rather than the owner.

Land tax assessments are the most used tax lists by genealogists as they survive better than others. Introduced in 1692, the tax was based on a person's land valuation. The landowners are listed, with the occupiers being listed from 1772. Most surviving documents date from 1780 when the records were used to prove a person's right to vote, acting as an early type of electoral register. From 1788, landowners were able to choose to pay their land tax in a one-off payment that freed their property from paying the tax. Their names still appear in the annual land tax records, however. If you have Roman Catholic ancestors, you will find that they had to pay double the going rate between 1693 and 1831. They could appeal against the double payment from 1794 onwards, with these records held at TNA. The following shows a transcription for the 1798 land tax record for Streethay.

Names of Proprietors	Names of Occupiers	Sums Assessed			Date of Contract
		£	s	d	
Rd. Holland	Himself	7	11	6	21 June
Mr Buckeridge	Geo. Wright	1	12	11	
Natl. Edwards	Jos. Middleton	-	7	9	
Thos. Oldacres	Himself	4	12	4	
Dr. Smallbrooke	Thos. Oldacres	-	8	-	

The Marriage Duty Act was a short-lived annual tax payable between 1695 and 1705. The government wanted to ensure it was taxing as many people as possible to fund the ongoing war with France. This meant the tax was payable by childless widowers and bachelors over the age of 25. There was also an additional tax on births, marriages and burials. Parish officials made lists of those residing within their parish boundaries in an attempt to ensure nobody evaded payment.

Oath rolls act in a similar way to tax lists, giving us names of people within a particular area of the county. The most well known are the Protestation Oath Returns of 1641/2. Every adult male within a parish was requested to declare his loyalty to the Protestant faith, in an attempt to discover any Roman Catholics living there. Those who refused to sign are sometimes listed, providing us with a mini census of adult males within the parish. Suffixes are usually given to differentiate between a father and son of the same name, but little other information is given. The Association Oath Rolls date from 1696 and were an Oath of Loyalty to the Crown, following an assassination attempt on King William III. These returns were less comprehensive than the Protestation Oath Returns, with only landowning males requested to sign the oath.

Locating the Record

TNA holds the land tax records for Staffordshire for 1798 in Series IR 23/79–81. These are also available to view on Ancestry in its 'UK, Land Tax Redemption, 1798' collection. Staffordshire History Centre holds sporadic land tax records for the county. These include records for Chillington for years 1699 and 1704–1711, Cuttlestone Hundred for years 1719 and 1728, Wetton for 1731, Stowe for 1750 and Offlow South Hundred for 1772. The best surviving records are between 1780 and 1832 when most records survive for the county. From this date, duplicate copies were kept among Quarter Sessions records and are also held at Staffordshire History Centre. There are later surviving land tax records post-1832 for Seisdon Hundred until 1846, Brewood until 1881 and Cheadle for 1875.

Window tax records do not survive well. Staffordshire History Centre holds window tax records for Leek Frith for 1704, Cuttlestone Hundred for 1711, Patshull for 1738–1759, Stowe for 1750, Fradswell for 1785–1787 and Brewood for 1801–1806. The William Salt Library holds the window tax records for Colwich for 1730. Eighteenth-century window tax assessments for Oakley are held by Cheshire Archives. Most of the surviving hearth tax records for the county are held at TNA in Series E 179/344. Miscellaneous tax records relating to taxes on hair powder, servants, dogs and horses (among many other examples) can be found at county records offices, often in estate record collections.

Staffordshire History Centre holds various lay subsidy rolls for the county. Search its catalogue for the term 'lay subsidy' to see if your parish of interest has survived for a year that your ancestors resided there. Examples of survivals include the 1557 roll for Totmonslow Hundred and a 1576 subsidy book for Offlow Hundred. Poll tax records tend not to survive well. There are some records from August 1641 relating to the Seisdon Hundred held by The National Archives (previously the Parliamentary Archives). The William Salt Library holds Stafford's poll tax for 1698/9.

Protestation Oath Returns are freely available to view via the Parliamentary Archives website, although its search function is not particularly user friendly. Visit **archives.parliament.uk/research-guides/protestation-returns** to see the collection. Some results are catalogued included people's names, whereas most are not. It is best to search by the name of the town or village you are interested in and then select 'Protestation Returns' in the left hand column, found under the 'Category' section. The image for each hundred is free to view. Alternatively, you can search by name via the Society of Genealogist's website (**sogdata.org.uk**). Surviving Association Oath Rolls are held at TNA in Series C 213.

Values of the Record

The main reason genealogists use tax lists and oath rolls is to locate a person within a particular parish. It can help to work out when a person may have moved between parishes, or perhaps see relatives with the same surname who also lived within their parish. These may be worth researching to see if they are related to your ancestor in some way. Finding a person in a list is also proof that they were alive at a particular time. This can help to narrow down when to look for a burial record. Many of the lists are comprehensive, giving the names of those who paid the tax or took an oath as well as those who were exempt or refused.

The tax records can give us information about our ancestors' financial status. If they lived in a large house with over ten hearths, this suggests they were wealthy. The exception to this rule is with innkeepers, where each person's room tended to have a hearth. You may discover a run of records, which can give you more information. If there is a good run of window tax records for example, you may note that the number of their windows decreased despite them residing in the same property. This is a common find, where people bricked-up their windows to pay less tax. The number of windows can hint at the size of a person's property. Seeing changing amounts of tax being paid by your ancestor within land tax records can also tell you how the size of their land increased or decreased over time. You may find evidence of land sale or purchase in other documents, with the tax records giving you a good idea of the date to look for these records.

As well as genealogical research, tax lists and oath rolls can be used for reasons of local history research. This can help you to add a greater understanding of your ancestors' changing environment. You can see over time how the wealth of the people in the parish changes and the number of people in the parish population. Land tax records might show a huge amount of land belonging to one estate owner with several different tenants.

The oath rolls tell us the religion of our ancestors, whether they were Protestant, Roman Catholic or other. The many miscellaneous taxes that appeared over time may tell you if your ancestor used wig powder or if they owned dogs. From 1780, land tax records can tell us if our ancestor had the right to vote. As with all records, we need to make sure we are being as thorough as possible when gathering genealogical information from these documents.

The exemptions listings of both tax lists and oath rolls can enlighten us to our forebears' disabilities or other reasons for exemption. For example, the Protestation Returns for Lichfield shows the exemptions of Nicholas Dale as he was 'an old man', John Jordan who was blind and John Sanders who was 'sick'. The lists also name parish officials including churchwardens and constables.

Limitations of the Record

We cannot learn as much from tax lists and oath rolls as we can from other sources. It is rare to find relationships stated and usually only one person per household is named. In the case of oath rolls, we do not know if any of those listed are related or if they are neighbours. All we can tell is that the people named reside within the parish at that time. Where we find a name in one of the lists, it can sometimes be impossible to prove it is even our ancestor. I have found the more common names of my ancestors listed in some documents, such as William Barlow, John Shaw and Thomas Marshall, but I cannot prove that it is them that the

> The names of all such persons
> Who have taken the protestation
> Within the parish of Pipe Ridware
> 1642.
> Michaell Lowe gent
> Thomas Edwards
> Edward Edwards
> Wm Edwards
> Francis Harvey
> Thomas Lea

record refers to as no other details are given. In some cases, there are duplicate names with no suffixes such as Junior or Senior to help with identification. In particular with my Marshall family, there are many people of the same name residing in the same area. This means there are a lot of Thomas Marshalls and Richard Marshalls but no way of knowing who are my ancestors for certain. There are some land tax records for Staffordshire that also only give a surname – which is not helpful. The above is a partial transcript of the 1642 Protestation Returns for Pipe Ridware showing the limited detail this provides.

Not everybody will appear in the records where you may expect them. There were many exemptions for taxes and the people who were excused from paying were not always named. People who were deemed to be poor were exempt from paying lay subsidies, hearth tax, window tax and tax relating to the 1695 Marriage Duty Act. The clergy were exempt from paying certain taxes, such as lay subsidies. It can be frustrating and time consuming to view the records and not have a positive result. Sometimes we can glean information from the records our ancestor doesn't feature in, as it may hint to us that they had a reason for exemption or were perhaps resident elsewhere.

Early records, such as lay subsidies, are written in Latin. As these tend to be fairly simple documents, all you really need to be able to recognise is your ancestor's name and parish. This is easier said than done when using earlier records and the writing can become very difficult to read. Unsurprisingly, many of the older documents are damaged through wear and tear, stains or flooding.

These documents are obviously very male focused. Women and children do appear at times; however, a large percentage of people listed are men. It can help to know who to expect to see in each record, but again this can be unpredictable. In the Association Oath Rolls, some areas record all adult males, whereas others only required the signatures of army officers and gentry. The Protestation Returns are almost all males. Some returns clearly state the names of Roman Catholics in their parish, whereas others do not. In the latter case, it may be hard to know if this means there were no Roman Catholics in the area on that date or if they just were not listed.

Staffordshire Examples

As a result of the Marriage Duty Act of 1695, many officials opted to take their own census of their parish to keep track of inhabitants and any tax they may be due to pay. An excellent example is the 1695 census of Lichfield. The names and ages of everybody in the household is given, including children. The relationships between the residents is noted, including children, servants and apprentices. Some occupations are stated, as well as anybody deemed to be a pauper. If a woman is widowed this is also mentioned. It is a rare find to discover an early census such as this which gives so much detail – in most cases it provides more detail than the 1841 census, so it is a huge boon to your research. Every adult's marital status is given along with the name of their street. A downloadable transcript of this document is available to purchase from Midland Ancestors (**https://midland-ancestors.shop**), with a bound copy available to view at Lichfield Library.

As previously mentioned, you will be lucky to find a window tax record naming your ancestor, but you are in luck if your ancestors resided in Wetton in 1754; a good record survives in Staffordshire History Centre (D1065/3/5). There are twenty-four property owners listed, with the number of their windows and the tax they were due to pay. The majority of those named are men including Laurence Fallows who had nine windows and William Robinson who had seven. Where women are named, their first name is not given and they are named simply as Widow Birch and Widow Bagshaw. The number of windows varies between seven and nine, with all property owners due to pay 2s each. The only hint of a family relationship between owners are with two men both named John Alcock and differentiated by the terms Junior and Senior.

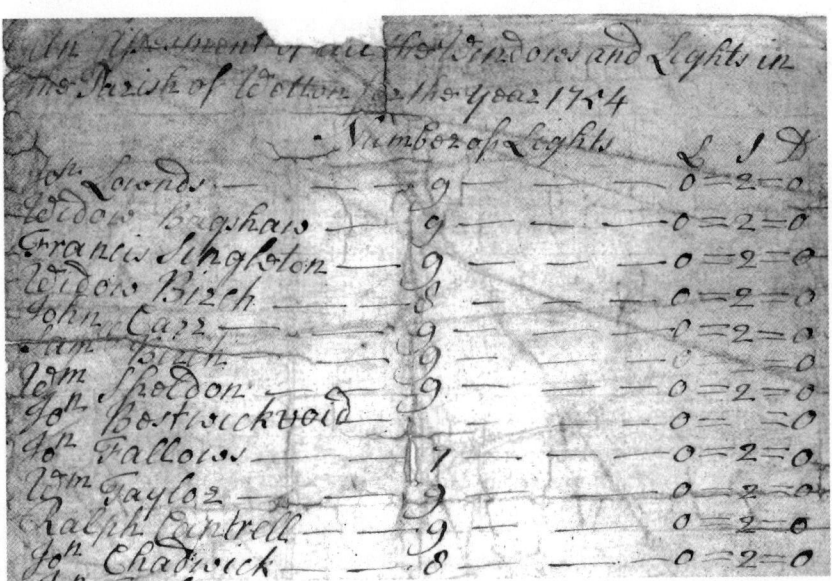

Crop of the 1754 window tax list for Wetton. (Reproduced courtesy of Staffordshire Record Office)

There are many excellent hearth tax returns for the Totmonslow Hundred held at TNA in Series E 179. Caverswall, sometimes recorded as Carswall, Careswall or Carswell, provides an interesting insight into the changing parish. In 1672 there were forty-eight householders listed with fifty-two hearths. Just two years later, in 1674, there are fifty-seven householders' names and sixty hearths. Caverswall Castle is, unsurprisingly, listed as the residence with the most hearths. The same series includes some individual certificates issued by parish officials. These are a rare find and you will be very lucky if you find one relating to your ancestor. One example includes a certificate from 1664 naming Thomas Cookes of Cookshill in Caverswall who has three chimneys, one of which is described as being used only for brewing. There are also surviving exemption certificates, including that of Ellen Wall of Caverswall who is listed as being exempt in 1664, having previously been found exempt in 1663. No reason for her exemption is given.

Chapter 12

TITLE DEEDS

About the Record

Title deeds are written records of legal proof that property ownership was transferred from one party to another. They are used by house historians to trace property ownership but are equally useful to genealogists. Many researchers do not realise the potential of title deeds in their genealogical research and decide not to pursue them. This is a big mistake, since deeds often contain the names of relatives, sometimes grandparents or uncles if our ancestor inherited the property from them. We can learn about our ancestors' forebears and descendants as well as details about their property and wealth.

Title deeds can be tricky to use. Many are very large documents with handwriting that is hard to decipher. Much legal jargon is used and it can sometimes be difficult to understand the words' meaning. The trick is to break it down bit by bit, word by word where necessary, to ensure you have gained as much information as possible from the record.

There are several different types of title deed and it helps to know which type of deed you are looking at, in order to understand what is being explained in the document. Due to the historical complex laws of selling property, the easiest way for many to sell was to create a fake dispute so the transfer in ownership was legally recorded in writing. The most common types of title deed you are likely to come across are:

Final Concord (Feet of Fines) – The record of a fictitious court case where the querent (plaintiff) demanded the specified property from the deforciant (vendor). A property value is stated but this is often inaccurate. Until 1733, the records were written in Latin.

Common Recovery – This was another fictitious dispute heard in court (usually the Court of Common Pleas) to transfer property ownership and to break an entail.

Bargain and Sale – Seen from 1535, this deed simply records the conveyance of property ownership between two parties for a set sum of money.

Lease and Release – This method of conveyance resulted in two documents being produced. Firstly, the lease was created. The following day, the release was produced which stated that the vendor surrendered his property ownership to the person he had previously leased it to. This method was abolished in 1845.

As well as different types of title deed, there are also different types of land tenure. These can be helpful to understand the conditions under which your ancestor held property. Each property may be described as leasehold, copyhold or freehold. These are described below:

Leasehold – A person with a lease did not have ownership of the property and instead paid rent to the owner for a set period of time. It could also be set in the form of 'three lives', such as a father, son and grandson. If the leaseholder was a married man, upon his death the lease would transfer to his widow. This may be mentioned in the man's will.

Copyhold – A person owned the property but with many restrictions. This can be found in manor court rolls, where permission from the lord of the manor was required if a person wished to inherit, sell or mortgage their property. Heritable copyhold allowed a tenant to pass the property on to their child, usually the eldest son. 'Copyhold for lives' meant the property could be passed between three people before ownership reverted back to the lord of the manor. Copyhold tenure was abolished in 1920, with all remaining copyhold land converted to freehold in 1925.

Freehold – Fee Simple – The simplest type of ownership, where the property owner had no restrictions on bequeathing his estate, selling it or gifting it. The property was the owner's outright.

Freehold – Fee Tail – This type of tenure ensured the property was passed down the male line to retain it in the family. The land could not be sold or bequeathed, meaning the property will not be mentioned in a will. It may be mentioned in equity court records, where property inheritance was disputed between siblings and cousins.

Freehold – Life Estate – A property belonged to a person for the whole term of their life. During their life, they could lease or mortgage the property; however, upon their death the tenure reverted back to the original property owner. Therefore, this property could again not be bequeathed and will not appear in a will.

After several voluntary deed registers failed to record much interest, the National Land Registry was established in 1862 and initially, registration was voluntary. It was not until 1899 that registering a property conveyance in a deed registry became compulsory.

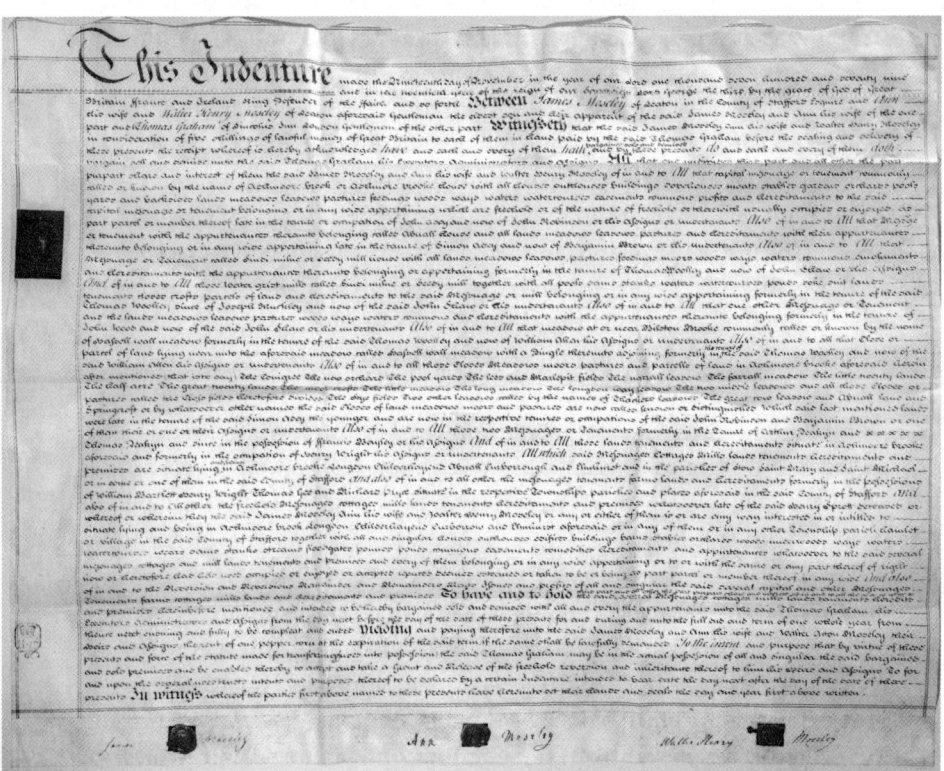

1779 title deed signed by James Moseley, Ann Moseley and Walter Henry Moseley of Leaton Hall, Bobbington. (Reproduced courtesy of Staffordshire Record Office)

There are key phrases used in title deeds that can help you to identify certain information. These are written in larger text so are easy to spot. The document usually begins 'This indenture' with the initial 'T' written decoratively. The names of the two or more involved parties comes after the word 'between'. 'Whereas' precedes information about previous transactions of the property which may name further family members. The document usually ends with 'In witness thereof', after which the signatures of the parties are given.

Locating the Record

TNA holds Final Concords in series CP 25 and Common Recoveries in series CP 40 and CP 43. It also holds a range of other deeds relating to Staffordshire although many are yet to be indexed, meaning a name search for your ancestor will not bring up a result. As well as the deeds themselves, TNA also has related court cases where the contents of deeds have been disputed. These can largely be found in its Chancery court cases collection.

The majority of surviving title deeds were deposited with local archives. In Staffordshire's case, most of these can be found in Staffordshire History Centre. Unsurprisingly, you can also find Staffordshire title deeds retained at neighbouring counties such as Derbyshire Record Office and Shropshire Archives. You can also find Staffordshire deeds held at Devon Heritage Centre and Herefordshire Archive and Records Centre.

To search all of these archives catalogues in one go it is best to use TNA's Discovery catalogue. You may wish to start by using an ancestor's name as a search term, perhaps along with their parish name. Some deeds are saved under a surname and a parish. Unfortunately, due to the sheer number of deeds held by archives, many have yet to be catalogued by name. Some are grouped together by parish and others are simply under a heading of 'uncatalogued title deeds'. You can choose to narrow the search results by looking at a particular archives or a certain date range. Be aware that searching for a parish or a name with the term 'title deed' may not bring up a result. Some titles do not contain the words 'title deed' and may instead be recorded as a 'bargain and sale'.

While some catalogue entries for title deeds give little information, others provide an excellent abstract. These can give you the full names of the parties involved, the location of the property and the names of neighbouring fields and who owns them. In these cases, use this information as guidance to be sure that you are ordering the correct deed to view. Never assume this is all the useful information the deed provides and always view the original document.

Copies of title plans and the title register can be downloaded for a small fee from HM Land Registry's official website at **www.gov.uk/government/organisations/land-registry**.

Values of the Record

Prior to 1925, it was a legal requirement for all property owners to retain all title deeds relating to their house and land regardless of date. This resulted in property owners passing on large bundles of deeds to each other after a conveyance was completed. After 1925, when the deeds were no longer needed, many people chose to hold on to them and these were later handed into county record offices. This means you can often find these bundles held in archives all relating to the same property. We can use these to see the deeds from when our ancestor purchased a property, when they sold it and read how the property changed while it was in their hands. We can also see the property's other transactions, which in some cases will be family members. Deeds can sometimes provide a date of death or the date a will was written for previous property owners.

Title deeds can tell us a lot about the property. Names of neighbours are often given, as well as the names of adjacent fields. This information can help you to find the property on a map. The size of the property may be stated which can hint at your ancestor's wealth and status. The deed will often give your ancestor's occupation. Where this is not given it is sometimes hinted at in the description of the property. This may be obvious if it is described as a wheelwright's yard or less obvious if other types of outbuildings are named.

Title deeds can give you the names of several generations of the same family. This may be due to simple inheritance, for example stating that the current owner inherited a freehold fee simple property from his grandfather, or due to the popular three-life leases where the lives were named. The latter usually named a man, his wife and their eldest son. Their names will be recorded, with their relationship and occupation, but it is uncommon to find more detail than that. Nevertheless, a title deed could be the one remaining documentary piece of evidence naming an ancestor that you can use to break down a brick wall.

Deeds were sometimes part of a bond, mortgage or marriage settlement, all of which can provide us with more information. If a property was inherited rather than purchased, you may find a copy of the will among the deeds. In some cases, you can also find copies of civil registration certificates and extracts from parish registers. The deed itself is signed by the two parties, providing you with a signature for comparison with other documents if needed for identification purposes.

Limitations of the Record

After the law changed in 1925, meaning that historical deeds no longer needed to be retained, a huge majority of title deeds were destroyed. Where they have survived, most have yet to be catalogued by name and so cannot be searched for easily. There are also many title deeds that have survived but are held in private hands.

When you do find a title deed relating to your ancestor, you may feel overwhelmed at the sheer size of the document and the difficulty in reading the text. Try not to scan through the document too quickly as it can be easy to miss a key piece of information. Deeds are full of legal jargon and can be repetitive. Historical documents, such as title deeds, often used very little punctuation. The meaning of the text can be hard to understand even once you have transcribed it. While this means they are time-consuming records to read, they are also one of the more rewarding documents. It can feel like a real achievement to read through a whole deed and understand exactly what was being conveyed and how this was to be carried out.

Until 1733, many title deeds, such as Final Concords, were written in Latin. This makes the task of extracting important information much trickier. It is best not to ignore the document in case it includes a vital detail relating to your ancestor. Firstly, try to understand as much of the document as you can. This may involve using an online translation app to translate key phrases into English. It is usually fairly easy to translate the names of the parties into English, such as Benedictus for Benedict and Georgius for George. Once you recognise your ancestor's name in Latin it will be simple to highlight this in the deed.

Staffordshire Examples

I was aware from viewing previous records, including addresses given in baptism registers and newspaper reports, that my fifth great-grandfather John Shaw resided and worked at Seedy Mill, situated south of Longdon. Searching for title deeds by using John's name brought up no relevant results. However, using Seedy Mill as a search term did. There were deeds relating to the property listed in the catalogue by date. Knowing roughly which date John was a resident there, I ordered the relevant document from Staffordshire History Centre. This was created on 19 November 1799.

From the catalogue and from a quick first glance at the deed, it seemed as though it may not be relevant to my family. The document is signed and sealed by James Moseley, Ann Moseley and Walter Henry Moseley. There was no mention of a Shaw in the catalogue entry. Reading through

An extract of the 1779 title deed which describes Seedy Mill and names John Shaw. (Reproduced courtesy of Staffordshire Record Office)

the deed, it became obvious this deed related to a wealthy family and several different properties. These properties all had different, named, tenants (albeit not in the catalogue) along with a good description of each piece of land that was being conveyed, including Seedy Mill.

The deed describes Seedy Mill as being currently inhabited by John Shaw and previously in the tenure of Thomas Woolley. The estate includes gristmills, watercourses, ponds, tenements and crofts. There are also meadows and pastures that were previously in the tenure of John Wood but now owned by the same John Shaw. There are many different parcels of lands described with several different tenants, both past and present.

Therefore, this deed is not only useful to descendants of the Moseley family named in the catalogue but also to the descendants of the tenants who are named in the record. The deed helps me to understand the tenure of John's property and its features.

Chapter 13

NEWSPAPERS

About the Record

Searching newspapers for mentions of our ancestors has become a lot easier since the increase of digitisation. Rather than searching page by page, we can type an ancestor's name into the relevant website and view the results in seconds. You may find mentions in the births, marriages and deaths column that confirms dates you already knew. You can discover new facts too – perhaps a birth announcement for a child you were not aware of. More excitingly, you can sometimes find out much more about an ancestor's character. This might involve reading the words they spoke in court, their involvement in an accident or an obituary. Newspapers can also help provide us with information that has been lost from an original source, such as coroners' inquest reports.

There is a bit of a knack to searching newspaper records to gather as much detail as possible. Once you have started searching for articles, you will find it addictive and there are possibly hundreds out there relating to your ancestors. They are my favourite record to search for as they have provided me with more of an insight into who my ancestors were than any other source. The articles provide so much more than names and dates. They add colour to our ancestors' lives.

Locating the Record

The best websites to search for newspaper articles are the British Newspaper Archive, known as BNA (**britishnewspaperarchive.co.uk**) and Findmypast, the latter of which has the records of BNA available on its 'Everything' subscription. A subscription is also required to view articles on BNA, although they are currently offering three free pages per registered user. Both have similar filtering functions so you can narrow results down by date, county or newspaper title. More newspapers are added each week so keep an eye on what new releases there are to see if you need to conduct a further search. There are also a number of free newspapers you can view on Findmypast.

There is a huge number of Staffordshire newspapers currently available online including *Cannock Chase Courier*, *Lichfield Mercury*, *Potteries Examiner* and *Staffordshire Chronicle*. The earliest records currently uploaded date back to 3 January 1795 in the *Staffordshire Advertiser*, with the majority of records from the nineteenth and twentieth centuries. For those researching more recent relatives, the latest newspapers currently uploaded date up to 31 December 1999 in the *Tamworth Herald*, *Great Barr Observer* and *Burton Daily Mail*.

To locate a particular ancestor in a newspaper record, start by typing their name in the search box. If your ancestor has a very rare name this may be enough to bring up relevant results without too many others to filter through. In a majority of cases you will need to add a further search term and filter the records by date and location. Adding the name of the person's parish is a good way of finding results, such as 'William Jones, Longton', as is narrowing the date down to when you know they were alive. You may also choose to search by adding their occupation, as people were often listed as 'William Jones, wheelwright' for example.

In some cases, people have their full name given, including middle names, such as 'William Henry Joseph Jones'. These may sometimes be given as initials, such as 'William H.J. Jones', 'W.H.J. Jones' or 'William Henry J. Jones'. All variants will need to be searched for separately, as well as any spelling variants of their surname. A harder case to crack is when people are named as 'Mr Jones'. The less detailed the name, the harder it becomes to know if we are reading about our forebear or a namesake. In these cases, research the people with the same name locally and see who matches the details in the article. For example, it may give a street address or occupation that can help you prove that it relates to your ancestor.

You may also choose to search by other terms, rather than a person's name. What you can search for is limitless, but good choices include a street name or workplace. You may wish to search by parish name to see what was happening in the area at the time your ancestors were there. Don't forget to also search for your ancestor's siblings to see if they got up to anything noteworthy.

There are other websites you can check for mentions of your ancestors in newspaper articles. A popular choice is the *London Gazette* (**thegazette.co.uk**) which can be searched for free. Despite its name, the newspaper published items relating to people across England rather than just focusing on London. The articles you may find vary greatly and include people receiving military awards, as well as those declaring bankruptcy. Heraldic notices were also placed where a coat of arms was changed. If your ancestor changed their name then an article may have been placed in the *London Gazette* so this is worth a look if you can't find any records about them before a particular date. *The Times* also has a great archival website of their previous editions (**thetimes.co.uk/archive**). Newspapers can also be accessed via **www.newspapers.com** where you can either choose to subscribe to the site directly or through Ancestry under their All Access membership. At the time of writing, there are twenty-three Staffordshire-based newspapers digitised there including *Burntwood Post, The Burton Observer* and *Chronicle and Staffordshire Newsletter*.

Not all newspapers are digitised and available online. The British Library's online catalogue (**explore.bl.uk**) has listings of every newspaper published in the United Kingdom. This includes over 34,000 titles. Similarly, you can also read *Local Newspapers 1750–1920* by Jeremy Gibson.

When you have found an article relating to your ancestor, save a copy of it and note down the name of the newspaper and its date so that you can find it again if you need to. The image that you save of this record will be covered by copyright or contract law so do not upload this to a public tree. Instead, extract the relevant information to type in yourself to bring life to your ancestor's story. You can also use the 'Saved' function on BNA or 'Add to Tree' on Findmypast to refer back to relevant articles.

Values of the Record

Newspapers are truly invaluable as a genealogical source. They can give us unique information about our ancestors that cannot be found anywhere else and a true insight into their lives. If this book inspires you to look at any record in particular, I hope it is newspaper articles. You never know what you may discover!

The birth, marriages and deaths column may seem self-explanatory in regards to their value. They will sometimes act as a secondary source to information we have already gained from GRO certificates. However, you can also find out new information from these published notifications. Sometimes the cause of death is given that goes into more detail than that stated on a death certificate. In the births' column there are sometimes notices of stillborn babies which are unlikely to be recorded elsewhere. The notifications also pre-date civil registration, so prior to their commencement in 1837 the article may be our only source of the event. For the earlier dates this is much more common for the wealthier members of society. In some cases, we may find that the information

BIRTH.

CORNELL.—On the 13th, Bore Street, Lichfield, the wife of F. H. Cornell, Esq., of a daughter, (stillborn.)

MARRIAGE.

THOMAS—MORTIMORE.—On the 17th inst., at St. Michael's, Handsworth (by the Rev. W. Kitchen), James Albert Thomas, of Pembroke, to Florence, youngest daughter of Henry Mortimore, Robert Road, Handsworth. No cards.

DEATHS.

LORY.—On Sunday, the 15th inst., at the residence of her sister, Mrs. Williams, Beacon Hill, Lichfield, Susan Heather, the beloved wife of the Rev. H. Coulson Lory, vicar of St. Mark's, Liverpool, formerly vicar of Cressing, Essex.

RYLATT.—On Feb. 11, at Chester Road, Erdington, Bertie, second son of George William and Marianne Rylatt, aged 12 years. Deeply lamented.

The birth, marriage and death column from the Lichfield Mercury dated 20 February 1885. (With permission from Reach plc)

provided in a newspaper article helps us to find the right certificate to order from GRO.

As well as these event columns, marriages often had a separate article giving great detail. This was not just for wealthy members of society. In fact, some of my poorest ancestors had their marriage details published. These articles often name the bride's and groom's parents, the best man, bridesmaids and flower girl. Details may include what the bride's dress looked like, what flowers she carried and what hymns were sung. The location of the couple's honeymoon may be given at the end of the feature.

Obituaries and articles about an ancestor's funeral are also very useful. Obituaries vary in length but can give a good outline of the deceased's life story. Funeral notices often include a list of those who attended, meaning many relatives are named, as well as friends. Less commonly, a photograph of the deceased may be included.

Crime was commonly reported on in the local newspaper and potentially, depending on its severity, in a national newspaper. Your ancestor may be named as the defendant, the victim, a witness or an official. If your ancestor was a policeman or a judge they will likely be named in multiple articles with regards to their work, giving a great picture of their day-to-day lives, as well as the chance to read many verbatim statements.

Articles about Coroners' Inquests can be very valuable, as the original reports have often been destroyed. Not all inquests were published in papers; however, when the highlights of the examination are given this can give us details about how our ancestors died. You may find from a death certificate that an ancestor died in a road accident from a broken neck and that there was an inquest. A newspaper report on the same incident is likely to tell you what happened, who was at fault and how the injury was sustained.

If your ancestor was involved in an accident this may be found in the newspapers. Even when there were no fatalities, they were still often noted as a piece of local interest. If the accident was on a larger scale, you may also find articles in national newspapers. Accidents may involve fire, drowning or the workplace among others. Newspapers used to go into graphic detail, explaining with gruesome description how fatalities occurred and the aftermath.

The *London Gazette* is great for finding official notices naming our forebears, including military and civil awards. An article dated 2 January 1914 tells us that Levi Jeffries, a sergeant of Wolverhampton Borough Police was awarded the King's Police Medal. Another article dated 11 November 1870 shows that Henry Browne had been appointed lieutenant of the 20th Staffordshire Rifle Volunteer Corps. Articles in the *London Gazette* date back to 1665, when it was under its original title of the *Oxford Gazette*.

As well as searching for specific articles about your ancestors, you may wish to look for pieces about notable events in their parish. Where large-scale incidents occurred, such as a natural disaster or a bombing raid, your ancestor is likely to have been affected by it in some way. It is therefore worth finding out a bit about the history of their parish and then researching articles about the occurrence. You may find that their street name is listed or a photograph may be provided. Examples include the Wheaton Aston Great Fire of 1777 and the RAF Fauld explosion of 1944. Even if your ancestors in the parish did not lose any loved ones, their lives would have been touched by the disaster.

An advert for Mason's Bread Factory in Burslem from Staffordshire Sentinel dated 18 September 1905. (With permission from Reach plc)

It is also of interest – and some amusement – to read advertisements placed in the newspapers at the time of your ancestors' lives. These include advertisements for doctor-recommended cigarettes, adverts for cleaning products entreating men to buy them for their wives, and adverts for medicinal concoctions with ingredients we certainly wouldn't find on the shelves today!

Limitations of the Record

Newspaper articles online are searched using a technique known as 'optical character recognition', where the pages are read digitally. This is much quicker than waiting for a person to transcribe the records; it is, unfortunately, prone to errors. Text in newspapers is sometimes blurry or too thick for a computer to interpret correctly. The older the paper is, the more likely errors are to occur. This is partly due to the higher presence of thicker text and partly due to an 's' appearing as an 'f' in the older way of writing, known as the 'medial s' or 'long s'. This means that some articles about our ancestors will be missed.

A popular way of filtering articles is by location. We may wish to filter by county so we only see articles published by Staffordshire newspapers. There are many examples where you will find articles relating to the county published elsewhere. I have found many of my Staffordshire relatives featuring in articles in Warwickshire papers. If an article is about something especially interesting or noteworthy then this is likely to be found in multiple papers across the country. In these cases, articles were essentially copied and pasted with little difference, but it is still worth checking all the articles to see if any extra detail is given. In many cases, filtering by county means we miss out on viewing relevant articles. Not filtering by county means we are often left with a mammoth task of searching through hundreds of records (or more). If an article is found in another county's papers, it is most likely to be a neighbouring county.

We must consider newspapers' reliability. As we see today, details in articles are often exaggerated to be more interesting. There may be a degree of bias and accounts of false reporting where an article is completely fabricated. Obituaries are often written with rose-tinted glasses of the individual, focusing on all their good qualities and ignoring the bad. With any verbatim statements from court proceedings, consider who is talking. A witness may be lying to sway the jury or judge into finding the defendant guilty or innocent.

It is worth being aware that reading some newspaper articles can be upsetting. This is particularly in the cases of more recent articles where we uncover something about someone we knew personally or where we read the details of a serious injury or fatality faced by our ancestors. You may also read less-favourable articles about your ancestor that are hard to stomach.

Staffordshire Examples

My fourth great-grandmother Eleanor Marshall died in Longdon in 1900 at the age of 94. People who lived to such an advanced age often made the papers upon their deaths which is the case with Eleanor. In the *Lichfield Mercury* on 12 January 1900, a short history of her life is given. This includes her birthplace of Seedy Mill, the name and occupation of her father John, her age, her nickname of 'Granny Marshall', the fact she had been married twice, the details of her second husband and how many children had outlived her. Brief details of her death are given which adds to detail from her death certificate. The main interest lies in the description of her character as a 'true lover of the country' and that she 'frequently took long walks in the fields'. These are pieces of interest that are unlikely to be found elsewhere.

My third great-grandfather Samson Barlow is an excellent example of some of the more minor cases you may find your ancestor involved in. In the *Lichfield Mercury* on 24 August 1883, it is noted that Samson received a fine due to two of his children's low attendance at school. In the *Staffordshire Advertiser* on 16 November 1901, there is a note that Samson had to pay 8s 6d for letting his dog run off lead without a collar or a muzzle. In *The Mercury* on 21 March 1902, the Longdon parish council meeting minutes state Samson's chickens had been a recurring nuisance on the parish's allotments and that he had ignored previous warnings of the damage they had caused. In the *Lichfield Mercury* on 28 May 1915, it is noted that Samson was fined 5s for keeping a carriage without a licence. There are further examples which show Samson was a frequent attendee of the Petty Sessions.

The obituary for Eleanor Marshall of Longdon in the Lichfield Mercury dated 12 January 1900. (With permission from Reach plc)

One of the most familiar figures, and the oldest inhabitant of Longdon has passed away. Mrs. Ellen Marshall, the person referred to, was born at Seedy Mill in the year 1806, at which place her father, John Shaw, was a miller and farmer; the deceased was therefore 94 years of age. During her long life she has been a true lover of the country, and throughout the whole of the summer months, and frequently in the winter, she might be seen taking long walks in the fields, and to this fact, no doubt to a certain extent, may be attributed her splendid constitution. Her illnesses have been few and far between, but it was thought about three years ago that her time was come, and that she could not linger many hours, but to the surprise of those who were watching over her, she asked for some bread and cheese and beer; this was given to her, and very soon after "Granny Marshall" was again seen taking her walks abroad. She continued in her usual health until early last week, when she was again taken ill. She lingered until Friday evening, and then quietly passed away. The deceased had twice married, her second husband being John Marshall, butcher, of Brookend. She leaves two sons and two daughters. Her remains were interred in the Parish Church on Thursday.

Chapter 14

MANORIAL RECORDS

About the Record

Most people have heard of manor houses, the lord of the manor, and are aware that some manorial records survive. Many people mistakenly believe that manorial records only cover the wealthy lord and his family, but this is untrue. Manors originated in the Middle Ages and were territorial and administrative divisions of land tenancy. Some manors covered more than one parish, whereas some parishes contained more than one manor. It is easy to see what records survive for each parish and manor, but not quite so easy to read and understand the records once you have them. Your ancestors will have lived within a manor boundary and many will feature in the manorial records.

One of the most helpful genealogical records in this category are the court records. Within each manor, there were two types of manorial court. The first court was the Court Baron which was held every three weeks. This court dealt with land transfer within the manor boundaries and often named generations of the same family or intermarriages between families, making them helpful at breaking down brick walls. The second court was the Court Leet which was usually held every six months. The Court Leet dealt with minor crime with some overlap between the Court Leet and Petty Sessions. You may be surprised to find some of your more law-abiding ancestors appearing as the accused in the Court Leet, however, as the offences were minor and in most cases were not really crimes at all. For example, if your ancestor's livestock escaped their field and blocked a roadway they may have been called to appear if it caused a nuisance.

Both the Court Baron and the Court Leet produced minutes, which are known as court rolls. Your ancestor may feature if they transferred land, appeared as the accused in the Court Leet, if they were appointed

The jury list for Longdon Manor dated 1753. (Reproduced courtesy of Staffordshire Record Office)

as a court official or if they were excused from attending. The jury of the court was known as the 'homage' and consisted of tenants of the manor. The homagers were all males who possessed property of a set minimum value. Your ancestor may feature in the homage list, although if father and son shared a name it may not be possible to know exactly who the person is. The minutes were written by the steward of the court who first made notes known as presentments, before writing them up into the court rolls. Sometimes presentments survive, whereas court rolls do not, and vice versa.

If your ancestor was appointed as an official of the manor, it may be helpful to understand what his role would have entailed. This is not always obvious from their title. A list of the most common roles is below.

Official Title	Duties
Steward	Stewards presided over the court and managed the manorial accounts. They were appointed by the lord of the manor and were known as the 'seneschal'.
Sheriff	Believed to have originated from the term 'shire reeve'; a chief officer of the manor court. Sheriffs collected fines and rent and managed the manorial court. They were also responsible for keeping the peace within the manor.
Bailiff	A bailiff collected fines and rents within the manor and are sometimes referred to as an agent or a sheriff's deputy.
Constable	A constable was a public civil officer whose duty was to maintain peace and order as a type of warden.
Hayward	Haywards protected the areas enclosed by barriers, such as fences, walls and hedgerows. To prevent theft of crops or livestock, they blew a horn to alert others of the presence of a thief.

Official Title	Duties
Pinder	A man who impounded stray animals found in the manor, for example dogs, sheep or cattle. They caught the animals and housed them in an enclosure known as a pinfold.
Catchpole	A catchpole, or catchpoller, was an assistant to the bailiff or sheriff of the manor, largely responsible for collecting debts. Originally, this involved taking tenants' poultry to pay the debt in kind.
Woodward	A woodward managed the timber of the manor and organised its sale. The name itself is believed to be a shortened term for 'wood warden'.
Ale Taster	Perhaps an enviable position, an ale taster tested the quality and measurement of ale within the manor to prevent fraud. Responsibilities could also include the testing of the quality or weight of bread.
Linkman	In the days well before street lights, a linkman or linkerboy would carry a torch through the streets during times of darkness to help illuminate the area and guide people through the manor.

Many surnames originated from the titles of the manor officials and you may recognise some from your tree. When an official was appointed, he was named in the court rolls and will appear within them on a regular basis thereafter.

Manorial surveys were taken, albeit on an irregular and unpredictable basis. Some surveys are very detailed giving the names of tenants, their fields and their payable rent, along with a map showing the boundary of each person's land. A majority do not have maps attached and where they do survive they are rarely accurately completed to scale. If you are researching the land of your ancestors, you may discover that a manorial map is the earliest surviving map of the parish.

There are four types of manorial survey.

- Rentals, sometimes referred to as rent rolls, list tenants' names and the rent that was due.
- Extents list the rent of each plot within the manor.
- Custumals give tenants' names and the obligations associated with their property or estate.
- Terriers are written descriptions of the manor in geographic terms. These can sometimes name fields and their owners but are quite rare to find.

Other manorial records include accounts detailing the income and expenditure as listed by the steward or bailiff. Call books may survive which list those present at a manorial court and who was absent. Fine books also have rare examples of survival, listing the punishments (known as amercements) handed out in court.

Locating the Record

The Manorial Documents Register is available on TNA website at **discovery.nationalarchives.gov.uk/manor-search**. Select Staffordshire as the historical county; there is either the option to search by manor name or parish name. You may have found the name of a relevant manor in other records. If not, the best way is to search by the name of the parish in which your ancestor lived. Some parishes, such as Caverswall, were encompassed by one manor known as Caverswall Manor.

On the other hand, some parishes contained several manors. It can be difficult to know which manor your ancestors' part of the parish was in. Wolverhampton appears in eleven different manors. In these cases, the best thing to do is to search each manor's collection holdings to see if there are any surviving manorial maps. These should help you to discover which manor your ancestor's land was in. Of course, to do this you will need to know from other records at least roughly where about in the parish your ancestor lived. This can be done using probate records, title deeds and estate maps among others.

When you select a manor, the results that appear show a listing of the surviving records for that manor. This includes the type of record, the dates the record refers to, which archive holds the documentation and its reference number. Sometimes using this information to search for the record on the archives' website can provide more information. For example, the Manorial Documents Register states that for Uttoxeter Manor there is a 1750–1751 rental held at Staffordshire History Centre. Using the provided reference number to search the archives' own catalogue tells us that the rental relates to the periods of Michaelmas 1750 and Lady Day 1751 and gives the name of the owner and occupier as well as a description of the property and the annual rent due. When you have found a record of interest you can then use this information to either view the record at the archives or order a copy online.

The number of surviving records for each manor varies, and they are held in several different archives. Longdon Manor has 230 collections held by 7 archives. Brewood Manor has 75 surviving record collections held over 4 different archives. Mitton Manor has one surviving record and there are plenty of others that have no known records available at all. These include Drayton Manor and Cheadle Manor. Audley Manor has manorial records dating from 1368 to 1839 held at Staffordshire History Centre, Derbyshire Record Office, Arundel Castle, TNA, William Salt Library, Cheshire Archives and Keele University Library.

While the Register is an excellent service it is not without its flaws. The archive names and reference numbers have not been updated for a while. This means that some archives appear which have since closed, such as Lichfield Record Office, whose collections were transferred to Staffordshire History Centre. Reference numbers have also changed, but searching the archives' catalogue using the reference number in the 'any text' field, rather than the reference number section, should bring up the relevant result.

Values of the Record

The records of the Court Baron can be hugely useful to genealogists. The previous and new tenants are both named and are often related. It is common to find a son inheriting land from his father. In these cases, their relationship is almost always stated. Where proof of relationship was needed for the court, documentation was provided to confirm this. This means court rolls may include extracts from records such as baptism registers and wills. Copyhold tenants needed the permission of the Court Baron to inherit, sell or mortgage their property. This can again give details of relatives. When a copyhold tenant died, the terms of his tenancy agreement was given alongside a brief description of the land in question. Details of his death may also be given.

The Court Leet rolls name people and list their offences. These are usually very minor such as leaving a gate open or not controlling the weeds on their land. The rolls can tell us our ancestors' occupations and their place of residence within a manor. They may feature in the rolls if they were appointed as an officer, showing they were in a position of trust within the community. If a person died while in an official position, this is usually stated in the rolls when a new person is appointed in their place.

There is no standard to how court rolls are set out so they will differ from one manor to the next; each official chose to record the events slightly differently but tended to stick to the same pattern. As a general rule, the type of court and date are usually at the top. The names of the jury and a list of those who could not attend tend to follow. The presentments will then be listed. This is a list of the issues to be raised in that day's court session.

Manorial surveys can also be very useful. Maps can show us exactly where our ancestors lived, who lived around them and any nearby notable features. The extent of their property boundaries is usually clearly marked. It is possible that a manorial map is the earliest map made of your ancestor's place of residence, with some dating back to the late sixteenth century. Surveys can tell us the rent that our ancestors paid and, where a run of records survive, they can be used to track when a person disappeared from the records. This may mean they moved out of the parish or died.

Manorial accounts are not usually quite as useful as other manorial records but may still be worth a look. They can provide names of tenants who were fined or payments given to named local tradesmen who were hired to work in the manor, such as carpenters. There is also a general interest to see how much rent they were paying or how much they were paid for a service.

Limitations of the Record

At first glance, manorial records are usually difficult to understand. Records were written in Latin until 1734, although set phrases can be recognised once they have been translated. It can help to know your ancestor's name in Latin so this can at least be recognised. The older the document is, the more difficult the handwriting is to read. Use online resources, such as the palaeography guide on TNA website (**nationalarchives.gov.uk/palaeography**) to help recognise different letters.

It is advisable to examine manorial records from 1734 onwards when they are recorded in English before you venture further back. This will help you recognise the format of court rolls and understand the type of language used. By familiarising yourself with a new document in a familiar language, you can gain confidence with a new record type rather than diving straight into Latin text.

Manorial maps are not always accurate. The reason for the creation of a map was key to how precise it needed to be. If the lord needed a very detailed map drawn to scale with exact locations of properties and geographical features within his land then he could hire a trained surveyor. If the lord just needed a rough idea of who lived where, it was not essential for a map to be drawn to scale or provide much detail.

As previously mentioned, the survival rate of manorial records is very patchy. It is down to luck as to what records survive for your manor of interest. Some manors can provide you with a steady stream of rentals and court rolls with a detailed map. Other manors may have one record from the thirteenth century that is too fragile for public viewing. A majority of manors have some records surviving but these have large gaps in their creation dates. It is believed that some manorial records still remain in private hands, unknown to the archives and the public.

If your manor has plenty of surviving records then this is great news. Your ancestor is more than likely to feature among them. The Manorial Documents Register makes it very clear where to find each record set. Where the records are held by a number of different archives, you will either need to travel around to view many different records or pay someone to do the research for you.

Staffordshire Examples

Jury lists are usually easy to understand, quick to read and affordable to purchase a copy of from the archives. The men on the 1753 jury list for Longdon Manor dated 25 October are all named as seen in the previous image. Underneath this is a list of men appointed to manorial positions. For example, John Westwood is noted to be a constable of Harbourne. Their manorial position gives insight into their daily lives.

Appointments listing from Longdon's manorial records dated 1753. (Reproduced courtesy of Staffordshire Record Office)

A list of amercements (monetary fines) issued to manorial tenants can be enlightening. An estreat summarised the amercements issued at a manorial court. One example is the 1756 estreat of Kings Bromley Manor. In this list, the name of the person being fined is given first, followed by an explanation of their wrongdoing and their fine. In many cases, the location of the 'offence' is given. The accusation for all men in this list is that they did not 'scour or cleanse' their ditches and all are charged the same agreed common fine of 3s 4d. The location of the ditches may be of particular interest to researchers so they can discover more about their forebears' land. For example, John Reynoldson was guilty of the offence at Clarks Close and John Saxelby at Shaw Lane. The only difference noted in the offences regards John Copestake who did not scour or cleanse his ditches at Croft End, despite a previous order at the last court session. Researchers may choose to view this as an act of defiance or a simple slip of the mind.

Estreats of Kings Bromley dated 1756. (Reproduced courtesy of Staffordshire Record Office)

Chapter 15

MEMORIAL INSCRIPTIONS

About the Record

Memorial inscriptions are what we find etched on our ancestors' headstones. This may seem like a subject unworthy of a whole chapter to some. Perhaps it seems self-explanatory to read the words on our ancestors' graves and gather meaning from them? There is much we need to learn to ensure we gain as much information as possible from this source.

There are many different types of memorial that may mark where our ancestors are buried, the most common being a headstone. This is an upright stone which will usually give your ancestor's name, year of birth and year of death. They can be many shapes, such as a cross, but are usually simple and rectangular with a rounded top. You may find a grave marker, a very small stone just giving the initials of the deceased. Grave markers were sometimes replaced by a headstone once enough funds had been raised and there are cases where both survive together. Ledgers are flat stone slabs laid into the ground with a similar appearance to headstones. If you find a ledger belonging to your ancestors, check that it wasn't once an upright headstone that has since fallen.

If your ancestors were particularly wealthy you may find they have a more elaborate memorial, such as a chest tomb. These can be found inside a church or outside in the churchyard. The deceased were buried beneath the tomb, rather than inside it. Only a small minority of memorials are found within the church. These are usually reserved for more notable members of the community, such as the clergy or the wealthy landowners. There are other cases where people are not buried inside the church, but have a memorial plaque on the interior church wall. There are examples of plaques found for church carpenters, organists and benefactors. You may also find there are memorials to soldiers of the parish outside the church, or a memorial roll inside.

Before heading out to find a specific grave, it is worth remembering that the majority of our ancestors will not have a surviving headstone. The further you go back in time, the less likely you are to find one. The oldest legible headstone in England is reputed to be that of Anne Green at Alstonefield who died in 1518 but this is a very rare find. Most of our ancestors would have been given a wooden cross to mark their burial spot, which will have since rotted away. Many researchers still like to visit the area to pay their respects or to try and find others with the same surname in the graveyard.

The first step when wishing to use memorial inscriptions is to find where your ancestor was buried. Sometimes this is pleasantly easy and you can find their name in the parish burial register online. If the graveyard is particularly large, you may wish to contact the relevant authority who often possess burial plans. This can pinpoint exactly where in the churchyard or cemetery you can find your ancestor. They may even be able to tell you if the headstone still exists.

It is not always obvious where to find our ancestors' memorials. Couples were sometimes not buried together, often being buried in separate parishes if the surviving partner relocated after they lost their loved one. People were not always buried in the churchyard you would expect either. For example, you may find them residing in a particular parish in the 1841 census and be aware that they died in 1846. However, in those intervening five years they could have moved and be buried in their new parish. As you browse the burial registers, you will also find the sad cases of burials of people with no name, often listed under a title such as 'unknown traveller'. If this happens to be your ancestor, then there will unfortunately be no named trace of their interment. Burial plots, therefore, cannot always be found.

The elaborate headstone of Phyllis, Ann and James Alcock in Ellastone churchyard. (Author's own)

If you cannot find your ancestor in a burial register, try to find the last record they appear in. This could be anything from a tax record, marriage register entry or newspaper article. It may be useful to locate their will, if they made one, as these were often written close to death and may give your ancestor's last known parish of residence. This hints where they may be buried, but is not a guarantee.

Staffordshire is home to the National Memorial Arboretum at Alrewas. You may discover that one of their 400+ memorials is relevant to your family tree. Examples of memorials include a tribute to the Women's Land Army and the Staffordshire Yeomanry Memorial.

Visiting the burial plots of our ancestors is a worthwhile task. It can be a tangible way to finish an ancestor's story. Even if no headstone survives, there is something special about being in the space that they lay and where our relatives may have visited to grieve.

Locating the Record

The best way to view memorial inscriptions is in person. A huge number of transcriptions and photographs are now available online, but the only way to truly ensure you have gathered all the possible information is to visit. You may notice a transcription error, text on the back of the stone that was missed when a person transcribed the information or perhaps other forebears' headstones located in the same churchyard. If you do choose to visit, choose a clear day and take photographs for your records. We are rapidly losing detail from memorial inscriptions with many now already illegible. Photographs are the best way of making sure the information on the stone is not lost. Make sure you also check the back of the stone in case there is more detail there.

If you cannot visit in person, there is a wide variety of websites you may wish to search to see if your ancestors' memorial inscriptions have been transcribed. Find a Grave (**findagrave.com**) is a fantastic free source where anybody can upload photographs of headstones, and transcribe them for others to search for. When visiting churchyards to see my ancestors' headstones, I also take photographs of other memorials and upload them to the website in the hope that they will help other people with their research. If you choose to do the same, my advice is to check first that nobody else has already uploaded the same images, and then focus on the headstones that are most at risk of becoming illegible. The number of burials that have been uploaded varies according to parish. For example, the churchyard of St Chad in Lichfield has over 500 memorials uploaded, whereas Penkhull has only 3. Billion Graves (**billiongraves.com**) and Deceased Online (**deceasedonline.com**) are similar sites although the latter requires a paid subscription.

Atlantic Geomatics (**agintl.org**) is currently in the process of photographing every headstone in Church of England churchyards and correlating each with the parish registers for the corresponding church. Maps will show exactly where every memorial is located, making the process of visiting the site ourselves much easier. As the company is using burial records not easily available to the public, its maps can also show us where our ancestors have been buried even if they have no surviving grave marker. This is being carried out on a county-by-county basis with Staffordshire not currently uploaded at the time of writing. The project is estimated to be completed in 2028.

Findmypast's collection 'Staffordshire Monumental Inscriptions' is available to view with a subscription and was originally transcribed by the Birmingham and Midland Society for Genealogy and Heraldry. The collection contains the basic information from the inscriptions, including the names of over 125,000 individuals, along with their place of burial, denomination and their year of death. Each transcription contains a link to the society's website Midland Ancestors (**midland-ancestors.uk**) where the full inscription can be purchased. Midland Ancestors has inscriptions available to purchase by parish and churchyard which are a small fee to download as a PDF file.

Ancestry's collection 'Records of the Removal of Graves and Tombstones, 1601–2007' contains the details of thousands of memorials which have been relocated. This is sadly a common occurrence. For Staffordshire, the churchyards include the Church of Holy Trinity in Burton upon Trent, Christ Church in Lichfield and Tipton Cemetery. The details given vary according to each place. For Burton upon Trent, the names of the deceased are given along with their date of death. The only other comments are with regards to the condition of the headstone at the time of removal, such as stating if it was damaged. For Tipton the full memorial inscription is given, an example of which is seen below.

**In loving Memory of
Ruth Annie Garness
Daughter of William and Susanna
Garness. Born Oct 3rd 1870
Died Oct 22nd 1873**

Values of the Record

The value of a memorial inscription lies within the information it supplies. The cost of engraving a headstone may mean that the inscription details are minimal; perhaps just a name and year of death. This may also simply be down to personal choice. Other headstones contain a large amount of useful genealogical information. This can include details such as the deceased's date of birth, place of residence and occupation. Names and dates of deceased children may also be given. Memorial inscriptions may be the only source we have of finding out a key bit of information, such as a date of birth. While this should be recorded, we must be aware of reliability issues where information cannot be backed up with another source.

Inscriptions can be used to trace a person's earlier details. If a year of birth or age at death is given, this can be used as a rough guide to find a birth certificate or baptism. Where an occupation is listed, this may lead us to discover an apprenticeship indenture or confirm a reference in a local directory.

Family members are often buried together in the same grave or close to each other within the same graveyard. Details of how they are related may be included, such as 'Elizabeth, wife of John' or 'child of the above'. When visiting an ancestor's burial place, it is worth having a walk around to note down any people of the same surname, or other familial surnames of interest, as you may find that these are relations at a later date. This will save a repeat journey. The deceased were often buried with their young children who may be mentioned, with rare occurrences of stillborn children also detailed. A married daughter may be buried with her parents, potentially giving you a missing piece of information such as her married surname.

The size of the memorial may hint towards the financial status of the deceased and their family. The wealthier members of a parish were more likely to be buried within the church or in a larger monument. The poorer members of society were almost certain to be buried without a headstone. There are some exceptions to the rule, for example when servants died some employers offered to pay for their headstone as a sign of gratitude.

You may discover that some of your ancestors have imagery etched into their memorial as well as text. This is usually fairly easy to interpret, such as a dove symbolising peace or a skull symbolising death. You may find images that hint at an ancestor's occupation, such as trade tools or a freemason's symbol. The imagery is often of a religious interpretation, for example a human hand pointing upwards towards heaven or a simple Christian cross. If you have a titled ancestor in your tree, you may find a coat of arms on the headstone.

Some inscription transcriptions were taken in the 1800s and these are particularly valuable as they are more likely to have details from headstones that are now illegible. Transcriptions are also valuable to those of us who cannot travel a long distance to see the memorial in person. Where a photograph is included along with a transcript, this is of a higher value as we can read the text ourselves and confirm the transcription.

Limitations of the Record

Many people believe that the details etched onto a monument are always accurate, but this is not always the case. It comes down to who instructed the headstone engraver and how much they knew. For example, if the deceased's age at death or birth year is included on the stone this is more likely to have been incorrect in earlier times when this information wasn't recorded as it is today. We will all come across ancestors whose age doesn't tally with their baptism, census returns and death records.

Memorials were sometimes erected many years after a person's death. After a person died, the family may have waited until their spouse also passed before erecting a permanent stone to replace a grave marker. This means that for the person who died first, their date of death is more likely to be misremembered and incorrectly recorded.

The number of headstones becoming illegible is ever increasing. Generally speaking, the older a memorial is, the more likely it is to be hard or impossible to read, although some headstones from the last fifty years are already difficult to read. This is largely down to weathering, but may also be due to vandalism or accidental damage. When faced with an illegible headstone, we may have to rely on earlier transcriptions if any were taken. Although these tend to be reliable, there is still a degree of human error so information should be backed up with other sources where possible. The increasing loss of detail from headstones emphasises the need to visit our ancestors' memorials sooner rather than later and to take photographs – at least one of the whole monument and one close up of the inscription. There are a number of cases where headstones have been legally removed, usually for building works. In this case we have no choice but to rely on any earlier transcriptions.

Lastly, the biggest limitation is simply that the majority of people were buried without a headstone. This means we have no memorial inscription for a majority of our ancestors, particularly the least wealthy members of the parish. Many were buried in mass graves, sharing their resting place with strangers rather than family. Commonly, an infant would be buried in the same plot as a stranger who died around the same time. In these cases, the infant is very unlikely to be named on the headstone.

Staffordshire Examples

My third great-grandparents, Samson and Rosanna Sarah Barlow, are buried in Longdon churchyard. Theirs is a basic inscription simply giving their names and the date of Samson's death and age of 80. It is presumed that Rosanna's date of death is also featured, although the stone has sunk too far into the ground to be able to see. It is therefore unknown as to whether any further details or quotations are noted at the bottom of the stone. There is a notable error within this inscription as Samson is known to have died in 1919 (proven via his death certificate), whereas the stone states he died in 1920. Rosanna died in 1921, hinting that the stone was most likely installed after Rosanna's death and the year of Samson's death was wrongly remembered – proof that memorial inscriptions cannot always be trusted and other sources should be sought where possible.

The headstone of Samson and Rosanna Barlow at Longdon churchyard. (Author's own)

The memorial for my fourth great-grandparents, John and Eleanor Marshall, can also be found in Longdon churchyard. This gravestone is in the form of a ledger, placed flat on the ground and features little decoration. The inscription is clearly readable, despite the stone's age, and, despite partially being covered by moss and grass at the edges, it has received little damage. The inscription gives both their names, dates of death and their relationship. John's birth date is given as 28 March 1803; this date has not yet been verified with another source and the inscription may be the only place this information can be found. As to how trustworthy the detail is, all that can be found is that John was baptised in December 1803 but no birth date is given. It is also unclear as to whether the stone was laid and inscribed after John's death in 1871 or after Eleanor's death in 1900. Eleanor's birth date is not given; however, it is stated that she was aged 94 at the time of her death. Her age has been verified using her baptism record from the same parish.

The ledger of John and Eleanor Marshall at Longdon churchyard. (Author's own)

Chapter 16

OTHER SOURCES

School Records

You are most likely to find school documents from the 1880s onwards when education in a school environment became compulsory until the age of 10. Admission registers are one of the more useful sources. These were compiled when the child was admitted into the school and give the child's name, date of birth, the name of their next of kin and their address. The address may be given as a specific numbered property, a road name or a parish name. There is usually a space for administrator comments among which it may be noted when and why they left the school. If a child left school due to moving parish, the name of their new parish is usually given, or at least a county name if this is outside Staffordshire. Siblings may be listed together when they were admitted on the same date, usually after a house move. Attendance registers and punishment books can be an eye-opening resource, showing how often your ancestor attended school, the reason they were absent and what they were punished for and how. Reasons of absence may be brief such as 'unwell' but are often more detailed noting the exact illness including measles and broken bones. They also note if a child was absent due to the death of a family member.

School log books contain information about daily events, often written like a short journal by the headteacher. These may tell you the weather that day, the number of children absent, the lessons that occurred, any new staff appointments and any notable events such as exam results. Log books are therefore useful to those researching a pupil or a member of school staff. Not all have been retained. Where school records have been digitised, admission registers are easy to search by pupil name, whereas log books will need to be browsed page by page. This is a lengthy process. Other school records include meeting minutes, photographs and architectural plans.

School records are predominantly held at local archives, with some retained by the schools themselves. Currently the only digitised collection is on Findmypast in its 'National School Admission Registers & Log-Books 1870–1914' collection. One example in the admission register for Butterton School shows Abel Armitt was admitted on 20 March 1882. His date of birth is given as 15 August 1869 and his father is named as Charles Armitt. They are said to reside at Butterton Moor. Abel's previous school is stated to be in the neighbouring village of Onecote and he left Butterton School on 15 September 1882, a month after his thirteenth birthday. The following is a partial transcript from the admissions register for Chapel Chorlton primary school dated 1911.

Date of Admission	Name	Date of Birth	Name and Address of Parent	Cause of Leaving	Date of Leaving
27/3/11	John William Cotton	18/2/06	Hensley Cotton, Butt House	-	21/3/13
16/6/11	Alice Turner	11/6/06	Elizabeth Turner, The Rowe	Death	Died 26/11/18
4/9/11	Ernest Randles	30/7/06	Charles Randles, Model HC	Labour exemption	17/10/17
16/10/11	Ciceley Williams	8/3/98	James Williams, Hill Chorlton	-	March 6th
23/10/11	Annie Florence Highfield	20/10/06	Harry Highfield, The Rookery Cott.	-	-

There are nearly 200 log books for historical Staffordshire within the same collection on Findmypast. One is that for Wordsley Mixed School dating 1904–1927. Some extracts include 2 December 1904 when severe snowfall led to 'seriously affected attendance'; 7 April 1905 when a new cookery class was introduced by Ms Willetts; and 28 November 1905 when Mrs Southall called to complain that Miss Yeomans had punished her daughter. The latter entry notes this was the third such similar complaint made by the mother and Miss Yeomans was reminded that she did not have the right to administer physical punishment to children.

Hospital Records

According to the Hospital Records Database accessed via TNA website (**www.thenationalarchives.gov.uk/hospitalrecords/default.asp**), there were fifty-two separate hospitals, asylums and dispensary services in the historical county of Staffordshire. This database is no longer being updated but still provides us with useful information. For example, the database shows that Meynell Ingram Cottage Hospital in Yoxall was founded in 1873 and closed in 1986. It was previously named Yoxall Cottage Hospital and its associated records are held at Staffordshire History Centre. As the database is no longer updated, be sure to corroborate any information found here with another source.

Stafford General Infirmary was founded in 1766 and is one of the oldest hospitals in England. Hospitals are a relatively new development in our history for a majority of the public. Only the wealthy were able to afford treatment from a doctor or surgeon. With the arrival of workhouses, the poorer communities began to be able to access care. Voluntary hospitals, so called because they were run by volunteers, were established and were funded by donations. These usually focused on particular health concerns, such as eye and ear conditions.

The records are rarely catalogued by name, meaning it helps to know what year your ancestor was admitted when viewing admission and discharge registers. Individual patient records survive in many cases. Some examples of what can be found include registers of patients assessed for mental health treatment at City General Hospital in Stoke-on-Trent 1926–1960, held at Stoke-on-Trent City Archives; a register of graves from Burntwood County Asylum 1867–1924, held at Staffordshire History Centre; and a discharge register for Cheddleton County Asylum 1907–1929, also held at Staffordshire History Centre.

When viewing hospital and patient records for our ancestors, it is important to remember the era they were written. Medical terms have changed and may require researching before you can understand what exactly your ancestor was suffering from. Women were admitted to asylums suffering from 'mania' after giving birth; what we would now call either post-natal depression or post-partum psychosis. There was very limited understanding of a huge range of illnesses, particularly mental health conditions such as post-traumatic stress disorder and schizophrenia. Those who today would be diagnosed as having learning disabilities or autism were labelled as 'idiots' and 'imbeciles'. These were not intended as derogatory terms and are examples of how language has changed meaning over time. You may also come across some shocking cases in asylums where homosexuals and dementia sufferers are 'treated' in a way that would be simply unacceptable today.

A patient database for the three historical Staffordshire asylums at Burntwood, Cheddleton and Stafford for the years 1818–1920 is searchable for free online via **www.staffsnameindexes.org.uk/default. aspx?Index=U**. You can search via surname, occupation, asylum and year of the record. The information provided usually includes the patient's name, occupation, union of residence, asylum they were admitted to, their year of admission and/or discharge and the date of their death if they died while in the care of the asylum. Many patients' diagnosis is also provided in brief terms, such as 'melancholia' or 'chronic mania'. Importantly, the source reference is provided for each person's details, meaning you can use the document reference number to find the record at the named archive to discover what extra information is held about the patient. In some cases, the database provides extra information, such as age at death and if any additional items are held for the person, including photographs and death notices.

Poll Books and Electoral Rolls

Poll books date from 1696 to 1872 and record a small minority of the population of England and Wales. Only the wealthiest members of society were allowed to vote in political elections. Poll books give the names of those able to vote, their qualification to vote and the name of the candidate for whom they voted. You may also find their address, district and occupation. Secret ballots were not introduced until 1872. Only men are featured in poll books as only men were allowed to vote. Some are digitised and available to view on Ancestry in its 'UK, Poll Books and Electoral Registers, 1538–1893' record set. Others are held in local archives including Staffordshire History Centre and Walsall Archives. The following shows an extract from the Newcastle-under-Lyme vote of 1812 where voters could choose between Earl Gower, Edward Wilbraham Bootle and Sir John Fenton Boughey.

Name	Occupation	Votes		
		Gower	Bootle	Boughey
Powys, Stephen	Feltmaker			1
Pye, Thomas, senr.	Hatter	1		1
Pepper, Moses	Bricklayer	1	1	
Plant, John	Shoemaker	1		1
Pendleton, John	Feltmaker			1

The qualifications to vote were gradually extended. From 1918, men aged over 21 and women aged over 30 were entitled to vote. The voting age for women was lowered to the same as men in 1928, reaching voting equality between the sexes for the first time. It helps to remember these key years so you know who to expect to find in the records for which date. There are some exceptions for women. They may be found from

1867 in municipal elections if they were the rate payer and from 1888 for local council elections.

Early electoral rolls from 1832 onwards are listed by surname alphabetically, with rolls from 1918 organised by street for larger districts. Many can be found online, such as on Ancestry and Findmypast with more found in local archives. The rolls show everyone in a household who was eligible to vote so can act as an adults-only census. There are gaps in the records to be aware of. No electoral rolls were taken in the war years of 1917–1918 and 1940–1944. There was an absentee voter list taken of soldiers on duty in 1918, which provides their service details. Electoral registers were compiled several months before publication, so in the meantime a person may have moved or passed away.

Until 1948, the rolls included letters as a code for each person to tell the reader why they qualified to vote. These are explained below.

1918–1927	
R.	Residence Qualification
B.P.	Business Premises Qualification
O.	Occupation Qualification
H.O.	Qualification through Husband's Occupation
N.M.	Naval or Military Voter

1928–1947 – Male Voters	
R	Residence Qualification
B	Business Premises Qualification
O	Occupation Qualification
D	Qualification through Wife's Occupation
NM	Naval or Military Voter

1928–1947 – Female Voters	
Rw	Residence Qualification
Bw	Business Premises Qualification
Ow	Occupation Qualification
Dw	Qualification through Husband's Occupation
NM	Naval or Military Voter

The word 'occupation' in this context does not refer to the person's profession, but instead to their occupation of a property. Be wary also when researching families that you know little about. A man and a woman seen residing together may not actually be a married couple. They could for example be father and daughter-in-law which may lead a researcher to add the female to their tree as his spouse or daughter erroneously. The following is an extract from the electoral roll for Burslem dating 1915 which can be found on Findmypast.

Name	Place of Abode	Nature of Qualification	Description of Qualifying Property
Dale, Albert Philip	186 Elder Road	Dwelling house	186 Elder Road
Bonsell, Thomas	21 Remer Street	Marine stores	Elder Road
Wheat, David	2 Sneyd Street	Dwelling house successive	14 Charles Street & 2 Sneyd Street
Blackhurst, William Henry	4 Sneyd Street	Dwelling house	4 Sneyd Street
Griffiths, Samuel	10 Sneyd Street	Dwelling house	10 Sneyd Street

Inquest Records

You may find, via a death certificate or newspaper article, that your ancestor's decease was investigated by the local coroner at an inquest. Inquests were held in the case of a sudden death, a death with no obvious cause, or death by suicide. Inquest records do not all survive and you are lucky if you can find one that relates to your family. Newspapers frequently gave summaries of the coroner's findings, including any notable injuries to the deceased, if alcohol was involved and the coroner's verdict on their cause of death. This may be a simple medical case such as a suspected heart attack, the result of an accident such as a fall, or murder.

Where a full inquest record has survived the information provided can be extremely useful to a family historian. The deceased's name, residence, age, occupation and place of death may be given. If the cause of death is a possible suicide then witnesses are likely to have been called to attest to the deceased's state of mind at the time of their death. Any known concerns that the deceased had are likely to be mentioned, such as the state of their marriage, financial situation and any health issues. If a death occurred at work then details of the conditions of their workplace may be given. Inquests tend to be filed with Quarter Sessions records from 1752 until 1860. Some are held separately in local archives and will appear with a name search of the catalogue. Those detailed in Quarter Sessions records are unlikely to be catalogued by name.

Staffordshire History Centre holds a collection of inquests for North Staffordshire dating from 1921 onwards, along with a register of inquests for Stafford dating 1861–1950. Inquest records are not available to researchers until seventy-five years have passed from the date of the inquest and most are destroyed after fifteen years. Wolverhampton City Archives holds inquests for the city dating 1870–2011 as well as entries included in Wolverhampton's Quarter Sessions records.

Overseas Travel Documentation

Despite being a land-locked county, you may be surprised to find your Staffordshire ancestors travelling abroad. This may have been to visit friends or relatives, as a tourist, to escape persecution or criminal justice, to work, to study or to emigrate. You may find that some of your ancestry hails from overseas with your forebears choosing to settle in Staffordshire, or perhaps some of your ancestors lived abroad for a while before returning. It is common to find families who relocate abroad returning home many years later.

UK-registered ships were only required to keep passenger lists from 1842 onwards, with a majority of records surviving from 1890 onwards. You may find your forebear in earlier lists if they were travelling on a ship registered elsewhere in the world due to differing legislation. The majority of surviving lists are for long-distance journeys, such as to America and Australia, rather than those within Europe.

Records for outbound passengers travelling from the UK between 1890 and 1960 are held at TNA in Series BT 27. These have been digitised and are available to view on Findmypast and Ancestry. Records for inbound passengers arriving into the UK between 1878 and 1960 are also at TNA in Series BT 26. These are available on Ancestry. The information supplied varies but may include the passenger's age, occupation, place of birth, name of employer or relative and their intended final destination.

When you have found an ancestor settling abroad, you can check the records to see what evidence survives of their time there. The documentation is likely to be the same as in the UK, including census returns, newspaper articles and civil registration records. Some passenger lists were also published in newspapers in the UK and abroad. The following is a partial transcript for incoming passengers on the 'Argentina Star' ship arriving at London from Buenos Aires, Argentina on 30 August 1948.

Names of Passengers	Class	Ages of Passengers	Proposed Address in UK	Profession or Occupation
ALLEN Alfred	1st	50	386 Sutton Road, Walsall	Engineer
ALLEN Mary	1st	44	As above	None
ALLEN James	1st	17	As above	Student
ALLEN Edward	1st	11	As above	Student
ROBSON Colin	1st	47	8 Archbold Terrace, Jessmond, Newcastle-on-Tyne	Engineer
ROBSON Elizabeth	1st	43	As above	None

Equity Court Records

The Equity Courts in London handled civil disputes originating from England and Wales. People travelled from all over the country to appear. The issues covered ranged from marriage settlements and contests of probate to boundary disagreements and trading disputes. There were many different types of Equity Court in Westminster, all with a different focus. The Court of Wards, for example, looked into cases of orphanage and the mentally ill, whereas the Court of Requests dealt with paupers. Most commonly, you will find cases in the Court of Chancery and the Court of Exchequer. The Court of Chancery initially largely dealt with land disputes; the Court of Exchequer handled financial disagreements. Over time, the lines became blurred and there was a lot of overlap between the types of case you would find in each court. Therefore, if you are aware that an ancestor appeared in an Equity Court, it may not immediately be obvious which one they attended even if you know the issue at hand.

All Equity Court records are held at TNA. Most are held together in bundles in a case-by-case arrangement. Unfortunately, the anomaly here is the Court of Chancery which also happened to be the most active court and therefore the one you are most likely to find your ancestors in. From 1876 onwards, the cases have not yet been indexed but are held in J Series. To search these records, it is recommended to first search newspaper records to find a reference to a case title. This can then be entered into TNA's Discovery search catalogue.

For Chancery cases prior to 1876, enter the name of your ancestor into the Discovery catalogue and narrow the results down to the 'C' series. Cases are often listed by surname only, such as 'Walbridge v. Turner'. Parish names are often entered into the catalogue also, so try searching for your ancestor's surname and their parish of residence. It is common to find cases involving close family members, so titles often appear as 'Davis v. Davis'. The catalogue sometimes gives further details, such as first names or what the dispute regarded. For example, the catalogue entry titled 'Fownes v Brecknock' held at C 10/486/71 tells us their names are Joseph Fownes and Francis Brecknock and the subject regards 'money matters' in Staffordshire in 1678.

The bill of complaint was given by the plaintiff and initiated the case as part of the pleadings. The bill should tell you the plaintiff's name, occupation and address and the name of the defendant. There may be more than one plaintiff or defendant. After the bill was received, the defendant issued an 'Answer' in response. You may also come across witness statements known as Depositions which can give their names, ages, addresses and occupations. The issue at hand will often influence how much genealogical information is found within the court documentation. Probate disputes and marriage settlements, for example, often name several members of the same family and can give a glimpse into their relationships. Supporting evidence was also often archived with the material, which may include copies of parish registers, wills or indentures.

There is little online aside from the Discovery catalogue, meaning once you find a case involving your ancestor you will either need to visit TNA in person to view the documents or order them to send to you digitally. There are two further indexes online; however, these give few details. Ancestry has the 'British Chancery Records, 1386–1558' record set which gives the name of the person in the record, the year of the case, the place and the catalogue reference of its location at TNA. For example, the 1515–1518 case of Georgius Oke of Stafford is held at C 1/433/16. The 'Charles I Court of Chancery Index, 1625–1649' collection on Findmypast gives even less detail as their location is not included. You may only search the collection by the surname of the plaintiff or defendant, making identification very difficult. Both of these record sets are transcripts only and should be used as a guide to find out more via TNA.

Divorce

Divorce is a rare find prior to the 1920s. This is largely down to the huge expense involved in obtaining an official divorce through a private Act of Parliament at the time, which was an option from 1668. The only other option was to request a separation from the ecclesiastical courts, although there were very strict rules for this, such as proof of an incestuous marriage. In 1858, the Court for Divorce and Matrimonial Causes was founded. This was transferred to the Probate, Divorce and Admiralty division in 1873. All divorce cases were heard in London until 1927 and were a lengthy process, taking years to authorise. The reason for the divorce means different information will be supplied for each case. The couple's names will be given, sometimes with a third party if adultery or bigamy is the reason for the divorce application. Their home addresses should be supplied, sometimes with their occupation. The names and ages of any children born out of the marriage are also likely to be given. Among the divorce papers you will find evidence where it was requested, including witness statements and marriage certificates.

Divorce records dating 1858–1937 usually survive and are held at TNA in Series J 77 and J 78. These are catalogued by name so should appear when you use the Discovery search engine. The wife will be listed under her married name rather than her maiden name. Most divorce documentation from 1938 onwards has been destroyed. Records of private Acts of Parliament dating pre-1858 are also held at TNA. As with most types of documentation, divorce records are held confidentially with no public access until seventy-five years have passed.

You can search the 'Divorce Index' set on Findmypast which will show if a person applied for a divorce between 1858 and 1903. Little information is given in the index but this is a good prompt to search for their names on Discovery. Alternatively, you can search Ancestry's 'England & Wales, Civil Divorce Records, 1858–1918' which provides images relating to divorce court cases.

One example shown on Ancestry is the divorce of John Thomas Adamson and Sarah Eliza Adamson (née Baker). John filed for divorce on 19 March 1884, with the final decree granted on 18 May 1886. Sarah was proven to have committed adultery with a butcher named Alfred Henry Craddock. The documentation states John and Sarah married 18 December 1873 at St Peter's Church in Wolverhampton. Alfred was called to court on 18 April 1884 but denied committing adultery with Sarah.

John's address is supplied as Oxford Street in Bilston. John stated he and Sarah resided in Bilston from the time of their marriage but had no children. He claimed that Sarah treated him 'with much cruelty', implied she suffered from alcoholism and frequently threatened to assault him. Upon returning from a trip to Manchester, John returned home to find his wife in bed with Alfred. Sarah's brother was sleeping next door and John called him in as a witness to the adultery, giving him the proof he needed for a divorce to be granted. John claims that since the incident on

In the High Court of Justice.

PROBATE, DIVORCE, AND ADMIRALTY DIVISION.

(DIVORCE.)

Before the Right Honorable SIR JAMES HANNEN, Knight, The President,

~~Before the Honorable SIR CHARLES PARKER BUTT, Knight, one of the Justices of the High Court,~~

sitting at the Royal Courts of Justice, Strand, in the County of Middlesex.

On the *11th* day of *February* 1885.

Adamson against *Adamson & Craddock*

An extract from the divorce papers for John and Sarah Adamson dated 1885. (With permission from The National Archives)

7 June 1881 he and Sarah had no longer been cohabiting and that his wife had been earning a living via prostitution. John and Sarah's marriage certificate is supplied among the papers.

Heraldry

Heraldry relates to coats of arms, the significance of their design and the method through which they are passed down and altered over generations. Family historians tend to either avoid using coats of arms altogether or overuse them in a way which is not relevant. After nearly twenty years of researching my tree I have yet to discover a genuine armiger; that is, a person who is entitled to a coat of arms. On public family trees you often see coats of arms attached to a person, usually incorrectly. Similarly, you can purchase merchandise bearing a surname along with a coat of arms. However, the chances that the arms are related to your family are very minimal. For people researching armigers, it is worth spending some time researching basic heraldry and its connotations as this can greatly help your research.

Arms were originally used in the twelfth century on the battlefield so that a helmeted person could still be identified. Each coat of arms, therefore, had to be unique. During this time, knights spoke Norman French in England, meaning that the language of heraldry had French derivations. It was important that people could describe a coat of arms through words, known as a blazon. At first glance, this appears difficult to understand. For example, *sable a fess argent* refers to a black (*sable*) shield, with a silver (*argent*) line across the middle (*a fess*). I personally found the easiest way to learn about heraldry was to memorise the names of the different colours first, followed by the different shapes, known as ordinaries and charges, you may find on the shields. From there you learn the order in which the description should be given.

This shield can be blazoned as 'sable a fess argent'. (Author's own)

There are many rules regarding heraldry and these help us with our research. Cadency marks prove useful in genealogy and are designed to quickly show a man's position within the family, such as whether he is the second-born son (crescent) or the seventh-born son (rose). Marshalling occurs when a coat of arms is passed down a generation and is altered. This happens when an armigerous man marries an armigerous woman and their shields are combined. How they are combined will tell you more information, such as whether the woman had any brothers and whether her father is still alive or not.

Between 1530 and 1688, heralds travelled the country on behalf of the College of Arms. They aimed to register and regulate the coats of arms being used and as a result produced many pedigrees. These trees are not entirely reliable but are still very much worth viewing. The Harleian Society has published the visitations for Staffordshire for the years 1583, 1614 and 1663–4.

Sport

You may find evidence of your ancestor playing a particular sport regardless of whether they played professionally or for leisure. Newspapers print articles about professional sports people, such as boxers and footballers, as well as local stories of friendly matches between village teams. Some people took part in bicycle races at weekends. This can be eye opening to researchers who were previously unaware of their ancestor's interests or sporting talents. Articles may appear with a basic name search. If you find your ancestor was on a particular team, you can then alternatively search for this team name in further reports as well as within archive catalogues. Some articles give very basic details, such as the surnames of those who took part in a football or cricket match, whereas others give more of a match summary, naming key players and their achievements during the game. You may also find advertisements for upcoming matches and rundowns of school games.

Some sporting documentation is held in local archives and others within the private hands of teams still in existence. Local archives hold various football programmes and sporting photographs. Specific examples include the 1950–1962 score books for Burton upon Trent Police cricket club and records of Leek Cricket Club for the years 1844–2012 both at Staffordshire History Centre. You may find that other descendants of your sporting ancestor have inherited related items, such as ticket stubs, trophies and photographs. These may also be found in a local museum.

> **UTTOXETER CRICKETERS SCORE WELL.**
>
> A cricket match in which several Uttoxeter players were engaged took place at Caverswall yesterday between the home team and Kingsley. The local men did splendidly, E. S. Rowley scoring 26 (making his total 500 for the season), W. Heasman 47, V. Dams 11, L. A. Hedge 26, and Rev. C. Dams 25, all of whom assisted Kingsley. C. Forrester, also of Uttoxeter, did not bat. Kingsley declared with 181 for nine, and then dismissed Caverswall for 84, Heasman capturing six wickets for 17; F. Walker (Oakamoor), who bowled well but had bad luck, several catches being missed off his deliveries, two for 46; and Griffin one for 7.

The report for the Caverswall v. Kingsley cricket match in Uttoxeter Advertiser and Ashbourne Times 25 August 1909. (Content provided by THE BRITISH LIBRARY BOARD. ALL RIGHTS RESERVED. With thanks to The British Newspaper Archive (www.britishnewspaperarchive.co.uk))

Photographs

There is an obvious general interest to finding photographs of our ancestors. When we have spent a long time researching someone's life, to be able to put a face to a name is a memorable moment. Many of us are lucky enough to have inherited a selection of family photos. Some of these are likely to have been carefully labelled with the person's name and perhaps a date or location. Others are left frustratingly unlabelled, leaving us to ponder who the person is and how they relate to us, if at all. Try not to fixate on the unlabelled photographs too much. Our ancestors held on to photographs of their friends and neighbours as well as their families, so you may not be related to them anyway.

It is important to digitise your family photographs to preserve them while also conserving the original. Make sure you record the names of any people you have confidently identified. It is your choice as to whether or not you wish to share your photographs with others, but be aware you may hold the only surviving photograph of an ancestor shared with many other descendants who would love to see a copy.

A photograph can tell us many things, aside from the interest in seeing a person's face. Outfits can give us an approximate date of when the picture was likely to have been taken. Different clothing styles went in and out of fashion as they still do today, so the type of dress, coat or hat that a person is wearing may narrow a timeframe. In the same way, hairstyles and facial hair can also help us to date an image. This is particularly helpful when we are trying to identify an unknown person in a photograph as it can narrow the selection of likely candidates. Make a note of anything of interest in the photograph, such as a family pet, any jewellery that is worn or how the people are positioned. It may be obvious from the background where the photograph was taken, such as if there is a landmark present. Alternatively, it may have been taken in a studio, whereby the studio information provided on the back of the image card can give you the address the photograph was taken.

A photograph of the Keep family outside Longdon post office c.1904. (Author's own)

As well as photographs of our ancestors, be sure to look into historical family collections of images that don't have any people present. These can still tell us much about our family history. You can find out what tourist attractions they visited, any vehicles or pets they owned and what their property looked like. Photographs of an ancestor's town or village of residence during the time they lived there can be especially eye opening; to see an important part of their world exactly as they would have seen it. If these are found within your personal collection, consider sharing them with local historians who are always on the lookout for new views of their place of study.

No matter how many photographs of our ancestors we have, we will always crave to find more. They are most likely to be held by other descendants of the same ancestor, so it is worth contacting cousins and second cousins to see what they have in their possession. Social media is increasingly being used for sharing old photographs so consider joining a Facebook group or Instagram page dedicated to your location of interest. Distant family members often make initial contact this way as not everybody is a member of a family history subscription site. Other potential sources to locate photographs of your ancestors include newspaper records, family history societies, criminal records, public family trees and local archives.

Chapter 17

STAFFORDSHIRE ARCHIVES

Before visiting any of the archive services below, please check their websites for opening hours and booking requirements. In addition to the sites mentioned below, also note that the Black Country History website at **blackcountryhistory.org** covers material held by the archives at Dudley, Sandwell, Walsall and Wolverhampton.

Staffordshire History Centre
Eastgate Street, Stafford ST16 2LZ
www.staffordshirehistory.org.uk
The Staffordshire and Stoke-on-Trent Archive Service runs both the county headquarters in Stafford and the Stoke-on-Trent City Archives. Newly opened in 2024, the Staffordshire History Centre holds a majority of the county's historical documentation and incorporates the William Salt Library buildings. It is at the Centre you are most likely to come across relevant records such as parish registers, parish records, manorial records, title deeds, maps and school records among many others. Search the holdings of the above archives at Gateway to the Past (**archives.staffordshire.gov.uk/CalmView**).

Stoke-on-Trent City Archives
The Potteries Museum & Art Gallery, Bethesda Street, Hanley, Stoke-on-Trent ST1 3DW
https://www.staffordshirehistory.org.uk/stoke-on-trent-city-archives
Relocated to The Potteries Museum in 2024, Stoke-on-Trent City Archives retains the historical records relating to the city and outlying areas. Its records can also be searched via the Gateway to the Past website mentioned above.

Wolverhampton City Archives
Molineux Hotel Building, Whitmore Hill, Wolverhampton, West Midlands WV1 1SF
www.wolverhamptonart.org.uk/wolverhampton-city-archives

This archive holds material relating to Wolverhampton and the surrounding area, including electoral registers, school registers, trade directories and poll books. It also holds a collection of Wolverhampton residents' wills, land tax returns and maps.

Sandwell Archives
Smethwick Library, High Street, Smethwick B66 1AA
www.sandwell.gov.uk/archives

The archive holds documentation relating to the six towns of Sandwell: Oldbury; Rowley Regis; Smethwick; Tipton; Wednesbury; and West Bromwich, the majority of which were previously within historical Staffordshire's border. Records include parish registers, maps, newspapers, education records and electoral rolls.

Dudley Archives
Tipton Road, Dudley DY1 4SQ
www.better.org.uk/library/dudley/archives-and-local-history-centre

This collection consists of material relating to Dudley and the surrounding area. Here you can find local newspapers, electoral registers, trade directories and business records, among many others.

Walsall Archives
Lichfield Street Hub, Lichfield Street, Walsall WS1 1TR
https://go.walsall.gov.uk/localhistorycentre

A part of Staffordshire until 1974, many of Walsall's records can be found at Walsall Archives. Its catalogue consists of a large number of historical photographs of the area, business records, council papers and church records.

Staffordshire Regiment Museum
DMS Whittington, Lichfield WS14 9PY
staffordshireregimentmuseum.com

Records held here include correspondence, newspaper articles, publications, information on the barracks and details of relevant memorials to the war dead. Research enquiries are welcomed for those looking into the 38th, 64th, 80th and 98th Regiments of Foot, the South and North Staffordshire Regiments and The Staffordshire Regiment. Note that it does not hold service, pension or medical records.

Birmingham Archives
Wolfson Centre for Archival Research, Library of Birmingham, Centenary Square, Broad Street, Birmingham B1 2ND
www.birmingham.gov.uk/archives

Here you can find Anglican and Nonconformist registers, maps, trade directories and local newspapers. Other examples of records include occupational records, such as those of the Birmingham and Staffordshire Gas-Light Company, local newspapers and a list of the county's jurors from 1734–1838.

Birmingham Archdiocesan Archives
Cathedral House, St Chad's Queensway, Birmingham B4 6EU
www.birminghamarchdiocesanarchives.org.uk/index.asp

This archive will be of relevance to you if your Staffordshire ancestors were Roman Catholic. Records include baptism, marriage and burial registers, documents from the now defunct Staffordshire Catholic History Society, and clergy papers.

Keele University Archives
Keele, Newcastle-under-Lyme, Staffordshire ST5 5BG
www.keele.ac.uk/library/specialcollections/

Keele University's Special Collections and Archives holds various manorial records for Staffordshire including for Keele Manor and Tunstall Manor. Documents include court rolls, amercements and rentals.

Cheshire Archives
Duke Street, Chester, Cheshire CH1 1RL
www.cheshirearchives.org.uk/home.aspx

The archive holds records relating to estates in North Staffordshire, among many other relevant offerings to the county. These include staff records of the North Staffordshire Railway 1884–1948, maps and a wide array of title deeds. Given the county border's location, the majority of Staffordshire records here relate to the north of the county.

Derbyshire Record Office
New Street, Matlock, Derbyshire DE4 3FE
www.derbyshire.gov.uk/leisure/record-office/derbyshire-record-office.aspx

As another county that borders Staffordshire, many of the records here relate to places close to the shared border. This includes estate records and title deeds. There are also records relating to the North Staffordshire Railway, apprentice indentures occurring across the border and various correspondence documentation.

Shropshire Archives
Castle Gates, Shrewsbury, Shropshire SY1 2AQ
www.shropshirearchives.org.uk

Its Staffordshire collection consists mainly of estate papers and relevant documentation such as grants and deeds. There are also marriage settlements, correspondence material and bonds.

The National Archives (TNA)
Kew, Richmond, Surrey TW9 4DU
www.nationalarchives.gov.uk

Home to millions of records, you will discover at some point in your research that TNA holds documents relating to your ancestors. Its online Discovery catalogue (**https://discovery.nationalarchives.gov.uk**) allows you to search its collection as well as those belonging to other archives across the country. Some of TNA's records are digitised and are available to view instantly online; however, a majority will either need to be viewed in person or have a copy request sent. At times, its digitised records are contracted to a particular genealogical subscription site, so you may find yourself redirected to pages on Ancestry or Findmypast.

TNA holds a large number of historical records relating to Staffordshire, including over 14,000 Chancery court records, over 13,000 Exchequer court records and nearly 9,000 probate documents. Some of the other items it holds are a selection of passports, timetables and accounts of the North Staffordshire Railway and documents of the county's Friendly Societies.

Other Archives
You could find material relating to your Staffordshire kin anywhere in the country, perhaps even abroad, typical examples being estate records and correspondence. Postcards and letters may have been sent from your family member to another county where they may now be retained in its archives. Try searching the TNA Discovery catalogue for any such results. Specific examples of what you can find elsewhere include the 1608 Kibblestone Manor survey held by Wiltshire and Swindon Archives; and an 1876 pedigree of the Parker family of Park Hall held by Hampshire Archives.

Chapter 18

STAFFORDSHIRE MUSEUMS

Visiting museums is a worthwhile task for anybody, but they have added interest for genealogists. By helping to educate us about general social history, we can better understand what our ancestors' lives were like, including topics we may not often consider such as hygiene, medicine and local politics. Museums can be focused on military history, a specific occupation, or the history of a town.

This chapter will focus on museums within Staffordshire, but do look further afield for others that may be of interest. For example, there may not be a museum in the county dedicated to your ancestors' occupation but there may be one elsewhere, which will still be worth a visit. Occupational museums, such as breweries and mills, can teach us what our forebears' daily lives would have involved. We can discover their likely working hours, any risks associated with the job and the working conditions. You may also find that the museum concerning your ancestors' military regiment is located outside of the county.

If you cannot visit in person, check out the museums' websites. Museums have become increasingly aware of the importance of improving online access; many now offer a chance to view their collections online. Some give you the opportunity to search their collections, such as by a person's name, a location or occupation. The Imperial War Museum's website (**iwm.org.uk**) is excellent for this feature and is well worth visiting.

Having worked in several museums, I know from experience that the staff are passionate about their work and are often keen to help genealogists with their queries. A significant part of a museum's collection is kept in its archives and these can sometimes be retrieved for personal viewings. You may wish to contact museum staff in advance of your visit to see if they have an item in their collection of relevance to you that is kept behind the scenes. Consider that museum staff are very busy so may not always be able to help you and payment may sometimes be required.

Ancient High House
Greengate Street, Stafford ST16 2JA
staffordbc.gov.uk/the-ancient-high-house

This remarkable building dates from the late Tudor period and opened as a museum in 1986. Previously inhabited by the Dorrington family, the house has many tales to tell. King Charles I was the property's most famous visitor and you can view the room in which he stayed. Rooms are set up in several styles according to different time periods, including Stuart, Georgian, Edwardian and Victorian. Upstairs, the house is home to the Staffordshire Yeomanry Regiment Museum. There is also a display on the building's construction and an art gallery.

Gladstone Pottery Museum
Uttoxeter Road, Stoke-on-Trent ST3 1PQ
www.stokemuseums.org.uk/gpm

The museum is housed in a Grade II* listed building with a striking appearance thanks to its bottle kilns. It is a working museum, which will be of added interest to those researching their pottery worker forebears. You can learn about every aspect of the pottery industry and discover exactly what your ancestor was doing. This includes throwing, moulding and decorating pottery. With much pottery on display, you can see the type of ceramics your ancestor worked with.

Ford Green Hall
Ford Green Road, Smallthorne, Stoke-on-Trent ST6 1NG
fordgreenhall.org.uk

The Hall is furnished as though it has remained untouched for hundreds of years. This clever method of displaying objects and furniture helps us to really imagine what life was like for our ancestors. The house is a beautiful timber-framed building dating back to 1624, with glorious beamed ceilings. Highlights include the parlour chamber, where you can see an example of wattle and daub construction, and the kitchen.

Samuel Johnson Birthplace Museum
Breadmarket Street, Lichfield WS13 6LG
samueljohnsonbirthplace.org.uk

While the museum is dedicated to the life of Samuel Johnson, known for writing *A Dictionary of the English Language* in 1755, there is much of interest here for genealogists. The period room settings are of particular significance; however, you can also learn much about the literacy of his time. Beautiful artworks adorn many of the walls including landscapes of the local area and portraits of the family. There is a brilliant virtual tour of the museum available via its website.

Staffordshire Regiment Museum
DMS Whittington, Lichfield, WS14 9PY
staffordshireregimentmuseum.com

As well as potentially helping your research as mentioned in the Archives chapter, this museum explains the history of the Staffordshire Regiment in an enlightening and often interactive way. There is a replica First World War trench outside and historical re-enactors help bring the scene to life during special event days. The museum has a large collection available to view, including many armoured vehicles from the Second World War onwards. This is a must-see if your ancestor was in one of the Staffordshire regiments.

The Potteries Museum and Art Gallery
Bethesda Street, Hanley, Stoke-on-Trent ST1 3DW
www.stokemuseums.org.uk/pmag/

This general interest museum displays a range of artefacts of interest from a wide time period, including items from the Anglo-Saxon Staffordshire Hoard, a Spitfire RW388 and a photographic collection of Longton photographer William Blake. Arguably, the main attraction is the collection of local ceramics including those by Wedgwood and Spode. Via their website you can search for photographs, maps, artwork and records about places within the Potteries area of Staffordshire.

Museum of Cannock Chase
Valley Road, Hednesford, Cannock WS12 1TD
museumofcannockchase.org

The museum is located on the site of the former Valley Colliery, which was later transformed into a mining training centre. There are exhibitions about mining the coalfield that will be of interest to researchers whose ancestors had a related occupation, as well as a gallery about the history of the Cannock Chase area. There is also a 1940s room which can show you how your more recent forebears may have lived. The museum is home to a lovely collection of children's toys and games, giving an insight into our ancestors' childhood.

Other Museums of Note
There are many other pottery-related museums in the area; if these are of interest to you, look at World of Wedgwood, Dudson Museum and Spode Museum among others. Other museums of note to genealogists include Redfern's Cottage Museum of Uttoxeter Life, Tutbury Museum, Apedale Heritage Centre and Kinver Edge Rock Houses. Be sure to research which other museums may be helpful to your research as there are too many to list here.

Chapter 19

VISITING STAFFORDSHIRE PARISHES

Our family trees cover a widespread area. This may be the county of Staffordshire, across England, throughout the United Kingdom or perhaps even worldwide. The number of your ancestors' parishes you may be able to visit depends on many factors, including the area covered, the time to travel, the costs involved and the willingness to do so. The latter is often influenced by how useful or interesting we believe the trip will be. You may think there is nothing to gain from viewing the places our forebears once lived, but please read ahead before ruling it out.

I have visited most of the counties that my ancestors are from, including Staffordshire, Dorset and Buckinghamshire. However, there are a few that I have yet to visit. When I think of the ancestors whose parishes I have visited, I feel I have a greater understanding of their lives. I have seen the houses that they lived in, the churches they attended and walked the same streets that they once did. I have a good idea of the atmosphere and the surroundings of the parish. I find it easy to remember these details when I have visited a place. When I have not visited a parish, I rely on historical and contemporary photographs and maps to help me build a picture in my mind. This information is not quite so easy to recall!

If you reside in Staffordshire, travelling is a lot quicker, cheaper and easier. You can easily cover multiple parishes in a single day and return home at the end. Those who live further away may require an overnight trip, making the need to plan ahead more important. Take copies of relevant maps to help you locate the places you want to visit. Mark the copy with exact locations, such as the church, their residence and school, to save you time when you are there.

You can also take any old photographs of the area with you to see how the area has changed over time. As with maps, it is best to take copies of these to avoid damaging the originals. Take your camera to take photographs of the sites so you can compare with old photographs; you may even spot further differences between the images when you get home.

Have a copy of your family tree with you so you can refer to it. This will best be done via a smartphone or tablet to view an online saved tree. This means you can quickly look up information such as names in a churchyard or addresses you forgot to note down. Take your time when you are there and, when possible, visit on a clear weather day.

Churches

Churches were a central part of our ancestors' lives. They were more frequent churchgoers, with all major life events – baptisms, marriages and funerals – taking place within the church space. Today, fewer babies are baptised and weddings and funerals often occur in non-secular locations. You may find from sources, such as churchwardens' records, that your ancestor worked in the church. This may have been as a carpenter or an organist and this will add extra interest to you as a visitor.

Cheadle Church. (Author's own)

You may wish to check the church's website before visiting, partly to check that it will be open but also to check that you won't turn up during a service. Many churches are kept locked due to the risk of vandalism and theft; however, if you contact them in advance they may be happy to unlock this for you. Every church will have its own system for visitors. I visited a church previously where the key was loaned out from the local village shop.

When inside the church, have a look at the architecture so you can see what your ancestors will have seen. Don't forget to look up – there are often fantastic details on church roofs. You will be able to see the very spot where your ancestors became husband and wife, as well as the font they baptised their children in. Some churches sell a small booklet inside with details of the history of the church. You may discover that the font has moved since your ancestor's day, that stained-glass windows have been replaced due to bomb damage or details about flood damage.

If you have clergymen or wealthy ancestors, check the plaques and tombs within the church to see if they are buried inside. There may be other information within the church, including memorial rolls of deceased local soldiers, lists of clergymen of the parish or names of previous benefactors. Etched floor slabs are particularly vulnerable to erosion and many are now covered.

If you have Nonconformist ancestors the above will still apply as, depending on the timeframe, your ancestors would still have needed to be married in an Anglican church for the marriage to be recognised. You may also wish to visit their former chapel.

Churchyards and Cemeteries

The Memorial Inscriptions chapter of this book can tell you why finding the headstone of our ancestors can be so useful to our genealogical research. The information supplied on their memorials could end up being just what we need to break down a brick wall and go back a further generation. As well as finding specific ancestors within the churchyard, it is useful to have a walk around and view other headstones. Family members are often buried close to each other. If you find a headstone with a familial surname, take a photograph of it and record the details as it may be that you later discover this is a relation.

For some memorials, depending on the type of stone, depth of etching and the light at the time you are visiting, photographs of the inscription may not be particularly clear. In these cases, you should write down your own transcription of the text. Check you can read the text in your photographs before you leave.

Where your ancestor has no surviving headstone there is still a general interest in viewing the churchyard where they are buried. The relevant church or authority may still be able to tell you where your ancestor is buried. If nothing else, visiting the churchyard shows you the area where your ancestors grieved for their loved ones and is a good way to put an end to their story.

Until space began to run out in the nineteenth century, most people were buried in their parish churchyard. From around the 1820s, cemeteries began to be created and gradually grew in popularity, especially for our Nonconformist or non-secular ancestors. There are many historical examples within the county, such as Eccleshall Road

Cheadle churchyard and Cemetery. (Author's own)

Cemetery in Stafford which has been in use since 1856 and Stapenhill Cemetery in Burton upon Trent which has been in use since 1866.

Some people choose to take flowers when visiting their ancestor's grave as a mark of respect. This is your choice. Please ensure that when you do visit a burial site that you act respectfully. There may be other people visiting their more recently deceased loved ones and they may not appreciate being disturbed. Take care where you walk and, most importantly, do not cause any damage. Cleaning your ancestor's headstone may seem like a good idea but this needs to be properly researched and permission will sometimes be needed. Many people have attempted to clean headstones using what they believe to be the appropriate materials and have damaged the stone beyond repair. Even grave rubbing using paper and a crayon is no longer recommended due to the chance of damage to the stone.

Residences

Visiting the homes of our ancestors is not quite as easy as you may think. The further back in time you go, the less likely it is that the house will still be standing as it once was. Even where streets have been left untouched, the numbering of the houses may have changed since your ancestor's day. This was very common as parishes grew. The street name may also have changed. You can check for any changes by comparing old and new maps of the area. In rural areas, you are less likely to find house numbers given in a census and more likely to find a description such as 'behind the school' or names of cottages that have since been changed.

Where their homes are still standing, note any modern obvious changes that have occurred, such as conservatories or garages, and picture the house as it would have been. Remember to respect the privacy of the current homeowner who may rightly find it a little suspicious that someone is looking at their house!

Viewing where an ancestors' house is located can help us understand their lives more. We can walk from their house to their workplace or to the local church and see the sights they would have seen along the way. We are more likely to notice features of the landscape that they would have seen when we are there in person, rather than relying on maps.

Workplaces

The more recently your ancestor was living, the more likely it is that their workplace will still exist. There are exceptions, for example some twentieth-century factories have been knocked down, whereas many eighteenth-century farms are still in existence. This is, therefore, another topic to research before your visit. It can help to gain some context before you go, such as imagining any pollution or knowing what other buildings used to be next door that are no longer there. Again, this is where old maps are so useful, as well as local history books.

I have visited many farms where my ancestors worked and walked through the fields in which they toiled. While doing this doesn't add a new 'fact' to your tree, it certainly helps to give a picture of what their lives were like. It also can help you to feel closer to your ancestors to see the sights that they would have seen every day while at work. Much of the farming landscape is beautiful and has remained unchanged for hundreds of years.

You may be surprised at what still remains from your ancestor's day. This may relate to farming, such as a surviving farmhouse, or another occupation. Railway stations have largely changed a lot; however, old features sometimes survive, such as an old signal box. Some old workplaces have been transformed into museums. There are many mills, breweries and potteries still standing today which are well worth a visit.

Pubs

There used to be many more pubs than there are today. It's not uncommon to find that even a village once had four pubs in the same street. They were thriving, bustling places-to-be and were likely to have been frequented by your ancestors. It is impossible to know which pub your ancestor would have visited; it would not always have been their closest one.

It may be more relevant to visit a particular pub if you know that your ancestor worked there. If the pub in question still survives, look inside to see if there any old features remain. Some are fantastically preserved with a true appreciation for their heritage. Others have been modernised beyond recognition. Whatever the case, pausing in the pub for a quick drink is a great way to have a break on a busy day of tracing your ancestors' footsteps.

Other Places of Interest
When looking at a map prior to your visit and planning where you wish to see, consider other locations in the parish that were a part of your ancestors' lives. Their old school may still be standing. You may wish to visit features such as the village green, canal or river where they probably played as children. Some places of relevance may be outside of the parish, such as the location where your ancestor committed a crime or where they were later imprisoned.

Many of us will visit multiple parishes where our ancestors lived to make the most of a journey and to see as many sites as possible. Many of our ancestors lived in more than one parish during their lives, often moving several times. It may be beneficial to think about the forms of transport available at the time they were moving and how this would have been possible. Were they likely to have used the railways or a horse and cart? Seeing the distance in person and any potential obstacles in their way, such as steep hills or fords, can help us comprehend what would have been an important journey for them.

Chapter 20

STAFFORDSHIRE OCCUPATIONS

Potteries

In the early seventeenth century, the north of Staffordshire became a hub for ceramic production. This was largely due to the materials naturally available in the area including clay and coal. The area known as the Staffordshire Potteries encompassed Burslem, Fenton, Hanley, Longton, Stoke and Tunstall. Some of the more well-known potteries from the area include Spode, Doulton, Aynsley and Wedgwood. Ceramic making also occurred throughout the rest of the county although never to the same extent as in the Stoke-on-Trent area. One such example is Armitage Shanks, founded in the village of Armitage in 1817.

By the late eighteenth century, North Staffordshire was the largest producer of ceramics in Britain, so chances are if you have ancestors from the Potteries area, some of them will have been involved in the industry. At this time, there were approximately 200 pottery manufacturers employing 20,000 people between them. Early pottery makers tended to work in small, family-run businesses with the secrets of the trade being passed from father to son. The opening of the Trent and Mersey Canal in 1777 saw business grow, although the pottery had already been exported from England since about 1740.

You may find a wide range of different occupational titles listed among your Potteries ancestors. These may include a placer whose job was to retrieve the wares from the kiln, a siever who would sift through clay in the sliphouse, and a smoother who would sponge the clay. Many are simply listed as a potter or ceramics worker. Confusingly, there are also job titles which may be misleading such as a muffin maker who created small bowls and plates and a table maker who was a creator of sanitaryware. Working in the industry was much sought after, with adult males among the best-paid manufacturing workers in England. Most worked a seventy-two-hour week, which was unfavourable but necessary to meet demand.

Child labour was common in the ceramics business. The first investigation into their treatment was in 1840 when the House of Commons commissioned Dr Samuel Scriven to investigate. His report highlighted the dangers that children faced in the workplace, including handling products with lead and arsenic content and being exposed to extreme differences in temperature. A further inquiry in 1863 found that around 6,500 children were working in the potteries, a majority of whom were aged under 13. It was not until 1898 that legislation was introduced preventing potteries employing anyone under 14 . Therefore, do not be surprised if you find ancestors working in the potteries from a young age.

The ceramics industry was seen as a reliable business to work in, with something for everyone no matter how skilled they were, with a chance of progression. It is not uncommon to find whole families working together in the same factory. The most common incidents tended to involve the heat from the kilns and fire but accidents were rare compared to other workplaces.

A wide range of records are held at Staffordshire History Centre including the collection of H&R Johnson of Tunstall, records of the Spode Museum Trust, and documentation belonging to sanitaryware brand Thomas Twyford.

Brewing

Brewing is strongly associated with Burton upon Trent where it has taken place since at least the eleventh century. The town is known to have transported its beer as far as Russia in the 1700s and India from the 1820s. The introduction of the railway network from 1839 made transportation of beer and other commodities easier. Often referred to as the brewing capital of the country, Burton once produced one in four pints of beer sold in Britain.

There were twenty-six breweries in Burton upon Trent in 1868, partly because of the water quality in the area but also helped by the transport links in the town, including being on the canal network from 1777. This was the year that William Bass opened his brewery here; it later became the world's largest brewery. Samuel Allsopp and Sons have been producing beer in Burton since 1807, and Worthington's Brewery dates back to 1761.

FATALITY AT BASS & CO'S. BREWERY.

A sad accident, attended with fatal consequences, occurred at Messrs. Bass and Co's. Shobnall maltings on Tuesday afternoon. A carpenter named Edward Fletcher was ascending a ladder at the tank near the washing-out shed, with a plane and chisel in one hand, and when he had reached an altitude of about twelve feet he fell backwards on to his head. He was at once taken in an unconscious state to the Infirmary, where he died at eleven o'clock at night without regaining consciousness. Deceased, who was only 27 years of age, resided at 25 Derby Road, and was the son of Mr. Fletcher, blacksmith, of Derby Street. He had only been employed by the firm a few weeks, but had previously worked at Mr. Gretton's new residence at Stapleford. It is stated that deceased was to have been married at Whitsuntide.

The article regarding Edward Fletcher's death at Shobnall in Burton Chronicle 27 May 1897. (With permission from Reach plc)

Of course, brewing occurred throughout the county. A notable example is that of Joule's Brewery, established in Stone in 1780. The company was later taken over by Bass Charrington before ceasing trading in 1972. You may also come across Bent's Brewery established in Newcastle-under-Lyme in the 1790s, which also became part of Bass Brewery.

Occupational titles you may come across within your brewing family include brewer, brewster, brewess and alewife. You may have maltsters or maltmen in your tree, as I do, who made brewers malt from local barley or 'broad coopers' who acted as a go-between for the breweries and the innkeepers.

If you know which brewery your ancestor worked for, it is worth searching the newspapers for the company name to see what notable occurrences happened during your ancestor's time while employed there. One such incident was featured in *The Burton Chronicle* on 27 May 1897 when Edward Fletcher was killed after falling from a ladder within the Bass Brewery maltings at Shobnall.

Most of the wide variety of surviving records relating to those that worked within the brewing industry are held at Staffordshire History Centre. Examples include records from the Lichfield Brewery Company Limited dating back to 1689, records from Allsopp's Brewery dating 1796–1955, and various employment agreements from Ashtead Brewery Company. You may also find related Chancery court records at TNA, including the 1828–1834 Salt v. Salt case regarding the management of their brewery.

Quarrying and Mining

Quarrying refers to the extraction of materials directly from the surface, whereas mining involves the process of extracting material from below the earth's surface. Both have been notable within Staffordshire, although you could argue that coal mining had the biggest impact in the county. Former coalfields can be seen all over the county, with Cannock coalfields sandwiched between the north and south coalfields.

You may find your ancestors working at Cauldon Low Quarry where limestone was extracted or Park Quarry in Tixall Park where sandstone was removed. The latter is often referred to as Tixall Stone and was used in the building of Stafford Castle. Quarrymen may be referred to as quarriers, diggers or rock getters. Those working in the mines had a wide range of occupational titles. Aside from the obvious 'miner', you may also come across hewers, wailers and hod boys among others.

Quarrying and mining were physically tough jobs involving working in awkward and uncomfortable positions for long periods of time, and both were very dangerous occupations. There was a threat of being crushed, whether from falling rocks or roof collapses, plus the additional health hazards of breathing in rock dust and incidents involving tools and machinery. It is common to come across men who suffered injuries in the work place, some more serious than others. The *Evening Sentinel* on 29 August 1938 reported that 59-year-old William Shilcock had his right hand amputated after it became stuck between the wall and a falling rock at Cauldon Low Quarry. Fatalities were also sadly common. The *Staffordshire Advertiser* reported on 2 January 1847 that 13-year-old John Cooper died at Shelton Colliery after falling 55 yards down the pit shaft.

> **COLLIERY ACCIDENT.**—On Saturday afternoon, a lad 13 years of age, of the name of John Cooper, who was employed on the bank of the Lady's Well Pit, belonging to one of Earl Granville's collieries at Shelton, accidentally fell down the shaft, a depth of 55 yards. He was brought out of the pit alive, though seriously injured, and was taken to the Infirmary, where he died in the course of the evening.

The article regarding the death of John Cooper at Shelton Colliery in Staffordshire Advertiser on 2 January 1847. (Content provided by THE BRITISH LIBRARY BOARD. ALL RIGHTS RESERVED. With thanks to The British Newspaper Archive (www.britishnewspaperarchive.co.uk))

The worst mining disaster in the county occurred at Minnie Pit in Halmer End near Newcastle-under-Lyme on 12 January 1918 when 155 men and boys were killed in an explosion and the resulting carbon monoxide poisoning. It was widely reported, including in the *Staffordshire Sentinel* on 14 January which estimated at least 75 women were left widowed and 200 children had lost their father. There were frequent reports in the papers whenever a new body was identified, as well as a list of those who contributed to the relief fund. Some local families lost multiple members. Frederick Henry Harrison of Halmer End lost his son, brother, six nephews and four other relatives.

Both quarrying and mining leave few records behind for us to trace our ancestors. The records that often survive tend not to name employees and include accounts and leases. If your ancestor was involved in an accident they may be named in the newspaper or a coroner's inquest may survive. If you know exactly where your ancestor worked, it is worth searching the newspapers for the place for the time that they worked there. Even if they are not named it can be interesting to see what was occurring on site while they were there. There may be comments about the site's working conditions or failures of management.

Agriculture and Farming

Even if you have only recently started your family tree research, you are likely to have come across an agricultural labourer, often seen shortened to 'ag lab'. This is just as likely to be found in Staffordshire as in any other county, with agricultural labourer being the most commonly found occupation in the 1851 and 1861 censuses. If (and when) you discover an agricultural labourer in your tree, make sure that you research this as much as you can. There is a tendency for people to dismiss this as a 'boring' occupation that leaves no records behind, but this is not the case.

You may find evidence of their work in newspaper articles. These may surround workplace accidents, livestock theft or locally organised competitions. The latter could involve ploughing, hedging or tractor driving among others. One example can be seen below in *The Staffordshire Advertiser* on 20 October 1866 where a ploughing competition was held at Acton with five prizes awarded. The winners are named along with their employer and their monetary prize.

Workplace accidents were common on the farm. The daily routine of an agricultural labourer was taxing with very long days and highly physical work. One accident reported in the *Staffordshire Sentinel* on 16 August 1927 involved 58-year-old farm worker Samuel Addison who was knocked over by a horse and suffered a fractured leg. Fatalities were not as common among agricultural labourers as with other occupations but did still occur. The *Staffordshire Advertiser* of 31 January 1846 reported the death of 52-year-old Thomas Sharratt of Hints. Thomas fell from a

STAFFORDSHIRE AGRICULTURAL SOCIETY.

THE NEWCASTLE DISTRICT PRIZES.

The competition for prizes for crops and ploughing in the Newcastle district took place on Thursday last; but, in consequence of the unfavourable state of the weather, the number of visitors was very limited. The ploughing competition was at Acton, on the farm of Mr. Chesters. The judges were Mr. Craven and Mr. Parlby, who commenced their inspection of the crops at eight o'clock in the morning, the farms entered for competition being occupied by Mr. Peake, of Bradwell Hall; Mr. J. Johnson, of Keele; the North Staffordshire Coal and Iron Company, Talk-o'-th'-Hill; and Mr. W. Hyatt, of Highfields, Wolstanton. The number of competitors for the five prizes for ploughing were ten. The field was a light turnip and barley soil, with a sloping surface: and the time allowed to each man for the completion of his work (namely, four-and-a-half hours for half-an-acre) was rather exceeded, owing to the rain and wind. The work was generally considered good, and the competition so severe that the judges bestowed considerably more than the usual time in the examination of each man's work before giving their decisions. The prizes for ploughing were awarded as follows:—

First prize of £2 10s., Thomas Berkin, ploughman to Mr. Dimmock, of Shelton-under-Harley; second, £2, to William Simkin, in the service of the North Staffordshire Coal and Iron Company, Talk-o'-th'-Hill; third, £1 10s., to John Boon, ploughman to R. Sneyd, Esq., Keele; fourth, £1, to John Silvester, in the employ of Mr. Dimmock; and the fifth, 10s., to William Podmore, servant to R. Sneyd, Esq. The ploughing of John Townshend, servant to Mr. Chesters, was highly commended.

An article regarding a ploughing competition at Acton in Staffordshire Advertiser 20 October 1866. (Content provided by THE BRITISH LIBRARY BOARD. ALL RIGHTS RESERVED. With thanks to The British Newspaper Archive (www.britishnewspaperarchive.co.uk))

cart which he was loading with straw resulting in a broken spine. He passed away the following day.

It is common to find your agricultural labourer ancestors moving frequently between villages. Many were hired on a casual basis, with some on annual contracts. Cottages tended to be tied to the job and were of a modest size. You may find some of your female ancestors were also hired as agricultural labourers. This is more likely if they were unmarried mothers who required an income.

Mechanisation hugely decreased the need for agricultural labourers and lead to the Swing Riots in the 1840s. Machinery and haystacks were set on fire in protest of the inconsistent work and low pay workers received as a result. Staffordshire was not as badly affected by the riots as other counties, but the impact of new machinery reducing the need for agricultural labourers was still an issue. It is common around this time to find our ancestors changing their occupation to one with a more reliable income.

Researching agricultural labourers in our family tree can be tricky as it is not always obvious which farm they worked at. We can sometimes find out through records such as the 1921 census, newspaper articles or personal memorabilia. If you do discover where your ancestor worked you may find it enlightening to visit the farm today. Much of the landscape remains fairly unchanged and it can be enjoyable to see the fields where your ancestor worked. For more recent ancestors, the 1940 National Farm Survey returns are worth viewing, described in the Maps chapter of this book. Staffordshire History Centre also holds other unique records including farming papers belonging to T.C. Brookes of Blymhill dating 1908–1953 and the farming accounts of L.J. Evans of Barlaston dating 1868–1915.

Shoemaking

Shoemakers are particularly associated with Stafford, with records showing they worked here from the mid-fifteenth century. Other occupational titles you may come across include cobbler, cordwainer and boot mercer. Cobblers tended to repair shoes, whereas others made new footwear. The best-known local shoemaker of the 1700s was William Horton who founded his business in Stafford as a teenager. His success as a businessman and craftsman led to him selling his shoes globally and he opened the first shoe factory in the town. Other examples in the county include Friary Shoes of Lichfield which formed in 1904, Bagnall's Boot and Shoe Makers of Burton upon Trent established in 1851 and Tipper Shoe Makers of Leek established in 1821.

As with agriculture, the mechanisation of the shoemaking business led to a lesser workforce need in the field. Sewing machines could complete work far quicker than even the most skilled shoemaker. For those who remained in the business, the work saw a change in environment. Many workers had previously worked from home; however, with the necessary machinery now in a factory, they were forced to head into the workplace. As with many industries, war increased production and forced craftsmen to develop new methods of mass production. One notable example was the Napoleonic Wars when large numbers of boots were required for the military.

The introduction of factories saw accidents in the workplace became more commonplace, although these were usually minor compared to other industries. There are newspaper reports of some of these, including some factory fires. Examples include the fires at Eatough's in Burton upon Trent in 1926 and 1930. Finding a large incident such as a factory fire may explain why your ancestor suddenly changed occupations if their workplace no longer existed. You may also find newspaper advertisements for the business where your ancestor worked.

Examples of relevant records held at Staffordshire History Centre are a minute book from David Hollins & Co of Stafford dated 1907–1931 and notebooks from shoe dealer Thomas Buttery of Brocton 1855–1868. The archive also holds the minutes of Stafford and District Association of Boot and Shoe Manufacturers 1871–1944. You may also find evidence of apprenticeships, although it was common for a shoemaking business to be kept within the same family. In cases such as this, you may find tools being bequeathed in the father's will.

Chapter 21

STAFFORDSHIRE SURNAMES

Originally, surnames were not passed on from parent to child in England. In fact, if you go far enough back in history, surnames weren't used at all and people were known by one name. There would have been no way of telling if two people were related when hearing their names – a practice which, thankfully, changed or genealogy would be a lot harder today. Hereditary surnames were initially adopted in the south of England with the trend spreading north in the mid-fourteenth century. So, what do we mean when we talk about Staffordshire surnames? To answer this question, let's look at the different types of surname by origin.

Type of Surname	Surname Origin	Surname Examples
Patronymic / Matronymic	A surname derived from a person's father's name (Patronymic) or mother's name (Matronymic)	Paul, Williams, Megson
Topographical	A surname taken from a feature of the landscape	Blackwell, Hill, Atwood
Characteristic	A surname used to describe a person's physical feature or character trait	Little, Armstrong, Smart
Occupational	A surname adopted due to a person's work	Smith, Carpenter, Carter
Habitational	A surname derived from a place name	Stafford, Lichfield, Blore

Looking at the above explanations, we can see why some surnames are very common today. Most of us will end up with the more common surnames such as Smith, Jones and Taylor in our tree. Indeed, these three names were the most common surnames found in Staffordshire in the 1881 census, but as they are found all over the country we cannot tell where someone with these names might originate from.

However, there are many surnames known to have been coined in Staffordshire and are found here more than anywhere else. These are what we can refer to as 'Staffordshire surnames'. It is easy to prove the origin of the habitational surname; others can be seen in a more general region.

To map where particular surnames are found, we can look at documents such as tax lists and oath rolls. By using multiple sources over a period of time, we can see how a name moves across the country and discover how it either grew in popularity or diminished. Many surnames have died out due to a lack of sons to pass the name on to their children.

Not all names have a known meaning behind them and their roots can only be speculated upon. These include names such as Grist, Singleterry and Seacole, which tend to be rarer than others. Having a rare surname can make it easier to trace your family tree. There may only be one person who has ever had a specific name who you can happily trace using historical records. However, the rarer names are more likely to be transcribed incorrectly so when searching online databases, you will need to use wildcard variants to find all possible spelling errors.

While some surnames can be pointed to a single point of origin, most have multiple sources. For example, the topographical surname of Atwood was given to someone who lived 'at the wood'. Occupational surnames obviously have multiple original uses. Habitational surnames can often be proven to have one original source, where the surname is heavily concentrated in one area of a parish, in or near to that of the same name. However, many place names are found several times across the country, such as Longton. This means that we cannot assume that everybody with the same surname is related back to the time when surnames originated.

Surname Anomalies

Many genealogists have a great passion for tracing the history of their surname. There is no harm in doing so, but do be aware that surnames are often not passed down in a straightforward manner from father to child. For example, adoption, illegitimacy and aliases are all common. In my experience, it is rare to find a tree without one of these instances. The most common is illegitimacy, where a child will usually take the mother's surname. This name will still be hereditary to you; however, many people like to trace their birth name through tracing their paternal line and become unsure of how to progress when they find an illegitimate birth. There is no right or wrong answer here and you are obviously free to research surnames in whichever way you wish.

My husband and I have surnames that cannot be traced back very far. My maiden name is Osmond. This name can only be traced as far back as my paternal great great-grandfather, George. He was born to an unwed mother with the surname Powell before being subsequently adopted by the Osmond family, taking on their name. My husband's name of O'Shea only goes back as far as his grandfather, Vernon. He was again born to an unwed mother with the surname of Cook. In this case, his mother later married Patrick O'Shea and he took on the name of his stepfather.

The above are two examples of how illegitimacy can change the course of a surname's path migrating down the paternal line. There are also many examples of how a surname is 'incorrectly' passed down through infidelity. If a married woman becomes pregnant as the result of an affair, she could state that her husband was the father of her child without the authorities or her husband being aware of the child's true paternity. The husband's name can therefore be found written on a birth certificate or in a parish register and we as genealogists would be ignorant to this incorrect 'fact'.

While DNA testing can help uncover more recent cases of infidelity, the more historical examples remain undetected and untraceable. The sad truth is we may spend a lot of time, money and effort in researching a tree that is not biologically ours. In rare cases you may find later documents that dispute a husband's paternity, such as divorce papers and court records.

Aliases were as common among criminals in the past as they are today – they were useful for evading capture by the authorities – but there are many other, less dishonourable, reasons for a person or family having an alias. I have an alias used for several generations in my maternal line that stems back to an inheritance claim, meaning the family had to take on the alternative surname of the deceased in order to claim their estate. In their records they are therefore known either as 'Janes alias Hopkins' or 'Hopkins alias Janes'.

In other cases, people may change their surname by choice, such as to avoid association with someone less favourable. There is often no official documentation of a change in name in these cases. Another common example is when an immigrant Anglicised their name to better fit in with the local community. For example, the French surname Mailloux could change to Mayhew or the Russian surname Tolmasoff may change to

Thomas. In these cases, a family historian may be unaware that they have ancestry based outside of the country until the changes are discovered.

The accuracy of spelling surnames has only become important in modern times. Today, it is hard to imagine spelling your surname in various ways as it is important that your name matches exactly on official documents, such as your birth certificate and passport. For our ancestors, this was far less important. Parish officials and registrars could record the names of people in documents such as parish registers however they believed it to be spelt. Illiteracy was commonplace so when a person was asked to put their mark next to their name, they may not have recognised the difference in spelling.

The manner of surnames changing makes it more difficult to be sure we are tracing the right family line. In my maternal line, the names Eggelton, Eggleton and Egleton are all seen in the same branch. Likewise, in my husband's tree, the Perceys become Pearcys in the early nineteenth century. It is important to remain open minded about spelling changes and be aware of any possible variants. Consider how the regional accent may have changed surname spellings. A common change is when an 'h' appears before a surname beginning with a vowel due to a person's pronunciation.

Staffordshire Surnames

Below is a list of surnames that originate from Staffordshire, are found most frequently in the county, or both. There are many more Staffordshire surnames than feature here so if yours does not appear below, search its history to discover more about its origins. If your name is similar to one mentioned here, consider that it may be a spelling variation, such as Jeavons and Jevons.

Allport

Thought to have been derived from the Derbyshire hamlet of Alport, around 6 miles from the Staffordshire border. Allports from the seventeenth century can be found in Tamworth, Wolverhampton and Shareshill. There are 274 Allports in the 1881 census in Staffordshire, compared with Warwickshire in second place with 129 people. By 1921, there were over 400 people with the name in Staffordshire.

Ashwood

This is both a habitational name from the hamlet in Staffordshire and a topographical name given to a person residing near an ash-tree wood. The name is first seen in Staffordshire parish registers in 1631 when

Robert Ashwood was baptised in Burton upon Trent. By 1881, the name had spread across a number of counties with Staffordshire in fourth place. However, of all the parishes in the country, Tamworth was home to the most Ashwoods.

Beardmore

A habitational name stemming from a place near Fawley in Staffordshire, recorded as Berdesmor in 1290, which no longer exists. As the name 'Beardless' has been attributed to men without beards, there is an argument the name may also have been given to men with longer, bushier beards, but this is just conjecture. Beardmores appear in the sixteenth-century parish registers for Swynnerton, Kingsley and Ellastone. Sixty-three per cent of all Beardmores were found in Staffordshire in the 1881 census, mainly in Stoke-on-Trent and Cheadle.

Beebee

Originally from the place name of Beeby in Leicestershire, Beebee is now overwhelmingly a Staffordshire surname. Of the 211 people with the name in the 1881 census, 171 of them resided in Staffordshire. The first parish register entries for the name in the county appear in Bilston in the late seventeenth century.

Blore

Another habitational name from the Staffordshire village of the same name, situated close to the Derbyshire border. Blore can be found in sixteenth-century parish registers in Betley, Keele and Audley. The name went on to be most prevalent in Lancashire by the time of the 1881 census. Over a third of Blores in this census in Staffordshire were residing in Rocester.

Brindley

A habitational name, with possible sources including Brindley Heath in Staffordshire and the parish of Brindley in Cheshire. Parish registers from the sixteenth century featuring Brindleys include Lapley, Kingsley and Trentham. Staffordshire was overwhelmingly home to the surname in the 1881 census, with 1,038 individuals, compared to 204 in Lancashire which was second. At the time, the most common parishes to find Brindleys were Stoke-on-Trent, Cannock and Willenhall. The name continued in its popularity within the county, with 1,334 people so-named found there in the 1921 census.

Bucknall
From the parishes of the same name in Staffordshire and Lincolnshire. Unsurprisingly, therefore, in the 1881 census these two counties were the most populated with Bucknalls, with 147 in Staffordshire and 93 in Lincolnshire. The name's earliest appearance in a Staffordshire parish register was the burial of John Bucknall in 1558 in Mucklestone.

Cooksey
While now identifying as a Staffordshire surname, this is actually a habitational name from a hamlet in Worcestershire. The first entry in historical Staffordshire parish registers can be seen in Rowley Regis when Katherine Cooksey was baptised there in 1616. By 1881, there were 208 Cookseys in the county, many of whom were living in Tipton and Wednesbury. By 1921, there were 436 Cookseys in Staffordshire.

Doorbar
A fascinating and rare surname whose origins remain uncertain. It is theorised that it may be a variation of the occupational surname 'Dauber'. The name is first seen in the parish registers for the county in Biddulph in 1727 when Richard Doorbar was baptised. Of the 97 people with the name in the 1881 census, 71 of these are in Staffordshire. Interestingly, more than half were found in Biddulph. The 1921 census shows a similar pattern with 127 of 171 Doorbars living in Staffordshire.

Ellerton
A habitational name from Ellerton in the East Riding of Yorkshire and Shropshire. The first parish register entry in Staffordshire is found in Bradley, when Alice Ellerton was buried in 1558. The name is found fairly equally between Staffordshire and Yorkshire in 1881, with the name being found most commonly in the Staffordshire parishes of Newcastle-under-Lyme and Burslem. The surname frequency has declined hugely over the last century, with it now being at risk of dying out.

Grocott
This is believed to be a variation of Grewcock, thought to have derived from the Middle English words 'grew' meaning crane and 'cock', the bird. This spelling variation was first used in Staffordshire in the Audley parish register when Peter Grocott married Anna Leak in 1701. Grocotts were most likely to be found in Stoke-on-Trent and Wolstanton in 1881. By 1921, half of all Grocotts were found in the county.

Horsenail

A very rare occupational surname for a horseshoer. There were only thirteen Horsenails in the country at the time of the 1881 census, with eight of these residing in Stafford. By 1921, there were no Horsenails left living in the county, although the census returns show Staffordshire as the birthplace for two of the twenty so-named people in other counties. There is now a small handful of Horsenails living in Staffordshire.

Jeavons

A patronymic name from the Welsh name 'Ieuan', or from the Latin word for young 'juvenis'. This spelling was first seen in Staffordshire parish registers in Kinver when Elenor Jeavons was buried in 1662. The name has tripled in popularity in the county since the 1881 census, when nearly 500 Jeavons were residing there, of which 150 were in Sedgley.

Keele

A habitational name from the Staffordshire village of the same name. The Keeles appear to have moved south to London and Hampshire fairly early on; the name declined in popularity in the county. Out of 139 nationwide, only 14 Keeles remained in Staffordshire at the time of the 1921 census.

Lichfield

An obvious habitational name from the Staffordshire city of the same name, this is undoubtedly where the name originated. However, like Keele, the name appears to have moved out of the county early on. There were no Lichfields living in Staffordshire by 1881, with most residing in neighbouring Derbyshire and Warwickshire. Early probate records show Lichfields residing in Tutbury in the late sixteenth century.

Limer

An occupational name given to operators of lime kilns. The name is first seen in Staffordshire parish registers in 1612 when Elizabeth Limer was baptised in Ellastone. The 1881 census shows Limers were most prevalent in Staffordshire. The name was spread fairly evenly between parishes including Stoke-on-Trent, Hollinsclough and Uttoxeter.

Maskery

The name comes from the word 'massacre' and was an occupational name given to butchers. The first mention in a parish register within the county is the baptism of Nicholas Maskery in Alrewas in 1548. Of the

278 people with the name in the 1881 census, 125 lived in Staffordshire, mainly in Stoke-on-Trent and Caverswall.

Sedgley

A habitational name from the town historically within Staffordshire's border. The name remained strongest within the county, being most prevalent there in 1881. Nearly half of all Sedgleys found in the county at that time were residing in West Bromwich. The earliest Staffordshire parish register entries for Sedgleys can be found at Colwich, with the first being the marriage of Galfried Sedgley to Elizabeth Phillippe in 1590.

Stafford

Another obvious habitational name from the county town, although there are other places in the country similarly named, such as Stafford in Devon and West Stafford in Dorset, where it may also originate. Despite its name, it featured more commonly in twelve other counties in the 1881 census, with just 2 per cent of Staffords being found in Staffordshire. The earliest probate record for the name in the county was in 1537 when Henry Stafford of Leek died.

Vodrey

A very rare habitational surname taken from Vaudrey and Vaudry in France. The name was first seen in the parish registers in Staffordshire in 1592 when Anna Vodrey married Johannes Barlowe in Norton Le Moors. In the 1881 census only ten people in England had the surname, nine of whom lived in Staffordshire. By 1921, the name had grown in prevalence, with thirty Vodreys residing in the county.

Wenlock

A habitational name from the town of Much Wenlock in Shropshire. The name was found most commonly in Staffordshire in 1881, with Shropshire second. In Staffordshire, the most common parishes to find Wenlocks were Lapley and Wolverhampton. The first appearance in the historical county was in Walsall when John Wenlock was buried in 1612.

Wildblood

A characteristic surname for a lively person, first seen in the county in 1570 when Joana Wildblood was buried at Stone. In 1881, the name was most prevalent in Staffordshire, with 77 out of 223 Wildbloods living there. Over a quarter of the seventy-seven were residing in Burslem. By 1921, the name had gradually increased in prevalence in the county.

Williscroft

A name of uncertain origin, perhaps stemming from the Old English referring to William's croft. Some argue it is a habitational name, a variation of Wooliscroft, located a small way out of Stone. Helping the latter argument is the fact that all of the earliest parish register entries for Williscroft are from Stone, the first being the baptism of Christopher Williscroft in 1583. The name remained most popular in Staffordshire in 1881 with nearly 60 per cent of Williscrofts found there.

Woolridge

A patronymic surname from the first name 'Wulfric'. It is first seen in the parish registers for the county in 1591 when Agnes Woolridge was buried at Stafford. The name was most commonly found in the county in 1881. The Woolridges were fairly evenly spread throughout six parishes in the county including Rolleston on Dove and Audley. It remains a strong Staffordshire surname today.

Wootton

A habitational name originating from several counties, with the name meaning 'place by a wood'. These places include Wootton village in Staffordshire and it is this spelling which is strongest there. The first entry of Wootton in the county's parish registers is in 1539 when John Wootton was buried at Ellastone. The name was found in forty-four counties across England, Wales and Scotland in the 1881 census, the most widespread of all the surnames viewed here. Staffordshire had by far the most Woottons at the time with 634 people, compared to London in second place with 244 people. The name became far more prevalent over the following forty years, with nearly 5,000 Woottons residing in England and Wales, with just under 1,000 of these living in Staffordshire.

Yoxall

Despite the name originating from the Staffordshire village of the same spelling, Yoxalls became more prevalent in other counties including Cheshire and Worcestershire. Shenstone features Yoxall's first appearance in a Staffordshire parish register when Elyzabeth Yoxall was baptised there in 1579. There were eighty Yoxalls in Staffordshire in 1881, mostly in Stoke-on-Trent, with a slight increase to eighty-eight in 1921.

Chapter 22

INTERNET SOURCES

For many of us, it is hard to imagine researching our family trees without the use of the internet, but some people try to do so exclusively now without ever setting foot in an archive, which is a huge shame. Nevertheless, nobody can deny that the internet has made genealogical research accessible to a much wider range of people. It is a huge time saver, with the ability to view millions of documents without ever leaving the house. We can see digitised documents created by archives hundreds of miles away, without the need to travel at all.

As well as accessing historical records, we can also use the internet to contact DNA cousin matches, join online genealogy groups, listen to talks by expert speakers and view photographs of ancestors. We can read books that have been digitised and watch films related to our research. Of course, some of the most useful websites are those of our local archives and TNA; however, as the usefulness of these has already been explained in previous chapters, we will focus here on some other highlights.

The internet is undoubtedly fantastic. Without it, our research would be thoroughly slowed down and limited to the financial and time constraints of travelling to archives. But not everything on the internet is correct and reliable. There are books published decades ago, freely viewable online, which contain factual errors – such as about the history of a town or person. The vast amounts of transcription errors online mean we may miss vital records or interpret them incorrectly. Arguably, the largest errors are found on other people's shared online family trees. Be wary of any information you find and, before you add a fact or a person to your tree, make sure that this has been proven with reliable sources.

Genealogy Subscription Sites

At some point, we may find ourselves joining one or more of the main genealogy subscription sites: Ancestry; Findmypast; MyHeritage; and The Genealogist. People often make the mistake of signing up to one of these sites without checking if the records they have are right for their research. Each site has an overlap of records such as census returns and modern birth indexes. Each also has exclusive rights to certain records and these are updated frequently. Findmypast posts a weekly blog about that week's new records. You can check the records it holds in its 'All Record Sets' page. The remaining sites upload records on a less regular basis. Check Ancestry's holding in its Card Catalogue and MyHeritage's holding in its Collection Catalogue.

It is important to consider that each site offers different levels of subscription according to the records you will be able to view. Many offer a free trial, which can be useful for you to see how beneficial the records are to your research. Most offer a cheaper, basic option where you can access essential UK records including modern birth, marriage and death indexes and census returns. As the subscription levels increase in price, so do the number of records you can view. The most expensive option is not always the one best for you. These usually contain many overseas records, which may be irrelevant. On top of your subscription fee, some websites often ask for an additional pay-per-view fee to view certain exclusive records. This is a rarer occurrence and was used when the 1939 Register and 1921 census returns were released.

Each website has its own benefits and drawbacks. Findmypast, at the time of writing, has exclusive rights to the digitised parish registers and probate records of Staffordshire held by Staffordshire History Centre. Ancestry provides some indexes for the county but no images. Ancestry has the best function for saving your family tree, with easy privacy options and it is very user friendly. MyHeritage has excellent overseas records, whereas The Genealogist has a Map Explorer which allows you to overlay historical maps to compare them. The Genealogist also has exclusive rights to the Lloyd George Domesday maps created between 1910 and 1915. These are still being updated on a county-by-county basis; at the time of writing Staffordshire has yet to be uploaded.

The biggest warning when using genealogy sites is the ability to view other people's online family trees. There are few comprehensively researched trees free from errors. A good family tree should have a wide variety of sources attached to each fact on a person's page. This does not include the current ability to quote 'Ancestry Family Trees' as a source. Family trees that should not be trusted include those with multiple coats of arms wrongly applied to people; other people's trees quoted as a source with very little other evidence of sourcing; and those with errors regarding dates (such as a mother supposedly giving birth when she was still a child herself or dying a year before her child was born). Many people take up free trials and believe they have gone back ten generations in a weekend and 'completed' their (always incorrect) family tree, but thorough genealogical research takes years. I have spent nearly twenty years researching my family tree and am nowhere near what I would ever call 'finished'.

Online family trees that belong to close DNA cousin matches can be more useful. These may contain photographs and scanned documentation belonging to relatives closer to home who the tree creator knew personally. These are much more reliable. Feel free to message the tree owner to share records and stories, although you may not always get a reply.

Professional Genealogists' Websites

There may be times when you need to hire a professional genealogist. There is no shame in doing so and even professionals often hire other professionals if they have a different speciality, such as the ability to read a foreign text. Visit the Register of Qualified Genealogists' (RQG) website at **qualifiedgenealogists.org** to see who is working in your area of interest. It may be that you wish to hire someone local to you who you can meet face to face, or it may be more useful to hire somebody living near a certain archive likely to be needed for your research. Everybody on this list will have been assessed by the RQG to ensure that they are fully qualified and accredited.

You may find that this site, or others, directs you to the website of a professional genealogist. It is the individual's decision to choose what they display on their site. Most will not openly post prices but will offer a free estimate. Some post examples of their own findings. My own website, The Past Revealed (**thepastrevealed.co.uk**), contains a monthly blog with each post focused on a different ancestor as inspiration to readers.

Town and Village Websites

Many towns and villages have websites run by parish councils or enthusiastic locals. These are used to keep residents up to date with the latest village news and upcoming events. There is a growing trend to provide information about local history which may be of genealogical use. There are also websites run by local history groups focused on a particular area. If your ancestors were based in a particular parish for a few generations, it is worth using a search engine to see if any such sites exist for that place.

Staffordshire has some great examples. Weston and Gayton share a site at **westonstaffs.org.uk**. This website has a page dedicated to the history of both parishes, with notes from the Domesday Book of 1086 as well as hearth tax information. Rolleston on Dove has a specific site for its history at **rollestonondovehistory.wordpress.com**. The site includes manorial court transcripts, a comprehensive analysis of the village in the 1921 census and pages on local families, including the Sweetloves. Brown Edge village has a site at **brownedge.com** which includes local family trees, information about public houses and a photographic archive.

Social Media

The use of social media is booming, with researchers from many backgrounds discovering the benefits of online networking. One such advantage is the ability to search for people and message them instantly. You may wish to contact a long-lost relative or a DNA match, but be aware of the caveats in doing so. The first is to be sure that you are contacting the correct person; never give personal information away in the first message to them if you are unsure. The second is that you may not get a reply. Many people are not interested in family history or connecting with distant relatives. This must be respected and pestering the person with messages will not result in a positive relationship with them.

Another benefit of social media in the genealogy field is the use of groups. These may be genealogy focused, look at local history, belong to a surname study group or concentrate on a particular interest, such as DNA testing. Facebook is especially useful for genealogy research. You can join a local history page belonging to your ancestor's parish of residence to receive updates when somebody posts something new. Photographs are regularly posted, meaning one of your ancestors could even feature. Seeing historical photographs of the parish where your ancestor once lived is of great interest. Many people upload images from their own family archives, meaning you will come across photographs that are not published elsewhere. If you are stuck at a brick wall, you can post a message onto a generic genealogy group page asking for help and guidance. Many people are willing to spare their time to point you in the right direction. Examples of groups include 'The History & Heritage of Leek and the Staffordshire Moorlands', 'Staffordshire Archives and Heritage' and 'DNA Help for Genealogy (UK)'.

If you are interested in images in particular, then Instagram may also be of use. This app shows images with captions and comments but uses less text than Facebook. You can use its hashtag search function to search for a particular place or genealogical term, such as an historical occupation or document type. You can also choose to 'follow' pages – similar to joining a group on Facebook. This will update your homepage with the pages' latest posts without the need to search.

Other Notable Websites of Interest

There are websites available to meet every genealogical need. The following list is far from exhaustive so do have a look at what else is available.

Free UK Genealogy is a registered charity which comprises three transcription sites:

- **FreeBMD (freebmd.org.uk)** focuses on civil registration indexes;
- **FreeREG (freereg.org.uk)** is concentrated on parish register entries;
- **FreeCEN (freecen.org.uk)** looks at UK census returns.

The transcriptions are uploaded by volunteers and are free to access.

GenGuide (genguide.co.uk) is an excellent educational resource. There are pages for different types of genealogical source, such as title deeds, bastardy bonds and inquest records. Each page helps to explain more about the sources, tells you where they can be found, for which dates they apply and also gives further web links to find out more.

GENUKI (genuki.org.uk) acts like an online genealogy encyclopaedia for those researching their UK and Irish forebears. You can search for specific source types, depending on location, and the website can tell you where these records are held. You can search by county, for example researching Staffordshire's archives, county maps and periodicals, or you can search by individual parish to see what records have survived. Changing population statistics and gazetteer transcriptions are usually added for each parish. The website is far from exhaustive but is great to use as an initial free guide.

DNA Painter (dnapainter.com) is a tool that can help you discover more about your DNA results. You can see which segments of DNA you inherited from each ancestor and discover how matches are related to each other. DNA Painter is also home to the **'What Are The Odds'** (WATO) tool which can help you to understand how a DNA match is most likely fit into your family tree according to how much DNA they share with your other matches.

The British Film Institute's National Archive (**bfi.org.uk/bfi-national-archive**) is an underused source and a personal favourite of mine. You can access over 12,000 historical films, dating from 1895, for free. You are very unlikely to be lucky enough to spot one of your ancestors in any of these films, but they are useful in several other ways. You can search by occupation to see what videos exist of a person at work in your ancestor's role to get an idea of what their daily life was like and the conditions they worked in. You may also wish to search by parish name to see if there is any footage of your ancestor's parish from the time they lived there. Some of the Staffordshire examples include a 1915 film *Christmas at Stafford* and a 1929 film *H.R.H. The Prince of Wales Visits the Pirelli Tyre Factory at Burton upon Trent*.

Chapter 23

FAMILY HISTORY SOCIETIES

There are many benefits to joining a Family History Society (FHS), including being part of a supportive network of people and access to resources and materials. Many FHS resources are also accessible to non-members for a small fee. The main FHS for Staffordshire is Midland Ancestors which also covers Warwickshire and Worcestershire. Other groups exist that focus on more local areas of Staffordshire, rather than the county as a whole.

As well as county-based FHS, there are others with a broader appeal that may apply to your research. These include the Huguenot Society of Britain and Ireland and the Quaker Family History Society. There is also a Romany and Traveller Family History Society which will interest those whose ancestors were Romany Gypsies, Travellers or Fairground people.

Costs to purchase transcriptions, books and other items from their shops are usually reasonable. They are generally run by volunteers who are passionate about the topic, so make sure to converse with them to see how their society may help your research. It may be they have a volunteer who is knowledgeable about a particular village or area of research who can help you.

You may also wish to consider volunteering your time for a FHS project. This may involve transcribing records from the archive, taking photographs of headstones in your local churchyard or creating indexes. Consider your particular strengths and what you would enjoy doing.

Midland Ancestors
https://midland-ancestors.uk
Midland Ancestors covers Staffordshire, Warwickshire & Worcestershire. It is known for its online shop, comprising a huge range of transcriptions

including monumental inscriptions and parish registers. It currently holds events including talks, monthly meetings and one-day courses in Birmingham, Kenilworth, Stoke-on-Trent, Stourbridge, Wolverhampton and London; the calendar is kept up to date with upcoming events so check to see what is happening near you.

Talk topics have previously covered local workhouses, military history and DNA testing meaning there is something for everyone. It also runs regular courses for beginners to family history which can be a great place to start out if genealogy is new to you. Members benefit from a quarterly magazine and there is a discounted price for joint membership.

The Midland Ancestors Family History Centre is situated in the Kingsley Norris Room at The Birmingham & Midland Institute, 9 Margaret Street, Birmingham B3 3BS. It has a recognised FamilySearch Affiliate Library, meaning you can access records on the Family Search website that are unavailable from home. You can also access Findmypast from its computers using the society's subscription. Members can also take advantage of the society's Names Match Service to discover if others share the same ancestors as you. This can be a great way of finding a research buddy to share your findings with.

Burntwood Family History Group
bfhg.org.uk
Formed in 1986, The Burntwood FHG is open to anyone with an interest in local and family history. It currently holds two meetings each month at Chase Terrace Academy in Burntwood, with non-members allowed to visit free for their first meeting. One of these meetings involves an outside speaker giving a talk on a relevant topic with the other meeting acting more as a drop-in session for queries. The upcoming events calendar can be viewed on its website.

Burntwood FHG produces a quarterly journal free to members (non-members pay a small fee). It also has transcriptions for local towns and villages, including census returns and school admission records. A long list of the areas covered is on the website – encompassing places such as Lichfield, Woodhouses, Longdon, Cannock and Chorley among many others – so do not be put off by the society name.

If you have an ancestor in your family tree from Burntwood who lost his life in either of the two world wars, be sure to looks at the Serviceman page on the website. Here are biographies of the many men who died while in service. These have been thoroughly researched with supporting sources available to view. These include photographs, medal cards, certificates and census extracts. Chair Keith Stanley states its biggest strength lies in the priceless local knowledge possessed by the enthusiastic volunteers.

Audley and District Family History Society
audleyfhs.co.uk

Of use to those with roots in the north of the county, is the Audley and District Family History Society, also formed in 1986. The society covers the parish of Audley and the neighbouring parishes of Wolstanton, Keele, Madeley, Betley and Balterley in Staffordshire, plus Church Lawton and Barthomley in Cheshire. The society publishes a quarterly journal and an annual publication and has two Facebook groups. Talks are held every two months at the Audley Methodist Church Hall. Previous topics have included clergymen, heraldry, and local surnames. Talks are free to members or a small fee for non-members. Membership also gives you access to the Members' Area of its website, the ability to contact people with similar research interests as you, and a research service.

The Member's Area contains previous newsletters, some of the previous annuals, extracts from the Audley Parish Church magazine from 1920 onwards and a funeral cards' database. The society also sells a variety of books. Its website has a page on coal mining, listing local colliery disasters with photographs of memorials, and a page on the world wars including photographs of cenotaphs in the area.

Family History Federation
www.familyhistoryfederation.com

The Family History Federation is an educational charity which promotes the membership of Family History Societies. Its website lists all the accredited Family History Societies in the country, as well as some based abroad. It also advertises upcoming talks and events provided by these societies and provides resources including research tips and links to free genealogy sites. The Family History Federation has two shops: one selling genealogy books, the other selling transcriptions and maps, among other records.

New societies are welcome to apply to join via an online form available on the website. There are certain conditions which must be met before you can be accepted, such as having a minimum of ten members and to have been in existence for at least one year. In return you will receive free advertising via the website, advice regarding data protection and copyright and the ability to state on your website that you are a recognised society with the Family History Federation. This acts as proof of legitimacy and can encourage potential members to sign up to your society.

Other Societies of Interest

All FHS vary in terms of what they offer. If you have ancestors from outside Staffordshire, consider looking into how other county-based FHS may help your research. Also consider what other non-county-based FHS may help you with, whether this is focused on a particular nonconformist religion or another country. You may be interested in joining a one-name study group if you are particularly focused on researching a particular surname. Many of these are also listed on the Family History Federation's website. Surnames currently being researched include Chandler, Metcalfe and Beresford.

If your ancestors were located within a specific location for several generations, you may wish to consider joining a local history society. This is also useful to people who wish to research more into their own parish of residence, such as those researching their house history. Local history groups are not focused on genealogical research; however, many of the resources that are used overlap so these can still be useful for expanding your tree. Visit the British Association for Local History at **www.balh.org.uk** to see a list of groups from Staffordshire. These include Cheslyn Hay and District Local History Society, Ingestre and Tixall Local History Group and Smethwick Local History Society. National and regional groups are also listed, including the Black Country Society and the Railway and Canal Historical Society.

Chapter 24

DNA TESTING

Many people interested in researching their family history have not yet done a DNA test. There are also many people who have done a DNA test but are not quite sure what to do with the results. For those of us who receive close DNA matches, it can be easy to see where the other tester slots into our family tree. Most of our DNA matches are to more distant relatives and each match can take a bit of time and sleuthing to work out how you are related. Doing so can help you to prove your tree research is correct, as well as leading to a potential new contact to share new information with.

There are many false assumptions about DNA testing. The most common assumption I have heard people say is that there is no point in them doing a DNA test as they have already proven their tree using historical records. This is inaccurate, as despite us meticulously tracing our family and technically doing nothing wrong, we can still not rule out the fact that there may have been a hidden infidelity in the family. Many testers have been surprised to find that there are no matches to them on a particular parent or grandparent's side and, with research, conclude that they are not actually related to them at all. We may also find that a male ancestor fathered a child before his marriage, possibly without ever knowing. Without DNA testing, we cannot be 100 per cent certain that the tree we are researching is ours.

DNA testing is especially recommended for people who have been adopted (or whose parents or grandparents have been adopted) or where illegitimacy has left a blank branch on their tree. You are more likely to be successful in breaking down brick walls if they are more recent. If you have an illegitimate ancestor born in 1700 for example, then DNA testing will not help you discover their father. Any problem further back than six or seven generations is very unlikely to be solved by DNA.

If you are new to the idea of testing, take your time to consider which test will be most helpful to you. It is also worth testing your oldest relative rather than yourself first. If you test your father, you will only receive DNA matches from his side but he will have matches relating back to further generations than you. You only receive 50 per cent of your father's DNA meaning a lot of people will match to your father but not you. DNA is not cheap, but it is worth testing as many relatives as possible if you can afford to. If you have already lost your parents, consider testing your siblings as they will have inherited a different 50 per cent of your parents' genes than you and may just lead to an important match.

Some DNA testing websites are more user friendly than others and you can upload your results to different sites to view more matches. I originally tested with Ancestry, but by uploading my result to MyHeritage I was able to identify a new match who was not on Ancestry and break down a long-standing brick wall. Don't dismiss the usefulness of testing. Those who do usually do not understand how to use their results to their full potential.

Types of DNA Test

There is more than one type of DNA test used for genealogy purposes. For the majority of people, an autosomal test will be best. This looks at DNA you inherited from both your mother's and father's side. It is the best way to get a comprehensive look at your entire DNA inheritance. Autosomal tests are the most commonly used and if the test does not state which type it is, it is most likely to be this. Currently, Ancestry only offers an autosomal test as there is more demand for this.

If you are only interested in trying to trace your paternal side, a Y-DNA test may suit you better. Only men can take the test so women will need to test a male relative such as their father or brother. A Y-DNA test will only look at results from the male line, i.e. your father, your father's father, your father's father's father etc. There will be no results from any female line as the information garnered from a Y-DNA test is gained from the Y chromosome which men pass down from father to son. You will receive far fewer results from a Y-DNA test as you are only looking at one specific branch; however, this may be just what you need if your paternal grandfather was adopted, for example.

Lastly, there is the option of a mitochondrial test, otherwise known as a mtDNA test. Men and women can take this test which looks at the female line. Again, this looks at a specific branch, i.e. your mother, your maternal grandmother, your maternal grandmother's mother etc.

mtDNA tests are the least helpful for genealogists and tend to be used more for looking at ancient heritage.

Where to Test

The most popular website to complete a DNA test with is Ancestry. It has the biggest database so you are more likely to have more matches on here than elsewhere. You can download your test results from Ancestry and upload them to other sites such as MyHeritage and GEDMatch to find more matches, but you cannot upload a test to Ancestry that has been completed elsewhere. For these reasons, many people choose to first test with Ancestry if they are looking for an autosomal test.

Other sites that offer autosomal testing include MyHeritage, Family Tree DNA, Living DNA and 23andMe. The features and layouts of all of the websites vary and it is worth looking into first to see which set up you are happiest using. If you are a confident user of MyHeritage but rarely use Ancestry, you may feel more comfortable testing with MyHeritage. Remember, however, the best thing to do even in this scenario is to first test with Ancestry and upload your results to MyHeritage. That way you will receive many more matches, but can choose to base your research on the MyHeritage page if that is where you are most comfortable.

Y-DNA and mtDNA testing is currently only available from Family Tree DNA. These are more expensive tests; however, it is worth it if you are tracing your male to male or female to female branch. Y-DNA testing is becoming increasingly popular but it is often down to luck as to how many matches you will receive. My father and my husband have both completed Y-DNA testing and my husband receives far more matches than my father.

Some companies offer other features as well as looking for genealogical matches. These include 'Traits' by Ancestry, where you can pay an extra fee to see which of your characteristics may be inherited. Examples include the thickness of your hair and sweet sensitivity. As it is a very new science, these are not accurate – and they serve no genealogical purpose. Other companies, such as Living DNA, offer health checks as well as genealogy DNA tests. These may include testing your metabolism or how well your body responds to vitamins. There is always an extra cost for health and wellbeing tests and they again serve no genealogical purpose. Some health tests are more in-depth than others so please be very careful when purchasing one of these tests. There are reports of people who have found out that they have an inherited condition through this testing and received no support. If you are concerned about your health, it is far better to see your doctor and receive results in an appropriate environment with trained people who can help you.

When considering where to test, cost will be an obvious factor. DNA-testing companies have frequent promotions, reducing costs around Mother's Day, Father's Day and Black Friday in November. The latter is usually the cheapest time to purchase. Postage is not usually included.

Ethnicity Results

The ability to find out about your ethnicity via a DNA test is for some the main selling point, whereas for most it is just an additional feature. You will find that many of your DNA matches have no online family tree connected to their results and may not have logged in for years. These people have usually either been purchased a test as a present and not had time or interest to pursue the results or they may have purchased the test purely to find out about their ethnicity. Since DNA-test marketing is often based around discovering ethnicity, it is no surprise that people lose interest once they have seen their results.

The science behind DNA testing and ethnicity is very new and more is being discovered all the time about how our genes relate to our heritage. You will find that your ethnicity results change over time, usually being updated once a year. This is because as the testing companies have more people that have tested with them, they have a larger database of people to use as a research sample. These results can then, in theory, be made more accurate each year.

As every testing website has a different sample group of people who have tested, you will find that your ethnicity results vary between them. On Ancestry, I am currently listed as roughly 70 per cent English, 10 per cent Norwegian, 10 per cent Germanic European with 10 per cent split between other regions. On LivingDNA, my ethnicity is recorded as roughly 60 per cent French and German, 35 per cent British and 5 per cent split between other regions. Ancestry is usually the most accurate with regards to ethnicity as it has the largest database and this is certainly true in my case. I have yet to come across a French or German ancestor, so any link to these countries would be distant.

Localised findings, known on Ancestry as ancestral journeys, are of more use to us than our regional ethnicity results. These were previously referred to as 'communities' and are based on our cousin matches and look at where people in their family trees resided. This feature tends to focus more on the last 50–300 years, whereas our ethnicity results will tell us where our more distant ancestors are from. If your parents were born in Staffordshire but their forebears were all from other counties or countries, then there will be no link to Staffordshire in your ethnicity results.

Interpreting the Results

Many people expect to receive their DNA results and to have a lot of very close matches, all with their trees publicly viewable and for any mysteries to be easily solved. This is rarely the case and the lack of willingness to learn how to interpret their results correctly often means they fail to unleash their DNA results' potential. Make sure you have an online family tree saved to the same website that you have your DNA tested with. If you upload your test to other sites, upload your tree here too. Many sites, including Ancestry, allow you to link your DNA test to the person in the tree who has taken the test, whether that is yourself, a sibling or a parent. If somebody else has taken a test, they can choose to make you a 'manager' of their results so you can view their matches in the same way as you view your own.

Whatever testing website you use, your results will show as matches to people based on the number of centimorgans (cM) you share. From this figure, most sites such as Ancestry and MyHeritage, will estimate your most likely relationship to this person, such as a second cousin for example. The more cMs that you share with a person, the closer you are in relationship. This is generally speaking, however, as there are overlaps. For example, a second cousin will usually share between 50cM and 590cM, whereas a third cousin may share between 0cM and 230cM. This shows a large overlap; however, by viewing each other's trees, it is usually possible to see how you are related.

To discuss how to interpret your results I will focus on the Ancestry website as it is the most commonly used. The principles remain the same

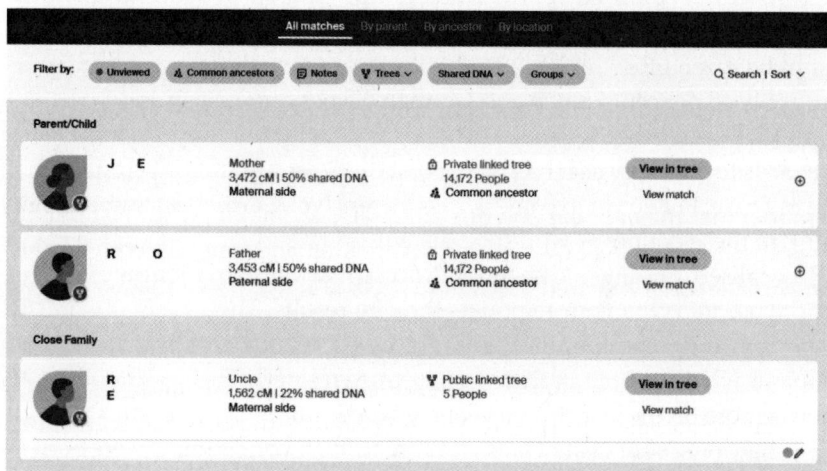

A screenshot of my Ancestry DNA Results showing my parents and uncle as my closest matches. (With permission from Ancestry)

for other sites. Your results will be displayed with the closest match to you at the top. This will be the person you share the most cM with. My parents and my uncle have all tested so they are my top three matches. It is best to first focus on the nearest matches outside of your close family. For each match who is present in your tree, you can 'link' their test result to your tree for future reference.

If you are disappointed by a lack of matches then don't worry. More DNA test results are uploaded every day and your matches will be constantly updated with these. You will probably find the biggest influx of results happens in January and February, when people who have purchased tests in the Black Friday sale or received them as Christmas gifts get their results.

There are many ways you can filter your results, depending on what you are most interested in looking at. You may opt to first view the matches you have a 'common ancestor' with. This is where Ancestry's algorithms have discovered you share an ancestor due to the similarities in your trees. This is not a perfect science so do take care to corroborate using records. You can also choose to view only your matches who have publicly viewable trees. This makes it much easier to see how you may be related. Other filters include filtering by maternal or paternal matches and by matches you have not yet viewed.

You can also filter by 'group'. These colour-coded groups are self-allocated, meaning you can choose to label them however you wish. Most people choose to either have four colours with one for each grandparent or eight colours with one for each great-grandparent. There is no right or wrong way and you can change your mind at any time by deleting a group and starting again. The colours will appear as small squares with the first letter of the group name next to each match as you browse your matches list, meaning it is quick and easy to see at a glance which branch you are related to that person through. These colour-coded groups remain private; nobody else can see them.

Your cousin matches will be able to see your test result in the same manner that they appear on your match list. By making your test public, it is easier to discuss how you may be related and you will both be able to see each other's shared matches as well. You may have already proven that you relate to a shared match through your maternal grandmother's side, meaning this is likely how you relate to the new match too.

As previously mentioned, not everybody will have completed a DNA test for genealogical purposes. You will have many matches who either do not have a family tree attached to their results or who do have a tree but have opted to keep this private. This can make proving how you are related very difficult. If you message the match, they may be happy to share their private tree with you. If not, have a look at the shared matches between the two of you and the amount of cMs you share to come to a likely conclusion. If their test is saved under their real name (some opt for an untraceable nickname) then you can search other genealogical sites to see if they have a tree saved elsewhere. While it may be frustrating to receive no reply from the person, please do be respectful. There is no point in badgering them with constant messages; just one or two messages politely and briefly introducing yourself is enough. If they are interested and wish to find out more then they will, otherwise it is likely they have no desire to find out more about their test results.

Remember that the more people who test, the more results you will receive. Try and get any relatives to test, starting with the older generations. This could be your parents, aunts and uncles, siblings or cousins. There are even reports where people have encouraged their friends and neighbours to test only to find out that they are related. Some researchers choose to purchase DNA tests for their loved ones as a gift. If doing so, offer to help them manage their results so you can use them for your research if they are happy for you to do so.

Staffordshire Examples

When looking at my own Staffordshire ancestry, it is better to focus on my mother's DNA test results as my father has no ancestors from the county. Using Ancestry's 'Common Ancestors' feature, I can see that my mother currently shares three matches linking us back to my third great-grandparents Samson Barlow and Rosanna Sarah Marshall of Longdon. There are likely more; however, these three people all have Samson and Rosanna on their family trees, meaning Ancestry can link our relationship back to these two people.

We are related to Samson and Rosanna through their daughter Rosabella. One of my mother's matches is the descendant of their son Samson John and is my mother's third cousin, matching at 56cM. I match with this person at 33cM. There are four further matches who are all descendants of Samson and Rosanna's son George. These matches are also all third cousins of my mother, with the amounts of cM being 16cM, 17cM, 22cM and 46cM. I, however, only match with two of these people. All of the cM figures are within the correct range for a third cousin.

If we go back a further generation to my fourth great-grandparents William Barlow and Mary Brindley of Cheadle, we can see further matches on that branch. As well as the previously discussed matches through Samson's line, there are six further confirmed matches. The ranges vary from 11cM to 38cM. I match with five of the six people, ranging from 10cM to 23cM. Had these matches not made their trees publicly viewable, I would not be able to confirm how I am related to them.

CONCLUSION

I hope this book has inspired you to discover new records relating to your Staffordshire ancestors. By using an assortment of record sources, we can gain a clearer image of who our ancestors were. Understanding more about the context of their lives can greatly help us to learn what the world was like when they were alive, so read up about the history of Staffordshire to see what events or changes our ancestors lived through.

It is common to get stuck when trying to research a particular ancestor. Sometimes it feels as though we have found everything out about them that is possible. Eventually, it gets to the point where this is somewhat true; when every parish record, court case, parish register entry, business record and manorial record has been scoured for mentions of this ancestor.

When you get to the point where you feel as though you are stuck with a particular person, try writing their biography. You may find that piecing together the records that you have and studying them in chronological order raises questions and opens new avenues of research. This may lead you to records that may not specifically name your ancestor, but will still teach you something about them. You may decide when writing their biography that you wish to know more about their life on-board a particular ship. While you may have gathered together all of the records that mention their existence on the ship, it is still beneficial if you can find a painting or a first-hand written history from someone else who was on-board at the same time. From these you can learn about the conditions your ancestor was living through and any notable battles or weather events that occurred. Similarly, if you are struggling to find many records about your ancestors' working lives, look at others who worked there to see what you can find about them. Their colleagues may have left documents behind that will give a fresh insight into what working there was like.

You can enhance an ancestor's biography by reading up about the parish that they lived in. There are many books available on the history of Staffordshire, some which focus on particular parishes. Search to see if there are any which look at the area where your ancestors lived. You can search newspapers for their parish to see what was going on locally. Just because an article doesn't mention people by name, doesn't mean the event in question didn't affect them. You may discover that their village was badly flooded or experienced an epidemic.

What we cannot know from this type of information is how our ancestors felt about such an event or how they reacted to it. Never assume their emotions or actions. It is human nature to want to see ourselves reflected in our ancestors or to want them to have reacted in a heroic way to an event. Try and stick to the facts when writing a biography but use it to further your research at the same time. Use the sources you have as prompts to discover more.

Family history is all about being resourceful. We have to stop and think what records our ancestor may appear in depending on when they were alive, where they lived, where they worked, their religion and their financial status. When people claim to have 'completed' their family trees, this usually means that they have found out everything they wish to know. Some people get to a point where they have got back as far as they are happy with and know enough about their ancestors to have satisfied their curiosity.

Others among us never reach this point. Assuming a family tree has no 'duplicate' ancestors (i.e. intermarrying cousins), we have 1,024 eighth great-grandparents. This number doubles with each generation we go back. The likelihood is that at some point you will find cousins marrying, even if they are distantly related, leading you to have 'lesser' ancestors. Still, to research all of these individuals would be more than a lifetime's work. Your research is personal to you and, as long as you do it methodically, you can choose to focus on whichever ancestors interest you the most.

People look into their family history for many reasons. Some people have a passion for history, some want to know where they get a certain trait from and some enjoy acting like a detective to uncover hidden historical secrets. Whatever your reason for wanting to find out more about your Staffordshire ancestors, I truly hope this book has inspired you to discover more about your family tree.

INDEX

Aliases, 77–8, 176–7
Alumni records, 80–1, 83, 89
Apprenticeships, 25, 28, 32–7, 81, 83, 85–7, 105, 133, 155, 174
Assizes, 32, 70–1, 75
Association Oath Rolls, 99, 101–104, 176
Audley and District Family History Society, 192
Autosomal DNA tests, 195–6

Banns, 5–6, 25, 29
Baptism Registers, 22–30, 34–5, 49, 94, 112, 125
Baptists, 49, 52–3, 55
Bargain and Sale, 108, 110
Bastardy records, 31, 34–9, 70
Birmingham Archdiocesan Archives, 54, 58, 154
Birmingham Archives, 53, 154
Birth certificates, 1–11, 17, 133, 177–8
Bishops Transcripts, 22–3, 28
Brewing, 106, 157, 165, 168–9
Burial Registers, 22–30, 50, 88, 130–2
Burntwood Family History Group, 191–2

Calendars of Prisoners, 71, 73, 75, 78
Canals, 17–18, 28, 82, 85, 91, 93, 166–8, 193
Census, 5, 7, 12–21, 76, 85, 98, 164, 171, 173, 176, 185, 188
Cheshire Archives, 101, 125, 155
Churchwardens records, 32, 37, 84, 162
Common Recovery, 108
Compton census, 50–1, 53, 55
Copyhold property, 108, 125

Coroner's Inquests, 1, 114, 117, 142–3, 171
Court Baron, 121–2, 125
Court Leet, 121–2, 125

Death certificates, 1–11, 30, 47, 116–17, 120, 135, 142
Death Duty, 45
Death penalty, 71–3
Derbyshire Record Office, 110, 125, 155
Divorce, 9, 145–7, 177
DNA testing, 8, 35, 187–9, 194–200
Dudley Archives, 24, 42, 85, 152–3

Ecclesiastical census, 51–3, 55
Ecclesiastical courts, 41, 70, 74, 80, 145
Electoral registers, 140–2, 153
Enclosure maps, 92–8
Equity courts, 109, 144–5
Estate maps, 91, 94–6, 124

Family History Federation, 192–3
Final Concord, 107, 110, 112
Freehold property, 108–109, 111

General Register Office (GRO), 1–11

Hardwicke's Marriage Act, 25
Hearth tax, 99–102, 104, 106, 187
Heraldry, 147–8
Hospital records, 59, 138–40

Illegitimacy, 25, 31, 34–9, 70, 176–7, 194
Inventories, 40, 44, 47–8

Jews, 25, 49, 52–4, 56
Justices of the Peace, 33–4, 71

Keele University Archives, 125, 154

Land tax assessments, 100–104, 153
Lay subsidies, 99, 101, 104
Lease and Release, 108
Leasehold property, 108
Levée en Masse, 60
Lloyd George Domesday records, 93, 95–7, 185

Manorial Documents Register, 124, 127
Manorial records, 121–28, 152, 154, 187
Maps, 82, 91–8, 111, 123–6, 152–5, 161, 164–6, 185
Marriage certificates, 1–11, 51, 146–7
Marriage Duty Act, 100, 104
Marriage registers, 22–30, 49, 131
Memorial inscriptions, 51, 53, 55, 129–36, 163–4
Methodists, 49, 52–7
Midland Ancestors, 5, 24, 54, 105, 132, 190–1
Military records, 59–69, 116, 118
Militia, 60, 63–4, 66–7
Mining, 84–5, 160, 170–1, 192
mtDNA tests, 195–6
Museums, 60–3, 149, 154, 157–60, 165

National Farm Survey, 93, 95, 173
National Land Registry, 109, 111
National Memorial Arboretum, 131
Newspapers, 52–5, 63–4, 69, 72, 74, 76–7, 79–80, 82–3, 86, 88, 90, 114–20, 142–4, 148–9, 169–74
Nonconformists, 25, 36, 49–58, 91, 154, 163, 193

Obituaries, 55, 114, 117, 119–20
Ordnance Survey, 93, 95–6
Overseers, 18, 32, 36, 38, 76

Passenger lists, 143–4
Period of Commonwealth, 28
Petty Sessions, 70–1, 74, 76, 78, 120–1
Photographs, xii, 60, 64, 74, 82, 117–18, 131–2, 134, 137, 140, 149–51, 153, 159, 162–3, 186–7, 192
Poll books, 140, 153
Poll tax, 99, 101–102
Posse Comitatus, 60
Prerogative Court of Canterbury, 41

Presbyterians, 49, 52–3
Protestation Oath Returns, 101–104

Quakers, 25, 49–55, 190
Quarrying, 82, 170–1
Quarter Sessions, 32, 37, 54–5, 70–6, 78, 85–7, 101, 142–3

Removal orders, 34–8
Roman Catholics, 49–51, 54–6, 58, 100–101, 103–104, 154

Sandwell Archives, 24, 152–3
School records, 52, 137–8, 149, 152–3, 191
Settlement records, 28, 31, 33–8, 86
Shoemaking, 173–4
Shropshire Archives, 24, 110, 155
Social media, 150–1, 187–8
Society of Genealogists, 54, 84, 102
Sport, 148–9
Staffordshire History Centre (SHC), 13, 34–5, 41–2, 53, 64, 74, 84–5, 95, 101, 105, 110, 112, 124–5, 139–40, 143, 149, 152, 168–9, 173–4, 185
Staffordshire Potteries, 115, 159, 167–8
Staffordshire Regiment Museum, 61–2, 154, 159
Stoke-on-Trent City Archives, 34, 53, 84, 139, 152
Surnames, 99, 115, 123, 175–83, 193

The National Archives (TNA), 13, 35, 41, 53, 60–4, 72–3, 78, 83–5, 94–5, 100–102, 106, 110, 124–6, 143–6, 155–6
Tithe maps, 92, 94–8
Title deeds, 107–13, 124, 152, 155
Trade directories, 81–3, 86–8, 153–4
Transportation, 71, 73–5

Vestry, 32, 35, 80

Walsall Archives, 13, 140, 153
Wills, 40–8, 54, 86, 125, 144–5, 153, 156, 185
Window tax, 100–102, 104–105
Wolverhampton City Archives, 42, 74, 83, 143, 153
Workhouse registers, 31–2, 35–7, 76

Y-DNA tests, 195–6